T0311594

Social Therapeutic Coaching

Combining social therapeutics with the practice of coaching, this book guides coaches and mental health professionals in how to coach groups and couples using this innovative method.

Drawing from the authors' combined 50 years of experience, *Social Therapeutic Coaching: A Practical Guide to Group and Couples Work* empowers practitioners to break away from focusing on individual change to focusing on groups and their emotional growth. Early chapters touch on the history of coaching and powerful discoveries of social therapeutics before diving into how to lead a social therapeutic group. Sackett and Dabby explain how to incorporate the concept of human relationality into coaching sessions, demonstrating how it extends group work beyond assembling like-minded individuals with similar goals into bringing together diverse people with diverse issues that they want to work on and grow around. It also brings a fresh lens to working with couples, in which the focus is on discovering what "the relationship" needs, rather than trying to get individuals to compromise, change or work towards a preconceived shared vision for an end goal.

Written in an accessible style and filled with extensive case studies and examples, *Social Therapeutic Coaching* provides a powerful toolkit for coaches, counselors, psychotherapists, social workers, HR and talent development professionals, community-based leaders and social entrepreneurs.

Carrie Sackett is the founder of ZPD Coaching and an IABC Gold Quill award-winning employee engagement professional. She serves as an Associate at the East Side Institute in Manhattan, USA.

Murray Dabby, MSSW, is the Director of the Atlanta Center for Social Therapy and co-founder of innovative group-based therapeutic programs—*The Couples College* and *Curtain Up, Anxiety Down*.

This is a rare book that succeeds in uniting theory and practice. Even rarer is doing it with such joy. As a practical-philosophical guide, *Social Therapeutic Coaching* brings the history, concepts and practices of social therapeutics to the field of coaching and, in the process, enriches both of them.

Lois Holzman, *PhD, Director, East Side Institute*

The innovations of social therapeutics inform my coaching practice every day. This book is a ground-breaking offering for co-creating trust, connection, belonging and community; and, most importantly, for supporting our clients to achieve their goals in life and work.

Elizabeth C. Hechtman, *MS, PCC, CPCC,*
Past President, ICF Philadelphia

Sackett and Dabby define a new niche in the modern coaching industry. *Social Therapeutic Coaching* introduces new/old knowledge so that coaches can help the masses during this rather difficult time of "humaning". This book is brilliant on so many levels.

Michael Tucker, *MA, PCC, CSM, CSPO*

I have experienced the power of social therapeutic group and couples work as a client. It has changed my own life and my practice as a psychoanalyst and psychiatrist. Sackett and Dabby teach tools for emotional closeness. I encourage practitioners of all types to read it.

Aneil M. Shirke, *MD, PhD, FABPN, FABP*

Social Therapeutic Coaching

A Practical Guide to Group and Couples Work

Carrie Sackett and Murray Dabby

Routledge
Taylor & Francis Group

NEW YORK AND LONDON

Designed cover image: © Getty Images

First published 2024
by Routledge
605 Third Avenue, New York, NY 10158

and by Routledge
4 Park Square, Milton Park, Abingdon, Oxon, OX14 4RN

Routledge is an imprint of the Taylor & Francis Group, an informa business

Library of Congress Cataloging-in-Publication Data
Names: Sackett, Carrie, author. | Dabby, Murray, author.
Title: Social therapeutic coaching : a practical guide to group and
    couples work / Carrie Sackett, Murray Dabby.
Description: New York, NY : Routledge, 2024. | Includes
    bibliographical references and index.
Subjects: MESH: Psychotherapy, Group—methods | Mentoring |
    Social Interaction
Classification: LCC RC480.5 (print) | LCC RC480.5 (ebook) |
    NLM WM 430 | DDC 616.89/14—dc23/eng/20231024
LC record available at https://lccn.loc.gov/2023032606
LC ebook record available at https://lccn.loc.gov/2023032607

ISBN: 978-1-032-35352-4 (hbk)
ISBN: 978-1-032-35350-0 (pbk)
ISBN: 978-1-003-32646-5 (ebk)

DOI: 10.4324/9781003326465

Typeset in Caslon
by Apex CoVantage, LLC

To Fred Newman and Lois Holzman and the early development community, whose members dedicated their lives to creating a new way of making a better world.

CONTENTS

ABOUT THE AUTHORS

Carrie Sackett is the founder of ZPD Coaching, a virtual and international practice specializing in group, couples and family work. Together with co-author Murray Dabby, she formed The Center for Group and Couples Coaching to train coaches and helping professionals in the social therapeutic method.

Carrie was searching for social innovators when she met social therapeutic founders Fred Newman and Lois Holzman in 1992. She went on to train under Newman and Holzman, graduating from their Therapist Training Program at The East Side Institute in Manhattan. Afterwards, she carried the tenets of social therapeutics into a Fortune 500 award-wining corporate career in change management and employee engagement (two areas that are today considered specializations within leadership and team coaching). About ten years ago, Carrie decided to return to her therapeutic roots and discovered the world of coaching—a place where social innovators are free to operate. She is one of the first of a growing generation of social therapeutically trained coaches, and is an accredited somatic coach. Carrie graduated from Duke University and received her Master's in Strategic Communications from Columbia University.

Murray Dabby is a nationally regarded teacher in the use of improvisation and theater performance in group and couples work. He serves as Director of the Atlanta Center for Social Therapy and co-founded *The Couples College*, a group-based skill-building training for couples and *Curtain Up, Anxiety Down*, an improv program to help people with social confidence and social anxiety.

Murray developed an interest in social therapeutics in 1978 after witnessing the limitations of diagnosis and traditional treatment methodology while assisting in psychiatric research on the DSM III at Cornell Medical Center. While training in social therapeutics in the early 1980s, he began working in diverse and multiracial communities. As a therapist, coach, improv leader and affiliate faculty member, Murray has worked with physicians, academics, university administrators, business professionals, entrepreneurs, minority youth communities, ministers, nonprofit leaders, artists, writers and people in entertainment. Murray regularly performs as singer and guitarist in The Way Back Band. He graduated from City College of New York, received a graduate degree in Social Work from Columbia University and trained with the Relationship Coaching Institute.

ACKNOWLEDGEMENTS

We would like to thank Lois Holzman for her pitch-perfect guidance and direction as we drafted this book. We are indebted to her and Fred Newman's groundbreaking discoveries and practices known around the world as social therapeutics. It has been a terrifying honor to follow their lead and practicalize social therapeutics for the growing industry of coaching as well as practitioners of all types interested in group and couples work.

We are grateful to the Colloquium, a set of social therapeutic colleagues of which we are part, that gathers weekly for discussions of issues related to our practices. One particular conversation on emotional growth helped us charter new territory in writing on social therapeutics.

Book writing advice from Dr. Omar Ali and Jackie Salit has been invaluable. Conversations with Joyce Dattner and Randy Wilson on couples work as well as with Jan Wootten, Thecla Farrell, Ann Green and Raquell Holmes helped keep the project moving. Elizabeth Hechtman and Judith Kolberg have been important bridges between social therapeutics and coaching. Special thanks to those who braved reading or listening to our early drafts: Lori Abramson, Jill Battalen, Jennifer Bullock, Dr. Jared French, Aurelie Harp, Warren Liebesman, Qazi Abdur Rahman and Pat Wagner. And special appreciation goes to the first-generation coaches who shared with us their experiences of working with Thomas Leonard and being part of the cohort that brought coaching mainstream recognition—Bill Dueease, Jay Perry, Cheryl Richardson, Michael Stratford and Sandy Vilas.

We would not be here without Heather Evans, former Mental Health Editor at Routledge, whose keen sense for innovation and the need for practical coaching resources led her to request our book proposal and move us to contract in short order. We deeply appreciate Judith Kolberg, book coach, in her review of the manuscript, Caroline Donnola for securing permissions and a most special thanks to Eliza Rudalevige, whose patience, encouragement and excellent editing took us to the finish line.

Our deepest thanks go to our clients, who first and foremost have made us better practitioners. They have informed how we have told this story of social therapeutic coaching. We are continuously moved by their willingness to stretch, take emotional risks and grow with us, their partners and fellow group members.

We celebrate the unexpected and delightful partnership we have formed while writing this book together. While we have admired each other as practitioners through the years, this is our first experience of uniting our talents.

Murray offers deep appreciation for his professional partners and friends, Allison Caffyn, whose passion for working with couples endlessly inspires him and Lesly Fredman, an improviser par excellence who has created with him a deeper appreciation for therapeutic play and performance. Finally, to Murray's life partner and wife, Lori Abramson, whose therapeutic eye provided continuous professional and emotional support.

A most loving thank you goes to Carrie's family and her *famiglia grande*, whose emotional support kept her going through the most difficult moments, her professional coaching colleagues who have welcomed her into the community and her Arizona friends whose enthusiasm and confidence in her kept her forging ahead.

INTRODUCTION

The old order is dead. It's imploding, it's not going to get better. Back
to normal is not an option.

Bob Anderson, panelist,
The 2022 Coaching Summit by Coaches Rising

Imagine a Life Development Group in which a dozen participants gather
weekly to listen, learn from and build with other group members who
are there to work on life issues different from their own. In the process,
with the support of a social therapeutic coach, they create the conditions
for their own growth. Together they produce a full range of experience
of belonging and being connected in the world. That continuous building
activity turbocharges emotional growth and development for the group
as a whole and the individuals in it. This book will show the reader how
to practice in a transformative new way with clients—in groups, teams,
couples and, by extension, with families, communities and individuals.

The 2020s are pushing us to live in completely new ways. Continuous uncertainty and the deeply uncomfortable fear of the catastrophic
hang over us. A perfect storm of global pandemic, environmental
crisis, extreme economic and racial inequity, random violence, threat
of nuclear annihilation, rapid technological change and loss of trust
in institutions (Edelman, 2021) feels nearly overwhelming. Millions

DOI: 10.4324/9781003326465-1

1

around the globe are seeking innovative, humanistic approaches for dealing with the fallout from the world we humans have created over these last centuries. That fallout is social, economic, political, environmental— and emotional. This book is offering a new way to relate to and build with emotional pain and distress specific to this moment in human history.

New approaches must emerge now if we are to thrive collectively and globally. Coaching researchers and authors Yossi Ives and Elaine Cox advocate that "there has to be a change in mindset" (2015, p. 3). Our modernist conceptual tools cannot carry us to a better world. Of course, those tools have produced incredible advances (think: penicillin; electricity; machines for rapid transit and communication). But they have also produced the messy, painful, unjust and lonely[1] world we all reside in now. In 1984, Black radical lesbian feminist and poet Audre Lorde put it like this: "The master's tools will never dismantle the master's house" (2007). Our world has shifted since then. Today, one does not need to be a radical to declare that we need new emotional, social and cultural concepts and tools to address the challenges of our unpredictable times. Or conversely, we are all becoming radicals!

Social therapeutics offers a radical conceptual and methodological shift, an alternative to relying on the fixed categories, labels and diagnoses that pervade our culture. Embedded in its method is a radical acceptance of and ability to create with uncertainty. Its distinguishing breakthrough is that of seeing collective human activity—group activity—as the unit of human development, rather than the individual. While group work is becoming somewhat more common in life coaching, team coaching, psychotherapy and social work, what sets social therapeutics apart (in addition to seeing group activity) is its practice of creating and conducting *heterogeneous* groups. By heterogeneous, we do not intend box-checking heterogeneity, though our groups are diverse by race, class, gender, age, religion, geography and sexual orientation. In social therapeutic Life Development Groups, it is those cultural/historical differences *in addition to* the diversity of what group members bring to work on that creates the stage for growth and transformation. Every week for 90 minutes, four to twenty people come together to do the activity we call "building the group." In doing so, the group grows and the group's participants grow.

Heterogeneity in this sense *is* life development for us. Clients get related to as creators of their lives, families, communities and our world.

Born out of a multiracial community-based effort to create a new psychology in the 1970s and 80s, social therapeutics requires other ways to measure and understand what is changing/emerging/developing. Similar to other forms of life—sex and learning to speak come to mind—it is experiential. And, like them, social therapeutics is not teachable in the traditional sense of learning a model and applying it onto people or situations. Nonetheless, we are writing this book to bring to life to a broader audience[2] what we believe to be a most powerful approach to emotional growth and social/cultural transformation. Tens of thousands of social therapeutic group sessions have occurred over the last 40 years, in both short-term and ongoing weekly groups.

As such, our clients come to embrace that emotionality—both our emotional pain and joy—gets created with and *in relation to* others. They begin to develop new ways of seeing, doing, communicating and feeling. The social therapeutic coach empowers clients with a conceptual/experiential toolkit for continuously transforming their lives and how they relate to others in it. And when people discover that they can build and create in the moment with whatever is going on for them, they discover their power.

In the last 20 years or so, coaching has exponentially expanded its global influence. On life coaching, one of the most successful businessmen of all times and leader of a billion-dollar philanthropy Bill Gates says, "Everyone needs a coach. We all need people to give us feedback. That's how we improve" (Fromell, 2016). We could not agree more that we all need others to help us grow. What brings coaching and social therapeutics together in *Social Therapeutic Coaching: A Practical Guide to Group and Couples Work* is three things: The focus on co-creation with the client; the openness to not-knowing and building with what is emerging in the work; and, the commitment to growth and transformation. We suspect that practitioners will recognize some of how they already work in the social therapeutic method and find value in having it voiced and shaped.

If coaching and social therapeutics are innovations tooled for the 21st century, social therapeutics offers the methodological magic of revolutionizing group and couples work. This unique practice of working with clients with diverse issues (rather than a single theme, e.g., weight loss) in a group setting is accompanied by an ambitious vision. The more coaches trained in leading social therapeutic groups, the more ordinary people everywhere can access the capacity to create growthful environments with others. The more people grow, the more they are building connection and community and the possibility of transformation at all levels—personal, societal, political, cultural.

Why Group *and* Couples

We are introducing social therapeutics as a method in which the unit of development is the group. So why include couples work? The short answer is that we see it as group work. Consider the material fact that there are three people participating—the two clients and the coach. Additionally, there is the "groupness" of what the couple wants to fix, which is *the relationship*. The coach helps couples identify what the relationship needs and then supports them to create that (even though they might come into coaching assuming it is the other person who needs to be fixed). Family coaching works similarly, though it resides outside the scope of this book. Social therapeutic practitioners even relate to individual work as group (of two) work. Group-oriented questions like, "How are we doing?" and "What are we creating together?" carry through all types of social therapeutic coaching sessions.

There is another reason we are focused on both group and couples work. We believe the particularities of each help illustrate different aspects of the social therapeutic method, thus offering the reader different roads into the material we are presenting. For group coaching, and group work in general, there are very few models of how they should operate and even fewer societal expectations of how group members should interact (with the exception of not talking over each other). By and large the debate on groups has centered on whether they are a positive or a negative force in a society which rests on the presumed fundamentality of the individual. Thus, there is a lot of open space for us to work in. And in the section where we look specifically at social therapeutic groups and how to coach them, we invest more heavily in illustrating the mechanics of its practice of method.

In couples work, the social construct of "the couple" is more obvious. Messages bombard us every day of what a romantic relationship/marriage should look and feel like. The playing field is already packed with off-the-shelf tools—psychological theories, games to create intimacy, quizzes which tell us which category of lover we are, rom-coms, etc. We come into relationships with pre-made scripts. When we turn our attention exclusively to couples work there is more emphasis, though not exclusively, on the culturally transformative aspects of social therapeutics. Drawing on the tools of theater, social therapeutics incorporates the metaphor of performance to empower clients to create their own script, rather than be overdetermined by the one already written for them. It takes what an actor does onstage and carries it offstage where the coach can encourage new performances by clients and suggest they try out new lines with their partner. This activity and the language employed while doing it supports the overthrow of societal expectations of who we should be.

Taken altogether—the fusion of new methodological concepts with the creativity and improvisation of performance—*Social Therapeutic Coaching* shows in practice how coaches can shift into "seeing groups" and support their clients to see themselves as—and become—creators and transformers of their lives, in relation with others. And it instructs on *how* coaches build with and direct their group. When the coach leads by way of focusing on this joint activity with the group, it catalyzes emotional growth and development for clients in ways that are inconceivable in one-to-one coaching.

We are writing this book exactly 20 years after edited transcripts of social therapeutic's co-founder and lead practitioner Fred Newman's consultative sessions with therapists and practitioners-in-training were published. That book, *Psychological Investigations: A Clinician's Guide to Social Therapy*, was edited by co-founder Lois Holzman[3] and pioneer social therapist Rafael Mendez and remains a valuable resource today (Holzman & Mendez, 2003). Since then, social therapeutics has expanded across the globe to many more practitioners of mental, social and community well-being. This has driven new demand for accessible training materials. That, plus the exponential growth in the number of coaches combined with interest in new forms of life coaching, has led us to write *Social Therapeutic Coaching*. In a field that "seems to be exceptionally open to adaptation of different ideas deriving from a wide range of disciplines, to a degree that might be considered unacceptable by practitioners in more traditional disciplines" (Abravanel & Gavin, 2017, p. 32), we believe this book will be well received. And, in line with the intersecting of social therapeutics and coaching, one of us—Carrie—is a coach and the other—Murray—is a licensed social worker. We have been practicing social therapeutics for a combined 50 years.

How to Read This Book

Perhaps it is every nonfiction author's dream to have the reader work through their book in the order of first page to last. We recognize that many may choose to head straight to the hands-on nuts-and-bolts chapters to see what this social therapeutic approach is all about. We have written this book as a weaving of social therapeutic concepts in the first half followed by practical snapshots of group and couples work in the second half. If we have done our job well, no matter where you dive in, you will want to move back and forth in it several times for an immersive experience. Hopefully, in the process you will find yourself bounced outside of contemporary societal assumptions and experience floating around in another world, unsure of where you are going. If you do, we will be elated! We will have done our job.

To take you somewhere new, we sometimes do unusual things in our writing. As non-dualists writing in a language founded on dualisms, we often employ the slash for conveying a unity of things which our culture sees as separate entities, like "mind/body" or "think/speak." We also sometimes utilize words not found in the dictionary, like "languaging," for which social therapeutics has formed a meaning. Rest easy that we will not write in gibberish, though we did consider it at times! On another language note, social therapeutics was developed in an era when anyone could practice as a therapist. Thus, early practitioners called themselves social therapists. To the extent there are quotes by Newman and Holzman included in this book that refer to social therapists, this is the reason.

While the focus of Part I (How Did We Get Here?) is conceptual, there are some practical elements incorporated. We include call-out boxes with examples of group and couples work. These are composites drawn from the many clients we have worked with over the years. We include comparison tables so that the abstract starts to take shape as a coaching practice. We also provide homework exercises at the end of each chapter, so that the experiential can begin immediately.

In Chapters 1 and 2 (A Brief History of Coaching, The Emergence of Social Therapeutics) we outline our perspective of coaching's history and its organic connection points with social therapeutics. Then we introduce social therapeutic founders Fred Newman and Lois Holzman, along with key concepts they developed, most especially by drawing on the work of 20th century developmental psychologist Lev Vygotsky and the tools of theater.

From there we make our case for shifting to seeing groups in Chapter 3 (Why Groups). This requires examining the myth of the individual and deconstructing the conceptual and philosophical tools bequeathed to us by the Enlightenment and modern science. It opens up a portal through which we can see who and how we are *in relation to others*. By co-creating environments, we can become both more of and other than who we are— we can grow and develop.

We carry questions of growth, emotions and emotionality into Chapter 4 (Seeing Emotional Growth as the Path to Transformation). This involves challenging certain assumptions, for example, that emotions live inside of us, that they are private and that we must manage them. We offer a refreshing understanding of emotional development and transformation. Here we layer in Newman and Holzman's deep appreciation for Ludwig Wittgenstein, one of the 20th century's greatest philosophers, and their fusion of both Wittgenstein's and Vygotsky's work. This unifies the elements of social therapeutics introduced previously and hopefully carries the reader towards appreciating it as a practice of method, rather than a method to be applied (onto people).

Parts II through IV (Coach as Social Therapeutic Group Leader, The Social Therapeutic Couples Coach, Applied Social Therapeutic Case Studies) move solidly into the practical. We begin with group work. In Chapter 5 (The Social Therapeutic Group Leader) we speak directly to the coach and suggest how they might begin leading groups. Through the lens of group-as-unit of growth, we offer recommendations of the kinds of things a coach might say in certain situations, what the performance of group leader can look like and what to be on the lookout for in the group.

We hope to offer helpful brushstrokes rather than formulaic prescriptions. In that spirit we offer multiple variations where possible. Chapter 6 (Group Coaching Nuts and Bolts) flips the camera onto the group-in-action and provides a nuts-and-bolts look at 12 group scenes based on a composite of the groups we lead. Within each nut and bolt we add our commentary of the scene, which usually directs back to a methodological point laid out in Part I.

From group work we follow the same pattern for couples coaching in Chapters 7 and 8 (Social Therapeutic Couples Coaching, Couples Coaching Nuts and Bolts). We begin by speaking directly to the coach on how to reframe couples work as a discovering of what the relationship needs. Next, we offer a dozen snapshots of couples sessions, again based on a composite of the couples we work with. These will feel different than the group examples, as in these cases the group is smaller. There is more obvious struggling with and challenging of societal roles. As mentioned above, the tools of theater lend themselves well to the drama of marriage, love and family. They will be more pronounced in this section than in the group section.

In Chapter 9 (Six Social Therapeutic Case Studies) we conclude the book with longer case studies of group work by other social therapeutic practitioners. These innovators are taking the method beyond the coach's chair, beyond rooms and Zooms, and beyond borders.

Writing this book, pouring out into words on paper what we have lived and practiced for decades, has been a deeply emotional process. It is our hope it can be read as a poem, as an invitation to go new places unknowingly, to make unexpected discoveries, to create previously inconceivable conversations with your clients and to venture into leading heterogeneous social therapeutic groups and couples work.

Our world is desperately seeking out new ways of being, feeling and doing in it. We give this social therapeutic roadmap to group-based emotional growth as an offer, a contribution, to our collective human journey.

Notes

1 Record numbers of people report feeling lonely. See Weissbourd et al. (2021, February 9, p. 4).

2 For the purposes of simplicity we will write to coaches, though we recognize that our readership will include therapists, social workers, counselors, HR professionals, team coaches and community-based leaders.

3 For more on social therapeutic's co-founders, see Chapters 2–4.

References

Abravanel, M. & Gavin, J. (2017). Exploring the evolution of coaching through the lens of innovation. *International Journal of Evidence Based Coaching and Mentoring*, 15(1), 24–41. https://www.researchgate.net/publication/317368184_Exploring_the_evolution_of_coaching_through_the_lens_of_innovation

Anderson, B. (Panelist) (2022, July 7). How Can We Serve Deeply in Times of Transition. *The 2022 Coaching Summit by Coaches Rising*. https://courses.coachesrising.com/courses/the-coaching-summit-2022/#teacher_136479

Edelman (2021). *2021 Edelman Trust Barometer: Global Report*. Retrieved January 15, 2022 from: https://www.edelman.com/sites/g/files/aatuss191/files/2021-03/2021%20Edelman%20Trust%20Barometer.pdf

Fromell, S. (2016, January 25). The Rising Popularity of Life Coaching. *Entrepreneur Middle East*. Retrieved July 25, 2022 from: https://www.entrepreneur.com/en-ae/growth-strategies/the-rising-popularity-of-life-coaching/269936

Holzman, L. & Mendez, R. (Eds.). (2003). *Psychological Investigations: A Clinician's Guide to Social Therapy*. Brunner-Routledge.

Ives, Y. & Cox, E. (2015). *Relationship Coaching: The theory and practice of coaching with singles couples and parents*. Routledge.

Lorde, A. (2007). The Master's Tools Will Never Dismantle the Master's House. 1984. *Sister Outsider: Essays and Speeches*. Ed. Berkeley, CA: Crossing Press. 110–114. Retrieved July 10, 2022 from: https://collectiveliberation.org/wp-content/uploads/2013/01/Lorde_The_Masters_Tools.pdf

Weissbourd, R., Batanova, M., Lovison, V., & Torres, E. (2021, February 9). Loneliness in America: How the Pandemic Has Deepened an Epidemic of Loneliness and What We Can Do About It. *Harvard Graduate School of Education & Making Caring Common Project*. Retrieved January 15, 2022 from: https://static1.squarespace.com/static/5b7c56e255b02c683659fe43/t/6021776bdd04957c4557c212/1612805995893/Loneliness+in+America+2021_02_08_FINAL.pdf

PART I
HOW DID WE GET HERE?

1

A BRIEF HISTORY OF COACHING

I have a vision that coaching will go around the world and change the way people communicate and interact forever.

Thomas Leonard, a founder of coaching (1995)[1]

If psychology was born to answer the question of why (for example, seeking answers from our past to explain the cause of our pain), coaching's mission is to ask the "how" questions while standing in the present and looking forward. This novel form of helping people burst into public view in the 1990s. By the end of that decade, coaching had established impressive industry infrastructure, including competing international professional associations, multiple coaching training programs and dozens of publications dedicated to advancing the field. More than 20 years later, coaching continues to evolve its innovative practice.

Social therapeutics, the subject of this book, holds a strong family resemblance to coaching and builds upon its core competencies—co-creation with the client, inclusion of the coach's subjective experiences, an aversion to fixing problems for the client and a focus on process rather than outcome. Coaching is grounded in "holding presence," that is, an in-the-moment presentness that requires the coach to improvise with the client. What social therapeutics adds is a method to support our human capacity for continuous life development and transformation, by way of

DOI: 10.4324/9781003326465-3

improvised and co-created *group* activity—hence the name Life Development Group for social therapeutic group work.

Both social therapeutics and coaching are part of a broad becoming-mainstream movement of approaches to mental health, wellness and community-building that are not reliant on cognition as the dominant form of help. These include meditation, somatics, yoga, mindfulness, performance activism, Buddhism and other Eastern spiritual practices and, most recently, psychedelic therapeutics. These practices all lean into the experiential and emergent. They offer different ways of relating to emotional pain. And they present challenges to some of the foundational dualisms of Western thought such as mind/body, inside/outside, brain/emotion and thought/language.

One way to understand the growing industry of coaching is as a search (on the part of both practitioners and clients) for new ways of living and growing in a rapidly changing world. Society is hungry for a new toolkit for addressing widespread languishing (a new term created during the pandemic (see Grant, 2021)), loneliness, despair and anxiety. There is widespread longing for community as well as searching for individual and collective meaning. These nonclinical conditions are affecting all of us.

One hundred forty years ago, one could have said that psychology was part of a broad becoming-mainstream movement tooled for the modern era of industrialization, colonization, public education, science and positivism. Among other things, psychology helped to both create and aid people in adapting to a culture of mass consumerism and the alienated individual.[2] In its quest to become a widely accepted practice, psychology positioned itself as a knowable, and later, quantifiable science, similar to those of the physical world such as biology and physics and to the medical sciences such as oncology, obstetrics and osteology. Today, psychology is so embedded into our culture and language that we hardly notice its presence. Consider how advertisers tap into our emotions, like humiliation and desire, in order to get us to buy their products. In everyday language, we consider it natural and normal to speak of changing our behavior, letting out a Freudian slip from our subconscious and demonstrating an understanding of our shadow self. Rarely do we consider that these concepts were invented by early psychologists B.F. Skinner, Sigmund Freud and Carl Jung.

But we are now living under very different conditions—both conceptual and material.

Over the last 35 years, dozens of psychologists have offered challenges to and critiques of traditional psychology in an effort to create a new one (de Shazer, 1982; Gergen, 1991; McNamee & Shawver, 2004; Newman, 1991; Newman & Holzman, 1996; Strong & Pare, 2004). Today, newer non-cognitive approaches like somatics, spirituality and therapeutic psychedelics are reaching a broader audience as they become more widely integrated into both psychotherapy and coaching. These possess an inherent radicalness by breaking away from the cognitive bias and measurement-focused paradigm of mainstream mental health.

Somatic psychologist Barnaby B. Barratt offers a contemporary critique of current psychology's rage to quantify in *The Emergence of Somatic and Bodymind Therapy*. He writes, "Evidence-based procedures cater to the agenda of adjusting individual behavior to fit the existing social order" (Barratt, 2013, p. 96). The challenge faced by traditional psychology is that the social order is disintegrating, so trying to adjust individuals to it is like grasping at straws. Yet it seems that the more uncertainty enters our lives, the more the establishment doubles down on its traditional institution and method.

In contrast, our task is to accept and adapt to the unknowability of our era *and* somehow keep innovating new ways of being, feeling and doing together—discovering new ways of producing our world that foster connection, inclusion, joy, community, wellness, fairness and growth.

Coaching was and remains an innovation, a remix of what came before combined with newly emergent, outside-the-box seeing, thinking, doing and feeling. It has rapidly grown into a global industry. This chapter provides our view on the roots and practice of coaching. Our interest is in pulling out the historical, cultural, conceptual and methodological threads that hold a family resemblance to social therapeutics.

Innovation Driven by Social Motion

Many have written on the history of coaching (Brock, 2009, 2014; see also Allaho & van Nieuwerburgh, 2018; Koopman et al., 2021; Wildflower, 2013). Its principal multidisciplinary influences are most often characterized as psychology, business (management, leadership, communications) and self-improvement. We were also delighted to discover a richness, a nuanced rebelliousness from coaching's early days that has not always surfaced in accounts of its history.

Coaching was born out of the remnants of the social, political and cultural movements of the 1960s and 70s. At that time, there were many diverse and creative attempts to build new forms of community—from Large Group Awareness Trainings (LGAT), communes, alternative communities, Be-Ins and massive antiwar and civil rights protests to new forms of theater which broke down the fourth wall and invited the audience to co-create the play with the actors (Friedman, 2021). Inherent in these movements was the belief in collectivity as having the power to accomplish something, to change the course of history. That era's appetite for mass-based social and political activities has markedly diminished in our times (with a few exceptions, such as the estimated 15–26 million Americans who protested the murder of George Floyd in 2020 (see Buchanan, Bui & Patel, 2020)). However, the counterculture, as it became known, birthed many forms of life that have carried well into our present day, such as the expansion of sexual expression, the eruption of new forms of music, the rise of vegetarianism and whole foods diets and experimentation with psychedelics.

As the counterculture was dying in the late 1970s and early 80s, a new era of self-discovery and self-help guides took center stage. The modern founding of the self-help industry occurred during the Great Depression with Dale Carnegie's 1936 classic *How to Win Friends and Influence People*. If his guide to confidently achieving financial success offered hope to millions of ordinary Americans living in despairing times, the *New York Times* bestseller *I'm OK—You're OK* (Harris, 1967) offered an idealized response, 36 years later, to the disillusionment many were feeling over their generation's failed efforts for social justice and change. Author and psychiatrist Thomas Harris directed readers to look to their social interactions, which he labeled transactions, and change their internal state in order to resolve personal issues. By taking responsibility for their life, a person could change it and experience freedom of choice. As the Vietnam War, racism and the threat of nuclear war with the Soviet Union raged on, many (former) hippies looked inward to find solace in discovering themselves as they began raising families and seeking the kinds of jobs that could support a suburban lifestyle. The political receded into the personal. This post-social motion cohort received its moniker—the "Me Generation"—and it was coming of age. It would fuel the rapid expansion of coaching.

Another genre of self-improvement established itself in 1974 by introducing the act of mental self-examination in athletics. *The Inner Game of Tennis: The Classic Guide to the Mental Side of Peak Performance* by W. Timothy Gallway became a bestseller as business professionals joined athletes in seeking out and sharpening their competitive edge. By looking inward into the mind, athletes could overcome obstacles to winning and professionals could work smarter to achieve individual and company success. In one fell swoop, Gallway laid the foundation for what we know today as sports psychology as well as executive and leadership coaching. Gallway went on to become an active and influential member in the circle of coaching's founders.

It is worth noting that in the 1960s and 70s, as people were protesting, experimenting with group work and innovating new ways to improve oneself, some took to challenging outright the institutions of psychology and psychiatry. For today's reader, it might be hard to imagine a mass societal, cultural and political protest of these powerful institutions. Yet critiques of mental illness—what it is, what causes it, who gets it, how it gets treated and the biases embedded in those treatment models—were widespread and widely read (Fanon, 1963; Foucault, 1965; Laing, 1965; Showalter, 1985; Szasz, 1974; Whitaker, 2010). There was open dialogue and concern over a profession whose object of study and practice rested on the pathologizing of human behavior.

Civil rights and early generation gay rights leaders helped carry those critiques into mainstream acceptance. In 1967, Dr. Martin Luther King Jr. admonished psychology's methods and its objective to help people better adapt to the world they lived in. At the American Psychological Association Annual Convention, King defiantly declared:

> There are some things in our society, some things in our world, to which we should never be adjusted . . . We must never adjust ourselves to racial discrimination and racial segregation. We must never adjust ourselves to religious bigotry. We must never adjust

ourselves to economic conditions that take necessities from the many to give luxuries to the few. We must never adjust ourselves to the madness of militarism, and the self-defeating effects of physical violence (King, 1968).

King's point was that psychologists had to take into account the world in which they practiced their profession. It was harmful to relate to patients as somehow living outside of the societal conditions that contribute to emotional pain. For the growing number of gay people who refused to stay in the closet and adapt to heterosexuality, a major fight was brewing with the American Psychiatric Association (APA), which pathologized homosexuality as an illness. After a prolonged and publicized protest campaign the APA finally removed the diagnosis from its Diagnostic and Statistical Manual of Mental Disorders (DSM) in 1973.

While this was happening, diverse groupings of lay people and professionals were busy establishing alternative psychologies that turned away from adjustment and toward empowerment. Some sought to modify the white, male Eurocentric focus of psychology. They created Black, feminist and gay therapies. Others sought to humanize psychology into a more positive and growth-oriented practice, such as humanist psychology and the Human Potential Movement (HPM). It was these latter innovations and their offspring that most attracted the attention of coaching's founders; over time, it has been those psychologies that have most embedded themselves in coaching.

Coaching's Founders

In 1971 in San Francisco, Werner Erhard began weaving together strands of humanistic psychology with elements of 1960s Zen Buddhist counterculture and American pragmatic individualism in order to create life-transforming workshops. They were designed to help people resolve interpersonal conflicts and emotional pain through in-the-moment personal responsibility, accountability, transformation and possibility. These workshops came to be known as *est* (see Wikipedia, n.d.). They typically numbered up to 250 participants and lasted four days.

Implemented as a group experiential process, *est* had more in common with the Be-Ins and Happenings of the 1960s than with the interpretation of one's dreams, analysis of one's childhood or diagnosis provided by a psychiatrist. A typical Erhardt declaration such as, "It is what it is, we are where we are" was not so much theory as it was a philosophical and spiritual claim challenging how traditional psychology operated. He was creating a sustainable model for emotional help focusing on the present and future, rather than the past—a radical acceptance of who we are, rather than an endless search for causes and explanations of our problems. Importantly, *est* sessions seemed to help people over a course of only a few weekends, rather than the years of weekly appointments it took to find relief with a psychotherapist. And they were popular, with an estimated 700,000 participants by 1984 (see Snider, 2003).

There were two key client bases with whom Erhard advanced his work: White middle-class countercultural types (many of whom were soon to or had already entered into mainstream white-collar careers) and incarcerated men—many of whom were poor and working-class African Americans. In the 1970s, *est* held government contracts with at least 23 corrections departments (see Tanji, 1979). This combination of clients— who sometimes came together for trainings held inside of corrections facilities[3]—along with the experiential and group-based nature of the workshops, made for controversy. So too did some of the ways in which Erhard worked.[4]

The two people who are generally credited for the birth of coaching, Thomas Leonard and Laura Whitworth, worked directly for Erhard's Bay Area companies in the 1980s. They adapted, pragmatized and expanded Erhard's work—sometimes working as partners, sometimes as adversaries disagreeing on points of practice. Together, Leonard and Whitworth popularized a new form of helping people to the extent that both life and executive coaching were making major media headlines by the mid-1990s (Newsweek Staff, 1996; Waldroop & Butler, 1996).

Thomas Leonard started out his career as a financial planner and became someone who helped people plan their whole lives. This activity became known as coaching. To distinguish his practice from sports coaching or mentoring, Leonard clarified, "We are not selling coaching services; we're selling a partnership in someone's life" (Newsweek Staff, 1996). His goal-oriented Laws of Attraction were designed to inspire individuals to do things that would bring them success and fulfillment in their career, life and relationships. Leonard went on to co-found key coaching organizations and training programs for coaches. His bestseller, *The Portable Coach* (today sold under the title *The 28 Laws of Attraction: Stop Chasing Success and Let it Chase You)*, hit bookstores in 1998. Leonard tragically passed away at a young age. He left a profound imprint on the groundbreaking coaching businesses and institutions he had helped to build and which continue to this day. His legacy is felt by the people whose lives have been transformed by knowing and working with him.

Laura Whitworth was an adventurer as a young woman, having lived in both Alaska and Nepal by her early 20s. She then pursued an MBA and started a lucrative career as a CPA only to drop out after a few years. During that time, she was introduced to Tim Gallway (author of the *Inner Game of Tennis)*, who later became her coach.

While living in the Bay Area, Whitworth participated in *est* workshops and was hired by Leonard into Erhard's accounting department. Not long afterwards, Whitworth began her own coaching business and recruited Henry Kimsey-House as a client and, later, a collaborator. By the early 1990s, the two of them, along with Henry's wife Karen, had created their coaching approach. Now in its sixth edition, their classic guide *Co-Active Coaching* was originally published in 1998 (Kimsey-House et. al, 2018).

Significantly for our story, both Henry and Karen Kimsey-House came from theater backgrounds. A through-line from their training in theater and Meisner acting techniques is evident in their contributions to the founding principles of coaching. For example, when a client expresses emotion, the authors of *Co-Active Coaching* advise the coach that "the cause itself is not important; accepting the feeling is important" (2018, p. 173). Similarly, an actor accepts and responds to their scene partner's performance. A director's eye orients toward how the scene unfolds, rather than its end point. Likewise, the International Coaching Federation[5] (ICF) defines an advanced coach as one who "trusts that value is inherent in the process" (2017, p. 4).

Whitworth, Kimsey-House, et al. again turn to the tools of theater when it comes to the crucial skill set of listening. They compare it to a live performance in which the actor is able to read the room and "adjust their behavior accordingly" (Kimsey-House et. al., 2018, p. 46). A high-level coach embodies an awareness of the other and the ability to improvise.

Being present in the moment, embracing the emotional impact of actors on each other as well as directing the collective creativity involved in making a theatrical production—these activities all have connections with the practice of coaching. In other words, the coach's role is to stay in the scene with their scene partner, wherever it goes. The coach is invited to include themselves, as appropriate to the scene, by giving their emotional responses, wonderings, thoughts, discoveries and personal history, and to do so without holding onto what they have given. (In social therapeutic coaching, the coach also takes on the lens of the director. For more, see Parts II and III.)

The entire industry agrees that coaching is a co-created "spontaneous relationship" in which the client is a full partner (ICF, 2017, pp. 3–4). It allows for the "space of vulnerability and focus on what's important RIGHT NOW [emphasis in original]" (Britton, 2022, p. 24). The International Association of Coaching (IAC) recognizes this partnership as "creating an environment that allows ideas, options and opportunities to emerge" (2022). Thus, in coaching the client actively participates in and takes responsibility for building the emotional/relational space within which coach and client are working. Like the fourth wall that got broken down in experimental theater in the 1960s (removing the barrier between performer and audience), the hard wall separating psychotherapist from patient was sent crumbling in the late 20th century by the celebration of co-creation in coaching.

The early coaches expanded out from the Bay Area, passing through and near to the paths, channels and relationships already formed by Werner Erhard. Similar to *est*, the pioneering coaches took their new approach to two primary places—the prisons, which at that time remained open to testing more humane and humanistic approaches to human development,[6] and to the corporate sector where, if coaching could successfully prove its impact, there would be plentiful funding.

How Coaching and Business Became Partners

After decades of post-World War II dominance, US industrial manufacturing companies started to face serious competition from the restored European and Japanese economies and the emerging Asian economies. At the same time, technological advances were driving new, more efficient modes of production. American management consultants began advising companies on how to implement these new technologies and enforce the subsequent operational efficiencies and resulting reductions in a company's workforce. The days of Americans living out their careers at one or two companies were ending (Reich, 1998).

Postwar hierarchical, command-chain forms of corporate leadership and organizational structure no longer matched conditions in the marketplace. Beginning in the late 1970s, executives faced the daunting challenge of learning new leadership skills in support of new business goals in a rapidly changing economic and production environment. They needed to do something they did not yet know how to do—learn new ways to communicate with and inspire employees as well as design new ways for employees to work collaboratively and nonhierarchically.

In this period, *est* was running its weekend intensive seminars in hotels. Participants included business professionals, though the seminars' focus was not necessarily on work performance. *est* did in fact procure some corporate contracts in those years, but it was the onsite one-to-one coaching model, engineered to produce more flexible and communicative leaders, that was best positioned to fill this growing corporate need.

One bestselling book of the era succinctly articulated this cultural shift in management style—Spencer Johnson and Ken Blanchard's *Who Moved my Cheese?* (1998). It addressed the subjective—emotional, personal—experience of change in the workplace by showing managers how to lead change and employees how to embrace it. The story was told simply through the perspective of two mice and two humans working through a maze to find (or not to find) cheese. By 2017, over 28 million copies had been sold.

The growing symbiotic relationship between executive coaching—whose origins were fueled in part by the countercultural movement—and the business world is illustrated by the partnership of the book's author and its chief collaborator. Spencer Johnson was a 1970s dropout physician with a psychology degree who started writing inspirational children's books. Ken Blanchard was a management consultant.

Ever pragmatic, entrepreneurial and competitive, the business community invested wholeheartedly in this emerging experiential product called coaching. Companies began to hire both external and internal coaches to help drive the business outcomes they sought.

What did they buy? They bought coaching's forward-looking, goal-oriented focus—something that traditional psychology, with its more rigid structure and commitment to uncovering and fixing someone's past-driven dysfunctions, was structurally unable to address. In addition, they also accessed a form of help that was free of social stigma, unlike psychotherapy. While executive and leadership coaching has evolved over the last 25 or so years, one thing has remained constant: Its vision of establishing a non-pathologized approach for getting help and improving oneself.

Table 1.1 Key differences between coaching and traditional therapy

	Coaching	Traditional Psychotherapy
Question type	How	Why
Unit of focus	Individual	Individual
Mode of understanding	Experience-based	Analytical
Methodology	Embraces subjectivity in its process, does not claim science, relies in part on psychology—mostly deriving from humanist psychology	Claims science, applies methods, measures, embraces objectivity
Role of coach/therapist	Co-create with client, inquiry towards discovery, cultivate the emergent and possibilities, check in regularly on progress toward a goal	Authority, expertise, knowing, diagnosis, relieving symptoms
Relating to the client	Client wants help making a decision/life change or achieving a goal, client has inherent intelligence	Client has an internal dysfunctional pattern or cognitive distortion that needs to be uncovered and understood, then changed through insight
Understanding of the problem	The problem is internal. It is non-clinical. The client can improve	The problem is internal, stemming from the past which causes a diagnosable pathology. The client can be cured
Activity of the coach/therapist	Questioning to identify a goal and achieve it	Questioning to clinically diagnose, to understand, to develop an insight

Coaching 2.0

So far in this chapter we have highlighted some of the historical and cultural drivers of the birth of coaching as well as the business drivers for redesigning how companies work and engage their employees. We have also articulated ways in which coaching, from its beginning, has distinguished itself from psychology as more experiential and future-focused, with little concern for proving itself as a science and even less concern with pathology.

Today the influence and impact of coaching is so widespread that it now influences psychology. The International Society for Coaching Psychology (ISCP) formed in 2008. It affiliates with the American Psychological Association and focuses on "enhancing well-being and performance in personal life and work" (ISCP, 2022). Psychologists now incorporate coaching principles into their practices.

While coaching freely borrows from psychology—especially the recently established descendants of the Human Potential Movement, such as positive and gestalt therapy—it is not overdetermined by it. According to researchers Michael Abravanel and James Gavin, coaching is a rapidly evolving field open to innovation in method as well as technique: "Coaching pushes the limits of eclecticism further than psychotherapy and counseling by embracing a wide range of disciplines far beyond the bounds of psychology, psychiatry and social work" (2017, p. 35). Somatics, religion and spiritualism, theater arts and Native American and Indigenous worldviews are just some of the other disciplines tapped by coaches today. And, as we have already seen, business communications, leadership and self-improvement techniques have been integral to coaching from its beginning.

Elaine Cox, a leading coaching researcher, author and founding editor of the *International Journal of Evidence Based Coaching and Mentoring*, is an advocate of the industry remaining free of rigid orthodoxy. She writes that coaching, "overrides a top-down, single school approach . . . [With its] pragmatic, empirical position . . . [coaching] takes the emphasis away from the individual as having some core inner 'truth' and extends . . . outwards towards a more comprehensive, socially constructed theoretical playing ground" (Cox, 2013, p. 2). Here, Cox articulates a democratization of theory and practice that makes coaching accessible to a broad range of practitioners.

Indeed, coaching is recognized as one of the most rapidly expanding industries globally, with expected year over year growth of 6.7% from 2019 to 2022. The estimated global revenue in 2019 was $2.849 billion US dollars,[7] a 21% increase over 2015 (ICF, 2020, p. 12). This demand for coaching signals that a cultural shift is already underway in how people are choosing to address their professional and personal well-being. With more practitioners comes a deeper influence into mass culture and the broader population. It has always been the goal of coaching to transform how we communicate.

Life coaching developed simultaneously with executive and leadership coaching. For example, Thomas expanded financial planning to helping clients achieve the quality of life they sought (satisfying relationships, leisure activities, etc.), a form of "life advice." Life coaching has grown exponentially in this most recent decade. Noomii USA, a professional coach directory, lists nine specialties outside of business coaching, with the combined number of life, family, Christian and relationship coaches greater than that of business coaches.[8] There are now numerous certified specialized life coaching training programs.

As the pressures in everyday life have increased, employees are taking their life issues into work. Today's managers also have to respond to obstacles to professional performance that derive from people's destabilized day-to-day lives. And as they do, the line between executive and life coaching, team and group coaching continues to fade. This is another factor driving interest in many additional areas of coaching.

Meanwhile, the industrywide growth has reinvigorated a debate within academic and coaching circles on whether coaching should become a licensed profession like psychotherapy, social work and counseling, all of which are regulated by government entities in the United States. Lane, Stelter and Stout-Rostron explored the case for licensure and concluded that the coaching industry, while producing self-organized associations and credentialing programs, does not meet the conditions for a formal, regulated and institutionalized structure. Those conditions include having a defined theory of coaching or offering specific career paths as well as uniform training or formalized education programs (Lane, Stelter & Stout-Rostron, 2014, p. 379). The authors conclude that the world is changing too rapidly for coaching to aim to become a licensed profession.

Furthermore, with the decrease of public trust in institutions and professions, it might be better to stay away from formalizing the industry.

The question of professionalization appears driven more by those situated in executive and leadership coaching who have a competitive interest in guarding access to the very lucrative corporate space. And, we imagine, there could perhaps be a rebellious disinterest in professionalization coming from those innovators who are expanding coaching's practice and methodology. It is worth noting that coaching co-founder Leonard Thomas was a "strong believer in giving things away, and was continuously searching for ways to make coaching accessible to the general population" (Dueease, 2009, p. 2).

The potential for coaching to continue to evolve and help move the world forward in this moment is exciting and hopeful—and we see an openness in the industry for further transformation. Indeed, some leaders in coaching are advocating for a Coaching 2.0.

The Dublin Declaration on Coaching identifies the need for the global coaching community to "respond to a world beset by challenges with no predetermined answers by using coaching to create a space wherein new solutions can emerge" (2008, p. 4). This appeal invokes innovative activity while also looking out into the world, a sentiment that rings close to the statement by Martin Luther King Jr. referenced earlier in this chapter.

There is a self-awareness within coaching that it has the potential to address issues specific to this moment in human history. Author and pioneer in the field of leadership development and research Bob Anderson spoke on the panel *How Can We Serve Deeply in Times of Transition* at The 2022 Coaching Summit and remarked that we need to "literally reinvent the future . . . to righten society altogether, from the ground up . . . Nobody knows how to do that. It's way beyond what any of us know how to do. It's un-figure-outable rationally. But that doesn't mean we can't . . . sit in the unknown" (min: 25:41–27:20).

Hetty Einzig, a leadership coach and author, entreated the profession in her book *The Future of Coaching: Vision, Leadership and Responsibility in a Transforming World:*

> We are seeing a new kind of coaching emerge: engaged, compassionate . . . in favour of committed partnerships . . . [in which]

coaches move from their common perception as technical help-mates to full partners—contributing their knowledge, experience, the fruits of their spiritual quests and reflexive skills, but also their vulnerability and their not-knowing to the new kind of leadership needed in a world too complex for leaders to stand alone (2017, p. 2).

Here Einzig offers a picture of the evolution of coaching from compartmentalized to holistic, in which the coach can include all of who they are with the client. And they do so in a world that has become too complex not only for leaders but also for everyone. It is no longer healthy (if indeed it ever was) for anyone to stand alone.

Thus, we of the 21st century are called up to seek answers to new kinds of questions, thrust upon us by the great uncertainty, unknowability and instability of our times. How can we embrace the unknown, as Anderson and Einzig invite us to do, allow space for the emergent to become visible and then incubate it? How do we create new forms of life together? What can we build together to stave off possible species and planetary destruction?

While these big questions are most often posited as "we" questions, upon close inspection, nearly all society's current responses—including coaching's—offer "me" models.

Moving beyond the "Me" Model

The nearly impenetrable working assumption of our society is that the individual is the unit of change, transformation and growth.[9] We are all so used to seeing the world through the "I" lens that we hardly consider the way that lens tightly frames how we see, feel, do and react to everyone and everything going on around us. It is time to take very seriously the fact that the societal construction of individuality is severely limiting our capacity to transform our circumstances—in the world, our families, our communities and our workplaces.

This brings us to a contemporary point of methodological contention with coaching. As it entered the mainstream, coaching understandably leaned into the one-to-one threads of its multidisciplinary origins—psychotherapy with its *individual* bias, *self*-help, *personal* responsibility, the intense *individuated* culture of competition in business and the *inner* mental workings of an athlete playing an individual sport (tennis). Even in most group and team coaching today, the individual still gets evaluated and measured against goals and objectives.

For all the ways that coaching has innovated and expanded, for all its flexibility and pragmatism, there is a factor in the origin story, in the radical roots of coaching, which has been abandoned and with which we encourage reconnecting: The power of group work. Wildflower reminds us in the *Hidden History of Coaching* that the countercultural workshops which influenced Werner Erhard and his followers made visible how people were handling the group experience. Erhard "began exploring what was happening inside the group; how people reacted; what issues got raised" (Wildflower, 2013, p. 14). Erhard demanded seminar participants take responsibility for their lives. In some alternate universe, perhaps that could have been extended to participants taking responsibility for the creation of the group experience. That is where social therapeutics begins.

With its group-as-the-unit method, social therapeutics can make a valuable contribution to coaching. It offers an accessible and practicable method (per Cox's appeal to coaching's pragmatism) for addressing the "we" questions. It invites coach and clients to *create with* the unknown together and therefore radically embraces and builds with the "un-figure-outable" as Anderson poignantly puts it. And, as we shall see, the more participants create and build the group, the more they grow—as a group and individually.

There were many self-organized groupings of people coming out of the 1960s that sought to create, incubate and then evolve new ways for humanity to live together in community. Social therapeutics is one of them and we are honored to share it with you.

Exercises

Exercises are designed to invite a non-cognitive, integrated playing with and responding to the content of each chapter.

1) What are your reactions and responses to our story of coaching? Were you provoked, surprised, bored? What are you left wondering about?

(*Developmental option*) Write a poem out of your response. Make up a song and sing it to your colleagues, or at dinner with your family—or send it to us to post on our book's website, www.socialtherapeuticcoaching.com.

2) Spend a day noticing the "we" questions you and others ask and whether the answers are "me" or "we" oriented. What is it like to be noticing these questions and answers?

3) When someone asks you a question, try responding with, "I don't know. How can we create the answer together?"

Notes

1 As told to Sandy Vilas, co-founder of the International Coaching Federation (personal communication).
2 We challenge the model of the individuated, isolated self in Chapter 3.
3 For a description of an *est* training at San Quentin State Prison see Woodard (1978).
4 *est* was enough of a success that it became threatening to authorities who did not like multiracial, cross-class groupings of Americans coming together doing something other than traditional psychology. They attacked *est* as a cult in an attempt to dismantle it, opportunizing off of Erhardt's excesses and eccentricities to make the claim stick. Ultimately Erhard stepped away from the business and it was retooled and rebranded into Landmark, which remains successful today. See Wakefield (1994).
5 Perhaps the largest and most influential association of coaches (https://coaching-federation.org). As of 2019, ICF estimated 71,000 coaches worldwide, with 33,000 having received credentialling from ICF (2020, p.7). As of 2021, the number of ICF credentialled coaches grew to 41,849 (2021, p. 5).
6 Whitworth continued to develop coaching programs for correctional facilities up until her death in 2007. See Brock (2009).
7 Executive and leadership coaching—both internal and external—make up the lion's share of the market's financial rewards.
8 6320 life, relationship, family and Christian coaches v. 4278 business, executive, leadership and entrepreneur coaches. See Noomii: The Professional Coach Directory. Retrieved October 13, 2022 from: https://www.noomii.com/family-coach-united_states
9 We will challenge the model of the individuated, isolated self in Chapter 3.

References

Abravanel, M. & Gavin, J. (2017). Exploring the evolution of coaching through the lens of innovation. *International Journal of Evidence Based Coaching and Mentoring,* 15(1), 24–41. https://www.researchgate.net/publication/317368184_Exploring_the_evolution_of_coaching_through_the_lens_of_innovation

Allaho, R. & van Nieuwerburgh, C. (2018). *Coaching in Islamic Culture: The Principles and Practice of Ershad.* Routledge.

Anderson, B. (Panelist) (2022, July 7). How Can We Serve Deeply in Times of Transition. *The 2022 Coaching Summit by Coaches Rising.* https://courses.coachesrising.com/courses/the-coaching-summit-2022/#teacher_136479

Barratt, B.B. (2013). *The Emergence of Somatic and Bodymind Therapy*. Palgrave Mac-Millan.

Britton, J. (2022). Reinventing the Business of Coaching. *Choice: The Magazine of Professional Coaching*, 20(1).

Brock, V. (2009). Coaching Pioneers: Laura Whitworth and Thomas Leonard. *The International Journal of Coaching in Organizations*, 7(1), 54–65. https://researchportal.coachfederation.org/Document/Pdf/abstract_2966

Brock, V. (2014). *Sourcebook of Coaching History*. https://libraryofprofessionalcoaching.com/wp-app/wp-content/uploads/2022/01/SOCH-2nd-Edition-Free-2021-01-31-Secure-1.pdf

Buchanan, L., Bui, Q. & Patel, J. (2020, July 3). Black Lives Matter May be the Largest Movement in U.S. History. *New York Times*. Retrieved from: https://www.nytimes.com/interactive/2020/07/03/us/george-floyd-protests-crowd-size.html

Carnegie, D. (1936). *How to Win Friends and Influence People*. Gallery Books.

Cockerham, G. (2011). *Group Coaching: A Comprehensive Blueprint*. iUniverse.

Cox, E. (2013). *Coaching Understood: A Pragmatic Inquiry into the Coaching Process*. Sage.

de Shazer, S. (1982). *Patterns of Brief Family Therapy: An Ecosystemic Approach*. The Guilford Press.

The Dublin Declaration of Coaching. (2008). Global Coaching Community. V. 1.4 FINAL. https://www.pdf.net/assets/uploads/DublinDeclarationandAppendicesFINAL English.pdf

Dueease, B. (2009, February 3). Increase the Power of Coaching by Understanding its History. *Peer Bulletin*, 173.

Einzig, H. (2017). *The Future of Coaching with Next Generation Coaching: Vision, Leadership and Responsibility in a Transforming World*. Routledge.

Fanon, F. (1963). *The Wretched of the Earth*. Grove Press.

Foucault, M. (1965). *Madness and Civilization*. Pantheon Books.

Friedman, D. (2021). *Performance Activism: Precursors and Contemporary Pioneers*. Palgrave Macmillan.

Gallway, T. W. (1974). *The Inner Game of Tennis: The Classic Guide to the Mental Side of Peak Performance*. Random House.

Gergen, K. (1991). *The Saturated Self: Dilemma of Identity in Contemporary Life*. Basic Books.

Grant, A. (2021, April 21). There's a Name for the Blah You're Feeling: It's Called Languishing. *The New York Times*. https://www.nytimes.com/2021/04/19/well/mind/covid-mental-health-languishing.html

Harris, T. A. (1967). *I'm OK—You're OK*. Harper & Row.

International Association of Coaching. (2022). *The Coaching Masteries*. Inviting Possibility section. Retrieved March 2022 from: https://certifiedcoach.org/certification-and-development/coaching-masteries/

International Coaching Federation. (2017). *ICF Core Competencies Rating Levels*. Retrieved March 2022 from: https://coachingfederation.org/app/uploads/2017/12/ICF_Competencies_Level_Table_wNote.pdf

International Coaching Federation. (2020). *2020 ICF Global Coaching Study Executive Summary*. Retrieved March 2022 from: https://coachingfederation.org/app/uploads/2020/09/FINAL_ICF_GCS2020_ExecutiveSummary.pdf

International Coaching Federation. (2021). *Annual Report*. https://coachingfederation.org/app/uploads/2022/07/ICF_2021_AnnualReport.pdf

International Society for Coaching Psychology. (2022). *What is Coaching Psychology*. Retrieved August 21, 2022 from: https://www.isfcp.info/what-is-coaching-psychology/

Johnson, S. & Blanchard, K. (1998). *Who Moved My Cheese? An A-Mazing Way to Deal with Change in Your Work and in Your Life*. G.P. Putnam's Sons.

Kimsey-House H., Kimsey-House, K., Sandahl, P. & Whitworth, L. (2018). *Co-Active Coaching: The Proven Framework for Transformative Conversations at Work and in Life*. Nicholas Brealey Publishing.

King Jr., M.L. (1968). The Role of the Behavioral Scientist in the Civil Rights Movement. *Journal of Social Issues*, 24(1). https://doi.org/10.1111/j.1540-4560.1968.tb01465.x

Koopman, R., Englis, P. D., Ehrenhard, M. L. & Groen, A. (2021). The Chronological Development of Coaching and Mentoring: Side by Side Disciplines. *International Journal of Evidence Based Coaching and Mentoring*, 19(1), 137–151. https://doi.org/10.24384/3w69-k922

Laing, R.D. (1965). *The Divided Self: An Existential Study in Sanity and Madness*. Penguin Books.

Lane, D., Stelter, R. & Stout-Rostron, S. (2014). The Future of Coaching as a Profession. In E. Cox, T. Bachkirova & D. Clutterbuck (Eds.), *The Complete Handbook of Coaching* (pp. 377–390). Sage.

Leonard, T.J. (1998). *The 28 Laws of Attraction: Stop Chasing Success and Let it Chase You*. Scribner.

McNamee, S. & Shawver, L. (2004). Therapy as social construction: Back to basics and forward towards challenging issues. In T. Strong & D. Pare (Eds.), *Furthering Talk: Advances in the Discursive Therapies* (pp. 253–270). Kluwer Academic/Plenum. https://doi.org/10.1007/978-1-4419-8975-8

Newman, F. (1991). *The Myth of Psychology*. Castillo International.

Newman, F. & Holzman, L. (1996). *Unscientific Psychology: A Cultural-Performatory Approach to Understanding Human Life*. Praeger.

Newsweek Staff. (1996, February 4). Need a Life? Get a Coach. *Newsweek*. https://www.newsweek.com/need-life-get-coach-179824

Reich, R.B. (1998). *Locked in the Cabinet*. Vintage Books.

Showalter, E. (1985). *The Female Malady: Women, Madness, and English Culture, 1830–1980*. Penguin Books.

Snider, S. (2003, May). est, Werner Erhard, and the Corporatization of Self-Help. *The Believer*. Archived from the original on August 6, 2007. Retrieved August 2, 2022 from: https://web.archive.org/web/20070806045536/http://www.believermag.com/issues/200305/?read=article_snider

Strong, T. & Pare, D. (Eds.). (2004). *Furthering Talk: Advances in the Discursive Therapies*. Kluwer Academic/Plenum. https://doi.org/10.1007/978-1-4419-8975-8

Szasz, T. (1974). *The Myth of Mental Illness: Foundations of a Theory of Personal Conduct*. Harper.

Tanji, J.H. (1979). *Erhard Seminars Training (EST) in Correctional Settings – A Review*. University of Hawaii. https://www.ojp.gov/ncjrs/virtual-library/abstracts/erhard-seminars-training-est-correctional-settings-review

Wakefield, D. (1994). Erhard's Life After Est. *Common Boundary*. Retrieved June 17, 2022 from: https://web.archive.org/web/20100512010211/http://www.wernererhard.com/boundary.html

Waldroop, J. & Butler, T. (1996, October 31). The Executive as Coach. *Harvard Business Review*.

Whitaker, R. (2010). *Anatomy of an Epidemic: Magic Bullets, Psychiatric Drugs, and the Astonishing Rise of Mental Illness in America*. Crown Publishers.

Wikipedia. (n.d.) *Erhard Seminars Training*. Retrieved April 12, 2022 from: https://en.wikipedia.org/wiki/Erhard_Seminars_Training

Wildflower, L. (2013). *The Hidden History of Coaching*. Open University Press/McGraw-Hill.

Woodard, M. (1978). The est Training in the Prisons: A Basis for the Transformation of Corrections? *University of Baltimore Law Forum*, 9(2), Article 2. http://scholarworks.law.ubalt.edu/lf/vol9/iss2/2

2

THE EMERGENCE OF SOCIAL THERAPEUTICS

> We should stop relating to people as sick, I think we have to do this in a positive way by creating a whole new understanding, a whole new methodology. We have to fundamentally transform psychology, transform therapy, to a way of life, a positive way in which human beings can help each other to grow and develop.
>
> Fred Newman, founder social therapeutics (1998)

Social therapeutics introduces a method to see and create with *collective* human activity, relationality and emotional development. The rest of Part I is an attempt to deconstruct what we mean by those three terms, and to take what is a seamless experiential process and shine a light on its parts so that the reader can put social therapeutics to work in their practice.

The social therapeutic approach relates to humans as environment builders, able to create the conditions for their own growth. Social therapeutic coaches empower clients to see themselves as active creators of their lives, their communities and our world. As *group* environment builders, it becomes possible for people to co-create challenges to notions our society clings to as central to who we are: For example, our separate and fixed individuality and our insistence that we can and must know what is really going on. On their best days, social therapeutic Life Development Groups create an emotional, energetic and improvisational space

DOI: 10.4324/9781003326465-4   33 out of which new forms of life can emerge—new kinds of conversations, new emotions, new ways of relating and new growth.

By embracing its capacity to create conditions that straddle/play with both societal assumptions *and* the borderland of the emergent, social therapeutics can offer direction to one of the conundrums of coaching. Vicki Brock, an early coaching practitioner herself, exhaustively documents the birth and evolution of the discipline in *Sourcebook of Coaching History*. She identifies one of the industry's professional challenges to be that "unlike its root disciplines, coaching lacks a fixed starting point and consistent core principles and theories that can be applied to all specialties within coaching practice" (Brock, 2014, p. 426).

As we outlined in the previous chapter, coaching was born on "not solid" (read: unmeasurable, unsystematized) multidisciplinary ground. That has been one of its strengths. In this sense, social therapeutics offers the industry a way to help make the "problem" Brock identifies disappear. Social therapeutics does not require a consistent core. It employs a new ontology—that is, a new way of seeing, doing, conversing, relating to and being in the world. It is a continuous practice of method, rather than a fixed solution. And while "therapeutics" is part of its name, this approach sits much closer to principles of coaching.

Family Resemblances between Social Therapeutics and Coaching

Coaching and social therapeutics share origins in the social, political and cultural movements of the 1960s and 70s. In these years, Americans came together to build collective attempts to transform the country: To end institutional racism, militaristic expansion, the threat of nuclear war; to expand rights for African Americans, women, LGBTQ+ folks and Native Americans; to revolutionize sexual expression, create new forms of community and liberate Puerto Rico.

In this environment of mass social motion, it would seem almost natural that both approaches emerged and advanced their practices while working in a group format (*est* seminars and social therapeutic groups). From the point of view of the psychotherapy establishment however, the birth of both coaching and social therapeutics was unauthorized and radical. Both grew out of experimentation by unlicensed practitioners operating outside of academic or scientific institutions.

More bottom-up than top-down, freed from having to rely on government funding or filing philanthropic reports to justify activities, both coaching and social therapeutics resided in the borderlands of existing ideas, untested theses, unstructured syntheses and market demand. As esteemed social constructionist and psychologist Ken Gergen noted of social therapeutics: "Truly creative work in any discipline takes place at the borders" where practitioners can "risk innovation" (1999, p. 1). Or, as coaches and coaching researchers O'Connor and Lages postulate, "The edge of chaos is not a bad place to be; it is continually creative" (2007, p. 5). It is from the outliers that big visions manifest.

In fact, coaching and social therapeutics both held ambitious globe-changing goals from their outset. Coaching founder Thomas Leonard had a vision for coaching to "go around the world and change the way people communicate and interact forever" (Cockerham, 2011, p. xi). For social therapeutics founders Fred Newman and Lois Holzman, the work is to usher in a culturally transformative conceptual revolution of the same magnitude as the scientific revolution—to go around the world and change how people *do, create and build together.*

Both social therapeutics and coaching see and relate to the client as a whole person who embodies the potential to grow and change throughout one's lifetime. Coaching derived this understanding from the Human Potential Movement (HPM). A precursor to today's positive psychology, the HPM was critical of reducing a person to their childhood experiences, or any one particular experience for that matter. It challenged traditional psychology's focus on "what's wrong" with someone. Psychologists Abraham Maslow, Carl Rogers and Rollo May each identified different processes of growth (a topic we discuss further in Chapter 4). Each created their own roadmap of sorts to help individuals become more open to new experiences, existential awareness, broader choice making, constructive behavior and creativity.

Social therapeutics is derived from some of the most radical thinkers in their fields—Karl Marx, Ludwig Wittgenstein and Lev Vygotsky (the latter two will be discussed later). Throughout the 20th century, hundreds of millions of ordinary people, movement leaders and social change organizations looked to Marx for guidance. Most drew upon Marxist ideas on economics, alienation and class struggle. However, Newman and

Holzman focused on Marx's often overlooked postulations on "all-round" human development. In this passage from Marx and Engels' methodological work *The German Ideology*, they wrote:

> We have further shown that private property can be abolished only on condition of an all-round development of individuals, because the existing character of intercourse and productive forces is an all-round one, and only individuals that are developing in an all-round fashion can appropriate them, i.e., can turn them into free manifestations of their lives (1991, p. 117).

Today we might characterize developing in an "all-round" fashion to be mind/body/spirit transformation and "abolishing private property" to be challenging the market forces of globalization and the environmental, social, political and emotional distress it fuels. Marx's point was that, in order to make a new world we would need to develop as a species, to grow in a holistic fashion.

In that spirit of embodied, holistic growth, social therapeutics and coaching also embrace the whole practitioner. Both permit—and indeed, invite—the coach's subjectivity (i.e., the coach's responses, feelings, worldview, perceptions, opinions) into their work with clients. The International Coaching Federation (ICF) core competencies state that "The coach easily and freely shares what is so for the coach without attachment" and "is willing to be vulnerable with the client" (2017, pp. 7, 3). This implies that the coach can give what is going on for them in the moment, as part of co-creating the coaching container, without a need to be right or speak a singular Truth. Newman and Holzman raised methodological alarms over psychology's insistence—in the name of science—on objectivity in clinical work and research.

Social therapeutics and coaching both arrived at their visions and practices of systemic change by drawing pragmatically on multiple disciplines. Importantly for our purposes, both draw upon fields as diverse as theater and the philosophy of language, while insights from those fields impacted each practice in differing ways. Some of the other influences on coaching were outlined in the previous chapter. We are turning now to the influences and discoveries that led to the emergence of social therapeutics. First, we would like to introduce social therapeutics' founders Fred Newman and Lois Holzman and its early history.

Newman and Holzman and Building Community

Fred Newman created social therapy in the 1970s in New York City. With a PhD in the Philosophy of Science from Stanford University, Newman's desire to innovate an approach to emotional well-being grew out of his curiosity of this paradox: As a philosopher he took much joy in critiquing the method of psychology, and yet, when he went into talk therapy himself, he found it helpful and even curative. What was going on in the process of talking to another human being that produced relief from emotional pain? Was it possible to create that outcome without relying on an objective, all-knowing authority figure placed in the therapist chair whose job is to explain to the client who they really are and what's really going on inside of them? The remainder of Part I will address the conceptual, methodological and therapeutic discoveries of social therapeutics. These revelations make a radical, ontological break that does not rely on using explanation, reductionism, causality and dualisms such as inner/outer and objectivity/subjectivity in order to make sense of reality/ the world.

Newman was the first in his working-class South Bronx Jewish family to attend college, his tuition covered by the GI bill for having served in the Korean War. His early intention at Stanford was to study Eastern philosophy and methodology. However, in the mid-1950s the hot areas in the field (and the seeds of postmodernism) were the philosophy of science and philosophy of language (Newman & Holzman, 1997, p. 16). Newman was mentored by renowned analytic and neopragmatic philosopher Donald Davidson, and most importantly for our story, began a lifelong intellectual connection with the famed 20th century philosopher— Ludwig Wittgenstein (more on Wittgenstein in Chapter 4).

In the early 1970s, Newman began experimenting with these philosophical wonderings on therapy as he turned his attention to becoming a political activist and what today we might call a social innovator/entrepreneur. It was the height of the Vietnam War and he had just left an academic career. (Once one of his students explained that he was required to hold a high grade point average to avoid getting drafted, Newman started giving an A grade to all of his philosophy students, male and female. This led to multiple universities firing him, and to his surprise and bemusement, other institutions hiring—and even rehiring—him.) When he walked out of the ivory towers of the City College of New York for good, several of his students followed him. Together, they went out into the streets of New York to attempt to create new social justice tactics. The emotional impact on those engaged in these activities were of great interest to Newman.

One early attempt to explore that contradiction of therapy that Newman identified involved an area he already knew a great deal about: Mathematics. He convened a group of his former students, now nascent activists, to teach them abstract math concepts. As he lectured, he asked participants to include their emotional responses to trying to learn something several levels above their mathematical understanding. Whereas on a societal level acquiring knowledge and feeling/expressing emotions get related to as separate entities, Newman designed a situation to see what might happen if they were not posited as an either/or dualism.

Together with the participants, Newman discovered that inviting and examining the emotionality of learning a new language (math, in this case) radically transformed the knower/learner relationship. While Newman continued to study and deconstruct traditional psychology, he carried this discovery into the therapist/patient environment. In the search for creating a method for all-around development, the group-based emotional growth roots of social therapeutics emerged.

Newman's journey to innovation came not through the counterculture, but through the experience of growing up poor during the New Deal (his middle name was Delano) and living through the Civil Rights era. For many Jews after the Holocaust, the post-World War II declaration of "Never Again" meant never again would there be a Holocaust for *any* people. In 1950s and 60s America, many Jews actively protested the structural marginalization and extreme violence perpetrated against African Americans. They saw it as just as dangerous and immoral as Kristallnacht, the Nuremburg laws and concentration camps by which six million Jews were murdered in the 1930s and 40s.

Lois Holzman met Fred Newman in 1976 while doing post-doctoral research at the Laboratory of Comparative Human Cognition at Rockefeller University. Having already earned her PhD in Developmental Psychology and Psycholinguistics at Columbia University, with a focus on the sociality of early child language and thought (and an implicit critique of experimental methods of developmental psychology), Holzman and the Rockefeller team engaged in research exposing the invalidity of experimental cognitive psychology. This work questioned the validity of studying humans in a laboratory setting, working from the idea that the assumptions of the laboratory severely limit what one can see and, thus, claim to be valid. Holzman proposed a practical critique of psychology's basic premises and methods. When she "met" therapy, its premise—that once clients knew the causes behind their feelings and behavior they would change how they were feeling and behaving—fell flat. As Holzman would write years later, "social therapy is a method of helping people with whatever emotional pain they are experiencing without diagnosing their problem, analyzing their childhood or interpreting their current life" (2005, p. 101).

Finding common ground through questioning psychology's method, Holzman and Newman went searching for other ways to understand human development. "Perhaps, rather than trying to rule subjectivity out of order, we need to accept our self-reflexivity and devise methods to study human life subjectively" (Holzman & Mendez, 2003, p. xiv). As Newman and Holzman would establish in *Unscientific Psychology: A Cultural-Performatory Approach to Understanding Human Life* (1996), the objectivity of science may function well when humans study something at a distance, for example, the motion and behavior of stars. However, scientific protocol cannot be followed while humans study the behavior of other humans. The activity of interpreting, explaining and naming causes of other humans' behavior occurs through our societal and subjective lenses. There is no objective neutrality.

By the late 1970s, the activists following Newman were predominately Jewish and Black. Black empowerment was core to the values and vision of this embryonic community. It was also inclusive of anyone who wanted to help build it. Working side by side with African Americans and Jews were people from the Latino and LGBTQ+ communities, white folks and people from poor to upper middle-class backgrounds who ranged from highly educated to high school dropouts.

The search—for new tools with which to collectively build a new kind of world—was inseparable from the people who were doing the searching. Many of these activists participated in social therapy groups, establishing such groups as heterogeneous by race, class, gender and sexual orientation as well as by emotional issue/presenting problem. It quickly became clear that for people to experience their collective capacity to reorganize the emotional pain and oppression embedded into modern life, the diversity within social therapeutic groups offered a much more powerful model than one structured around single issues or identities.

While social therapeutics was incubated, tested and fueled by this burgeoning grouping dedicated to community-building and creating radical social and political transformation, members of the broader public were beginning to participate in ongoing weekly groups. By the early 1980s there was clear evidence of marketplace demand for social therapeutic group work. Centers opened in affluent areas in Long Island and Manhattan's Upper East Side, working-class Black and Latino neighborhoods in Harlem, and the Bronx and artistic neighborhoods like Chelsea.

Newman and Holzman collaborated for 35 years, discovering, articulating and advancing social therapeutics. There was a continuous, inseparable loop of Newman leading social therapy groups, Newman and Holzman looking at what was happening in those groups and them metabolizing the intellectual work and research of key intellectuals/academics/thought leaders as part of showing the powerful impact of the practice of social therapeutic methodology, in the therapy room and beyond (see Holzman, 2017). Social therapeutics was born of and evolved as a unified theory/practice, what Newman and Holzman came to call a "tool-and-result" method.

An international center for training and research

In 1985, Fred Newman and Lois Holzman co-founded the privately funded nonprofit East Side Institute (ESI).[1] It continues to operate today as an international training and research center working with hundreds of therapists, educators, coaches, business professionals, community-based social justice and performance activists every year. It also holds international conferences and has spawned numerous initiatives for human, youth and community development.

Social therapeutics was created outside of existing educational, research and funding institutions. Although it remains an independently funded and primarily volunteer-operated enterprise to this day, it has influenced those in mainstream academic and research institutions worldwide. The creation of a global social therapeutic network comprising of both grassroots and academic voices fosters a rich environment for continuous innovation and discovery.

Since 1993, Newman and Holzman have authored or edited 14 books and dozens of articles on social therapeutics. Their work has been translated into Chinese, Spanish, Japanese, Portuguese and Serbian. Over the years, they have introduced social therapeutics to social constructionism, cognitive behavioral therapy and critical, radical and sociocultural psychology, and partnered with many academics holding those orientations. Holzman continues to direct the East Side Institute, publish, lecture and converse with prominent public intellectuals and international activists who are challenging hegemonic institutions like psychology and education. Newman passed away in 2011.

Social therapeutically trained coaches and therapists now practice in several countries. They continue to innovate group work by establishing couples' groups and family groups, groups focused on dementia with both caregivers and people with dementia, health team groups formed to support someone with a serious illness, emotional support groups for women dealing with the uncertainty of a pre-cancer diagnosis, international youth and adult emotional support groups via WhatsApp and groups of international performance activists. Some of these efforts are showcased in the final part of this book.

Introducing Social Therapeutic Methodology
(Recasting Development)

From its earliest moments, psychology sought to bring the mechanics of scientific method to development. Both Sigmund Freud (1856–1939) and Jean Piaget (1896–1980) identified stages of childhood development through which every child passes linearly in a clearly defined and explained fashion. Freud's formative three stages were psychosexual and completed by age five. For Piaget, a child's cognitive development occurred in four stages and was fully developed by age 16. Others considered that development could occur in adulthood. Lawrence Kohlberg (1927–1987) focused on stages of moral development, while Erik Erikson (1902–1994) focused on psychosocial development. Abraham Maslow's (1908–1970) hierarchy of needs described five levels layered into a pyramid shape, culminating in an end point to one's development. These theories became the constructs which psychologists (and the growing psychology-aware public) could measure against an individual's progression in development.

While the giants of psychology tapped scientific reasoning and method to identify how babies develop from irrational creatures to logical, well-adapted adults, another psychologist of the same era—Lev Vygotsky—was asking different questions about child development and making different discoveries. Newman and Holzman found his discoveries of enormous value in helping to articulate what they were seeing in social therapy groups.

Lev Vygotsky

Lev Vygotsky (1896–1934), a Soviet psychologist, saw child development as an inherently social and cultural process. His discoveries offered a completely different view on both method (how to study development) and how children grow. Banned by Stalin in the 1930s, Vygotsky's work became accessible in Russian in the 1950s and only surfaced in English translation in the 1960s. It has become widely disseminated in education (Holzman, 2017; Lee & Smagorinsky, 1999; Moll, 2013; Wells, 2009), but much less so in psychology. Newman and Holzman embraced and advanced Vygotsky's work in *Lev Vygotsky: Revolutionary Scientist* (1993) in which they share their understanding of the stunning innovations by Vygotsky and then advance them to ground social therapeutics as an approach for continuous human development and a practice of method.

Vygotsky is most well-known for his radically different understanding of how children learn and develop, and in particular for our purposes, how they become language speakers. Rather than an *internal* biological development that instigates the physical process of making accurate, meaningful sounds, language acquisition for Vygotsky is a social and cultural activity. That is, a baby learns to speak through joint *activities* with more developed language speakers—*making* sounds, *looking* at each other, babies *imitating* adults and adults *cheering* them on, *playing* around with the words and sounds.

Vygotsky came to call this social/cultural activity a Zone of Proximal Development (zpd). The zpd is a co-created environment focused on *process*, rather than a spatio-temporal entity (Holzman, 2010, p. 33). In language development, the baby babbles, forming sounds that have no meaning in their native language. And yet, the mother—a language speaker—responds as if she has understood her daughter's babbling, as if it does make sense. "Brianna would you like some milk?" she might say after Brianna says something like, "goo goo ga ga." The baby—not yet a speaker—*performs ahead of herself* by engaging in this back and forth, imitating how she sees adults interact.[2] This exemplifies the essentiality of the social and cultural to human development. The mother relates to the baby not only as if she could speak, but also as an accepted member of the community. For Vygotsky, this way of seeing and understanding development, based on collaboration and imitation in community, is "the source of all specifically human characteristics of consciousness that develop in a child" (1987, p. 210). This differs greatly from the individualistic understanding of development and its dim view of imitation. To see imitation as rote copying misses the collaborative activity involved and reduces it to an instrument to be used for a fixed outcome, rather than a co-created, generative, creative process out of which something new can take shape.

These reframings of development might seem almost obvious in regard to babies' language acquisition, in the sense that most of us have participated in moments like this. Without even thinking about it, we adults relate to babies *as if* they could become a speaker, or to use Vygotsky's phrase, "a head taller" than they are (Vygotsky, 1978). Generally, we do not respond to a baby babbling by saying, "Come back and talk to me when you can get it right." However, we might not see that we are part of the unit—the zpd—that inseparably created both the *conditions* for becoming a language speaker as well as the material growth itself. Vygotsky called this qualitative transformation a "collective form of 'working together'" (2004, p. 202). These activities are simultaneous to the creating of an environment in which it is possible for the baby to become a speaker. Being able to see the building of the zpd as a "both/and" (rather than either/or) environment is key to seeing and leading groups.

Newman and Holzman took their understanding of Vygotsky's zpd and extended it into the therapeutic space. The social therapeutic practitioner:

> Works with the group (rather than the individuated selves that comprise the group) to organize itself as an *emotional zpd*. The various members, each at different levels of emotional development, are encouraged (invited, supported, challenged) to create *the group's* level of emotional development. This ongoing and ever-changing activity, it turns out, is developmental for all—including those who are most "individually" developed [emphasis in original] (Holzman, 2017, p. 35).

The social therapeutic emotional zpd is premised on diversity—in this case, different levels of emotional development. (We will take another look at the power of heterogeneous groups in the next chapter.) Rather than the group being an oppositional or conservatizing force to individuals' growth, it is a complimentary and necessary prerequisite. Individuals contribute to building the group and, as the group grows to create new things together, so too emerges the possibility for individual members of the group to grow. This is consistent with the both/and activity that Vygotsky illustrated as core to language acquisition.

The building of the group *is* the creating of the zpd, an environment in which group members are permitted and encouraged to:

- Imitate the therapist and other group members in how they do group (speak, listen, create)
- Relate to people's *activity with each other* as central to building the group (more central than the content of what people say)
- Babble in group without trying to get it right
- Question assumptions embedded in how we speak
- Not assume that people are understanding each other
- Ask curious questions
- Be playful, especially with language

Another way to articulate the mission of social therapeutic group activity is: To create with everything people give and make use of all of who they are at all their differing levels of development and unique histories. Newman and Holzman passionately insist that we all have the human capacity to reignite development, to break out of the societal scripts we have been handed—and what is required for doing this is the unit of the group.

As Newman and Holzman went about developing their understanding of Vygotsky and advancing his concepts to show the method of social therapeutics, they were impacted by another discipline that helped to make social therapeutic formulations more accessible to mainstream culture: Theater.

Performance, Being and Becoming

In midlife, Newman became a theater director and playwright. He would conclude social therapeutic group sessions for the evening and then head to theater rehearsals. He saw the "groupness" of the theater troupe. In that institution, the unit is called "the ensemble." In creating and producing theater, everyone in the ensemble is attentive to each other and the totality of the theatrical performance. This had a significant impact on Newman's thinking. "I've come to see life more as a play. Not in the sense as fictional or necessarily theatrical, but as a joint creation," he told an audience in 2010 (March 28, min: 30:55–31:10).

Performance entered into the lexicon of social therapeutics as another way to see what people are doing when they are not being themselves. Newman and Holzman carried their understanding of Vygotsky's "performing a head taller" in child development to everyone's capacity to perform onstage *and* offstage. Different from "fake it 'til you make it" or pretending, this concept of performance drew from the experience of actors on stage. For example, Maria is the actor who rushed to get to theater rehearsal on time, who worries about her credit card debt, who loves her partner and child *and* Maria the actor *performing* as Blanche in *A Streetcar Named Desire*. On stage, Maria is simultaneously who she is, and who she is not.

Newman and Holzman took that paradox off the theater stage, embraced it and brought it into social therapeutics: "Performing is what allows human beings to develop beyond instinctual and socially patterned behavior" (Holzman, 2015, p. 127). Development, then, can be created anywhere and at any time in our lives. It is not dependent on a pre-known, stagist, linear model like Piaget, Kohlberg or Erikson's. Rather, it is a process in which we are both who we are in this moment (a baby who can't speak) and who we are becoming (a baby who performs as a speaker on the way to actually becoming one). We are who we are (e.g., humiliated) and, if we so choose, who we are becoming (someone who is working to perform as other than humiliated even as we are feeling so). Holzman transported the early childhood activity of "performing a head taller"—which occurs before there is a formed recognition of "I" or of "knowing" how to do something—into adulthood. "Performing as someone else is an essential source of development" at any age (Holzman, 2010, p. 18). Once again, with the unit as the group in social therapeutics, the individual gets the most help by giving their felt experience (in this example, humiliation) to the coach and the couple or group for them to build with. This in turn creates possibilities for clients to "create a new performance" in their life and relationships, to grow beyond where they are.

Making a different performance choice

As told to the group by client Mira: "I was in a meeting with my manager regarding a corporate client. I needed to make a big ask for resources in order to complete the client's project on time. You all know me—I would rather take on things myself than ask for what I really need. However, with all of our work together in group on performing in new ways, I decided to try doing something different. So as this conversation with my manager was happening, I had the experience that I was floating above, watching myself be two things at once. I felt my usual pull to ask for little to nothing. And, at the same time, I decided to *perform* bigger, and take the risk of asking my boss for what I really thought the project needed. I saw old Mira and new Mira. I experienced feeling powerful as I did this new performance, and that felt great. I have been dying to share this with the group. And my boss agreed to my request!"

The shift to seeing ourselves and relating to others as both being and becoming opens up spaces of possibility. In a social therapeutic group or couples session, it acts as an invitation to group members and the coach to participate in someone's becoming. Rather than a cognitive exercise (of identifying what one should do or how one should think), it is an ongoing co-created performance. It was Vygotsky's non-dualistic view of thinking/speaking that helped Newman and Holzman extend his concept of completion into social therapeutic group work.

Completion

When we consider thinking and speaking, we assume they are separate things which operate in a simple order: We think and then we speak. If we can think hard enough, we will create the right thoughts which will then be spoken in the right way to someone. If these spoken words are not received in the right way, perhaps it is because we did not line up our thoughts properly before we spoke.

This understanding fits nicely into a rational, objective, measurable and dualistic worldview, but it has little to do with how we actually communicate. An obvious example that debunks this thought-first-speech-second idea is how we alter what we are saying when we notice our listener's reaction to us as we speak. If a listener frowns as we deliver bad news, we might omit some of the worst details. If a listener looks pleased as we deliver good news, we might linger on details or even exaggerate. What we say transforms as we take in the listener's response, the environment, how we are feeling and other external factors.[3]

Vygotsky questioned assumptions about the relationship between thinking and speaking. Through the zpd, he had come to see that individual language acquisition was co-created by people with differing speaking abilities. Always grounded in human activity and already having claimed that development is a social and cultural process, Vygostky posited that thought and speech are neither separated nor linear. He writes:

> The structure of speech is not simply the mirror image of the structure of thought. It cannot, therefore, be placed on thought like clothes off a rack. Speech does not merely serve as the expression of developed thought. *Thought is restructured as it is transformed into speech. It is not expressed but completed in the word* [emphasis added] (Vygotsky, 1987, p. 251).

"Completing" for Vygotsky is a term/activity to convey that we are in continuous motion, co-creating in the moment within a relational, cultural and social context. The environment cannot be removed from what we do, see, feel *and speak*. Thought transforms as it gets expressed through speaking (per the examples above), or we might add, through writing. We are experiencing this as we write this book. What you are reading here definitely does not correspond to the thoughts printed in our original outline. The act of writing (and writing and writing!) has completed—or transformed and advanced—our thinking, sharpening our message to the reader.

Newman and Holzman connected this understanding of completion—the non-dualistic experience of thought/language—with Vygotsky's understanding of language acquisition. If speaking as a completion of thought could be understood as an activity, did it have to reside solely inside one individual? Was it possible that a different person's speech could complete someone else's thought? Vygotsky's examples of a baby's language acquisition started to look like examples of completion. The baby babbles and the mother responds with, "Brianna, would you like some milk?" The baby speaks, the mother completes. The baby then imitates the completion (repeating the word "milk"), and so on. That is the social/cultural package. Thought/speech forms out of the unfolding co-created cultural, historical, relational activity.

Thus, what is said can be related to as something to be created with, by and with others. Newman and Holzman went further. If a mother completes a baby, then, they posited, could not other people complete us? Could not other people take what we are saying and make something with it? Holzman puts it like this: "If speaking is the completing of thinking, if the process is continuously creative in socio-cultural space . . . then it follows that the 'completer' does not have to be the one doing the thinking. Others can complete for us" (2017, p. 40). She and Newman built upon Vygotsky's insight focused on an individual, interior act, and unified it with the "exterior"—others who are participating in the conversation. Our speech becomes an offer, or a "giving" as we like to say, to others in the group or the relationship. Someone else might come up with the next line in the play entitled, *Today's Group Session*. What clients give is material to build with, to create with, to be completed. In other words, if transformation unfolds between thought and speech, then "[others] are no more saying *what* we are thinking than *we* are saying what we are thinking when we complete ourselves" (Holzman, 2017, p. 40).

This has significant implications for the role of the coach. Much of traditional coaching philosophy relies on the client working to figure out for themselves how they feel and behave and what help they need. The coach is a supportive questioner, guide and sometimes taskmaster of goal achievement. A coach completing the client is a more radical or advanced practice of co-creation. They are not just co-creating the structure of the session. An example of this might be a couple asking the coach, "What are you hearing and seeing in what we are saying/giving?" A typical coaching response might be to repeat back the words just uttered by the clients, followed by a question that pushes the couple to imagine how they would like to be. In social therapeutics, the coach might take in the full context of the couple's relationship as well as their relationship with the coach and respond with, "What I am hearing is that you love and respect each other. You started this work with me to see if your relationship has a future. And you each have been lukewarm on taking the kinds of emotional risks here in session that might build up your toolbox for communicating in new ways and transforming your relationship." In response to this, the couple might feel completed emotionally/socially/historically. They might say, "Yes, we hadn't been thinking about it that way, but we are lukewarm about being more vulnerable here and in general." And that could open up a new, unexpected direction in the work.

We can complete each other emotionally as well, and in the process create an emotional zpd—the core of social therapeutics. Often a client gets their first glimpse of completion when they experience being the completer, i.e., giving emotionally to someone/the group and having it be received/accepted. That act of giving and the content of what they gave is not about themselves. Many clients discover that activity as a relief from their usual inner self-critical loop or tendency to be competitive with others—and they want more of it. In addition, having discovered that they can be givers/completers, a client usually becomes more open to being the one given to/completed by the group/spouse/coach.

An example of completion and the emotional zpd

A client, Taylor, speaks in group, without emotion, of having been abused. Someone in the group shares how saddened they are in hearing both the content and Taylor's deadened delivery. Another client voices their anger that this happened and disbelief that Taylor is not angry himself. In this conversation, Taylor gives to the group. The group both accepts his lack of emotion and creates the space for other possible emotional expressions that perhaps the client is not able to do. It is both a completion and a zpd for emotional growth.

Group members giving those responses to the group has an impact on both the group (of which Taylor is a part) and on Taylor. For Taylor it opens the possibility to experience, see and learn other emotional expressions that he could not conceive of or experience individually. It simultaneously transforms the group's process to a form in which people could collectively share the emotionality of the experience of abuse.

Completion deprivatizes the individual experience of emotions as things living inside of a body that only the person feeling them can possess, which we will explore further in Chapter 4. Through completion, new spaces are created, new possibilities of how to be in the world can be seen and new meanings can be made, all of which contribute to both the group's and the individual's growth. Creating new, unexpected meanings is foundational to a very popular performing art form: Improv.

Improv

These days, improv is everywhere. There are improv trainings for business professionals, lawyers, doctors and families. They take place in the classroom, boardroom and living room. The core tenet of improv that has carried it into so many personal and professional arenas is, "Yes, and . . ." This exercise entails fully accepting "the offer"—i.e., whatever is said by another performer/colleague/family member ("yes") and adding to it ("and . . ."). In any given life and professional situation, we can choose to "Yes, and . . ." what has been said by others. The work is to stay in the moment and listen for offers to build upon. The TV show *Whose Line is it Anyway* brilliantly showcases the creativity that arises out of improvisationally accepting what the performers give (say) to the activity of building an improv scene. It is a form of completion. In the performance of an improv scene, the activity is transparently non-rational, unplanned, unknowable, sometimes nonsensical and always unpredictable. We often employ phrases like, "listening for the offer to build with" in our work with clients. (This will be brought to life for the reader in Parts II and III.)

In improv, when it is your turn to speak, there is not time to think through what you say. Often you have no idea what you are going to say, but you start talking all the same. Thankfully, the agreement is that your scene partner will catch you, will accept what you have given to the scene and carry it forward. An improv scene gets built out of no more than a suggestion from an audience member, or a one-word scene title from a slip of paper pulled out of a hat. This ability to create with what is present in the moment is becoming a highly prized skill in the workplace and beyond. In coaching, the skill is called "presence." Though not formally connected with improv (that we know of), we see a family resemblance in the coach and improv performer.

In contrast to improv, our everyday speech is often competitive and/or truth driven. This approach works relatively well with transactional conversations. For example, when we order a sandwich at the deli, we expect to be handed that sandwich, not a cup of soup. In general, however, we use that very same way of talking to each other to try to get some emotional outcome for ourselves. The results are usually less than satisfying, most obviously when we are trying to discuss feelings, vulnerabilities, wants and conflicts. It is in those moments in a conversation that it is the hardest to "Yes, and . . ." with others. We are much more comfortable blaming, judging, comparing or waiting for our turn to speak and letting loose our anger or frustration. We tend to believe that getting our thoughts out of our head, regardless of what else is going on or to whom we are speaking, will get us to where we want to go or what we want to acquire. These forms of speaking typically negate or ignore what is being said by the other person in a "Yes, but . . ." or "No, but . . ." manner.. Responding in a "Yes, and . . ." way opens up unexpected connections and directions of the conversation.

Yes, and-ing *to build connection*

During their second couples session, Hany and Jennie brought up the sensitive topic of going on a trip together. After several years of conflict and fighting with one another, they were starting to enjoy each other's company again. Hany, a creative professional who enjoys designing with others, wanted to take his regular trip to Burning Man. Jennie, who can be adventurous and did go to Burning Man once, did not want to return. She also wanted to take a trip with him that they could plan together.

Normally their conversations devolved into accusations and defensiveness. "You never take me on the great trips you take with your friends" or "You don't include me when planning a trip" etc.

In this session Jennie asked the coach if there was any way of doing the conversation differently. The coach suggested they plan a fictional trip right there in session using "Yes, and . . ." skills. Jennie started with a first line, "Let's go on a trip to Venice together." Hany added, "Yes, and . . . let's visit the sites where our favorite movies were shot." Jennie continued, "Yes, and . . . let's find a charming Airbnb to stay in," and Hany responded, "Yes, and . . . let's go when the gondola races are happening." The couple found relating to each other in this way energizing and intimate. They recognized that they could plan a trip together in a new way. The next week they shared with the coach that together they had come up with a terrific vacation plan and had already booked it.

The coach's performance posture is one of an improv performer, working to "Yes, and . . ." the group. To listen in such a way as to "Yes, and . . ." the couple or the ensemble. Or, listening for offers to build with. Or, creating the zpd in which group members can create with what is being given to the group.

Social therapeutic groups and couples work is grounded in the "Yes, and . . ." posture. It is critical to building the group and creating an environment in which new possibilities, new ways of talking, new kinds of conversations can emerge. At their best, social therapeutic groups radically accept what members give to the group and build with it, creating something that no one knew would be created. It also gives the sense of being heard.

Table 2.1 Key differences between social therapeutics, coaching and traditional therapy

	Social Therapeutics	Coaching	Traditional Therapy
Question type	How	How	What
Unit of focus	Group	Individual	Individual
Mode of understanding	Relational	Experience-based	Analytical
Methodology	Embraces subjectivity in its process, new ontology, does not claim science, embraces socio-cultural transformation	Embraces subjectivity in its process, does not claim science, relies in part on psychology—mostly deriving from humanist psychology	Claims science, applies methods, measures, embraces objectivity
Role of coach/ therapist	Co-create with client, not-knowing, playing with language, discovery, cultivate the emergent and emerging possibilities, continuous life development	Co-create with client, inquiry towards discovery, cultivate the emergent and emerging possibilities, check in regularly on progress toward a goal	Authority, expertise, knowing, diagnosis, relieving symptoms
Relating to the client	Client as creator of their life, the group, the couple. Creating occurs with others	Client wants help making a decision/life change or achieving a goal, client has inherent intelligence	Client has an internal dysfunctional pattern or cognitive distortion that needs to be uncovered and understood, then changed through insight
Understanding of the problem	There are no problems! Our emotional pain was created socially, the cure to our emotional pain is also created socially	The problem is internal. It is non-clinical. The client can improve	The problem is internal, stemming from the past which causes a diagnosable pathology. The client can be cured
Activity of the coach/therapist	Questions that move around and about philosophically	Questioning to identify a goal and achieve it	Questioning to clinically diagnose, to understand, to develop an insight

Listening as a Creative Act

As coaches and therapists, we work hard to listen to our clients. We are aware that listening is an active process, it is not something to take for granted. Often, we will check in by offering, "I am hearing you say . . ." as a way of giving the client the experience of being seen.

Recall that in Chapter 1 we introduced how early coaches Henry and Karen Kimsey-House brought their acting training into coaching. They define the highest levels of listening as the capacity to adjust to where the client is at, similar to the ways that performers adjust to their in-the-moment conditions: "Stand-up comedians, musicians, actors, training presenters—all have the ability to instantly read a room and monitor how it changes in response to what they do . . . [Level III listening skills are] awareness and impact and the ability to dance with whatever just happened" (Kimsey-House et al., 2018, p. 46).

As a director, Newman learned that leading and co-creating with an ensemble required a lot of listening—to the cast, the tech crew, the sales and marketing teams. In his final public speech, given at New York University on March 28, 2010 and entitled *How to Talk*, Newman attributed learning to listen as a theater director to a breakthrough in his understanding and practice of social therapeutics (slightly edited for context, emphasis added):

> I learned that what it meant for me to listen, was to listen as part of a process of creating something with the person to whom I was listening. That it wasn't enough to want to really, really, really hear what someone else or some group of people were saying . . .
>
> *If you want to listen to someone, you have to create something off of what they are saying . . .*
>
> I don't want to just hear what you think, I want to work with what you think, I want to create with what you think, and I want to see where that goes. And I want to be a participant in your conversation. I don't want to simply wait for my turn to say what's on my mind. I want to work to help create something new that is neither yours nor mine but ours (Newman, 2010, March 28, min. 29:44–36:00).

In drawing attention to the *activity* of listening, Newman showcases the act of creating with others. In establishing the coaching agreement, the ICF looks for the coach to be a co-creator of the session with a client such that the client sets a goal and then measures success against it. In this scenario, the coach listens actively, though the underlying assumption remains that there are two discrete individuals in conversation taking their turns speaking, with the coach helping the client get somewhere (to their goal). Here, Newman suggests we view all of life as jointly created with others (ensembles, if you will, or groups), listening in a way that could produce an unexpected turn, something more/other than the sum of its parts. Thus, the unit of growth, of focus, in social therapeutics shifts to the ensemble and away from particular moments, particular statements or the individual.

This brings us finally to Newman and Holzman's completion of Vygotsky's innovation of method.

Tool-and-Result Method

We referenced earlier in this chapter that Vygotsky offered another method for understanding development, one that offered an alternative to the dominating dualistic paradigm of psychology. We have provided a glimpse into it through highlighting some of his discoveries—the unity of thought/speech and the unity of the zpd. How Vygotsky got there was through a "search for method . . . simultaneously the tool and the result of study" (1978, p. 65). This search is a continuous process of discovery grounded in actual material conditions that cannot be separated out from the activity underway.

Newman and Holzman built on Vygotsky's unification of "the tool" and "the result" to establish the contrasting phrases "tool-for-result" and "tool-and-result." Tool-*for*-result is how most of us live our lives. It is instrumental and pragmatic. We do something (use a tool) to get something (a result). I take a hammer, pound it onto nails and the result is a new wooden mailbox. I wash the dishes (tool) so that my partner will feel guilty to stay even on the chores and therefore take out the trash (result). What is in it for me (result) in this new corporate policy (tool)? As Newman points out in *Let's Develop* (2010), this way of operating can be limiting emotionally and relationally.

Tool-*and*-result methodology is simultaneously process and product. Rather than a "do something to get something" mindset it is a "give-and-create" activity without knowing beforehand what will get created.

Newman, a tool and die maker in his youth, practiced tool-and-result methodology in his life and was a brilliant architect of many projects.

Our discussions of group and couples work in this chapter attempt to show the activity of give-and-create, for example in Newman and Holzman's understanding of completion as well as the inclusion of the tools of theater and improv. They illustrate the power of social therapeutics' tool-and-result method in *Lev Vygotsky: Revolutionary Scientist*:

> The activity of building the group is what is curative (Newman 1983; 1989b). People come to therapy seeking hardware store tools to use; [in social therapeutic groups] they are offered the chance to be toolmakers, to take the predetermining elements of their life space and create something entirely new out of it, to define collectively for themselves what and how their . . . emotions are to be (Newman & Holzman, 1993, p. 156).

The activity of building and creating with others *is* what breaks us out of our patterns and conventional ways of thinking, relating and doing. This pathway to growth is unmediated. That is, it does not require imposing theories, ideas, labels or explanations onto what is happening in order to make meaning. It is in and of the moment, with the meaning created by those involved in building the group. We attempt to bring this tool-as-result activity to life in Parts II and III where we provide numerous examples of groups and couples attending to how the group/relationship is doing even as individuals get help with their issues.

We have another intention in sharing this quote. It is to relate to you the reader as a head taller. The dialectical, holistic nature of social therapeutics makes it difficult to capture and explicate in parts. Yet to write a book requires breaking it into parts. This quote is inclusive of what we have written so far and introduces additional elements of the approach that we address ahead.

The Importance of Play

We conclude this chapter by returning to Lev Vygotsky. In his studies of child development he identified play as opening the door to growth: "In play a child always behaves beyond his average age, above his daily behavior; in play it is as though he were a head taller than himself" (Vygotsky, 1978, p. 102). We mentioned "a head taller" earlier in this chapter when we discussed the dialectical relationship of acquiring language and the creation of the zpd. Here we expand the unity (inseparable parts) of the zpd, completion, imitation, being and becoming, tool-and-result and the tools of theater to include play.

Why would play be important to coaching and emotional growth? Consider how young children play. They are creative and curious. They create the rules of a game as they go along. They perform ahead of themselves and imitate others (by playing mom or doctor or dad). They are unconcerned with knowing, nor are they worried about how they look (for example, whether they are acting "ridiculous"). This kind of free play occurs before and as children acclimate and adapt to societal rules of behavior. Social therapeutics embraces this type of play as an activity that liberates us out of our societally overdetermined adult roles (Holzman, 2017, pp. 50–53).

Dr. Stuart Brown, founder of the National Institute for Play and author of *play: How it Shapes the Brain, Opens the Imagination and Invigorates the Soul* notes how play nourishes adults—grounds us in the moment, frees us from self-criticism and allows us to "even be a different self" (2009, p. 10), i.e., invites and permissions us to try new performances. Brown goes so far as to say that when we adults stop playing, "we stop developing . . . we start dying" and the quality of our relationships become endangered (Ibid., pp. 76, 166). We could not agree more.

Let's take another look at how young children make up a game to play, right on the spot. A never-before played game. They just start and add the rules to the game as they go. This is a helpful metaphor for Newman and Holzman's tool-and-result method. Nothing is pre-known. The playing informs the rules, which then inform the game-playing, and the cycle continues. There is no standing outside the game and evaluating it; there is no objectivity. And when we are not standing outside observing, then the game that gets created includes all participants at all levels of development (those who are good at making up rules, those who look out for the team, those who have no attention span, etc.). Added to the other concepts introduced in this chapter, play helps both practitioner and client to better see and build with the emergent.

This chapter introduces new possibilities in coaching method: Responding to others' babbling with a completion that takes us someplace new; building a zpd and collectively creating emotional growth, i.e., "all-round" development; embracing we are both who are and who we are becoming; tool-and-result unity; doing a new performance; incorporating improv and play to help us be present and break away from knowing and explaining (our adapted-to-society adult performance); and, moving beyond seeing individuals, dualisms and particulars.

Now that we have introduced some tenets of the social therapeutic practice of method, let's look deeper at the inherited conceptual constructs of the Enlightenment and the modern era, so that we can work to be free of them. First up, examining the social construct of the individual and shifting to seeing groups.

Exercises

1) Try this improv exercise with someone.

   Part I) Somatic. Have your improv partner say out loud three times slowly—"No, but . . ." Notice how your body responds. Then have them do the same thing saying, "Yes, but . . ."; and finally, "Yes, and . . ." Does your body react differently to these three formulations? Does it close down? Do you feel tension? Does it open up?

   Part II) With your partner, spend two minutes planning a party. The first time you and your partner respond to each other starting each sentence with "No, but . . ." The second time, respond to each other starting with "Yes, and . . ." What were the experiences like? What did you discover about what you could or could not create together? How close were you feeling to your partner?

2) Without telling your friend, family member or colleague, try listening with the intention to build with what they are saying. What do you discover/experience in communicating in this manner?

Notes

1 www.eastsideinstitute.org
2 For an excellent example, see this father/son conversation on video with over 100M views, www.youtube.com/watch?v=0IaNR8YGdow

3 While these examples might make the point obvious, unifying thought and language overthrows roughly 1600 years of Western philosophical thought about language. For more, see Newman & Holzman (1996).

References

Brock, V. (2014). *Sourcebook of Coaching History.* https://libraryofprofessionalcoaching.com/wp-app/wp-content/uploads/2022/01/SOCH-2nd-Edition-Free-2021-01-31-Secure-1.pdf

Brown, S. (2009). *play: How it Shapes the Brain, Opens the Imagination and Invigorates the Soul.* Penguin Group.

Cockerham, G. (2011). *Group Coaching: A Comprehensive Blueprint.* iUniverse.

Gergen, K. (1999). Forward. In L. Holzman, (Ed.), *Performing Psychology: A Postmodern Culture of the Mind* (pp. 1–3). Routledge.

Holzman, L. (2005). Performing a Life (Story). In G. Yancy & S. Hadley (Eds.), *Narrative Identities, Psychologists Engaged in Self-Construction* (pp. 96–113). Jessica Kingsley Publishers.

Holzman, L. (2010). Without Creating ZPDs There is No Creativity. In C. Connery, V. John-Steiner & A. Marjanovic-Shane (Eds.), *Vygotsky and Creativity: A Cultural-historical Approach to Play, Meaning Making, and the Arts* (pp. 27–40). Peter Lang Publishers.

Holzman, L. (2015). Relating to people as revolutionaries. In D. Loewenthal (Ed.), *Critical Psychotherapy, Psychoanalysis and Counselling: Implications for Practice* (pp.125–137). Palgrave MacMillan.

Holzman, L. (2017). *Vygotsky at Work and Play.* Routledge.

Holzman, L. & Mendez, R. (Eds.). (2003). *Psychological Investigations: A Clinician's Guide to Social Therapy.* Brunner-Routledge.

International Coaching Federation. (2017). *ICF Core Competencies Rating Levels.* Retrieved March 2022 from: https://coachingfederation.org/app/uploads/2017/12/ICF_Competencies_Level_Table_wNote.pdf

Kimsey-House H., Kimsey-House, K., Sandahl, P. & Whitworth, L. (2018). *Co-Active Coaching: The Proven Framework for Transformative Conversations at Work and in Life.* Nicholas Brealey Publishing.

Lee, C.D. & Smagorinsky, P. (Eds.) (1999). *Vygotskian Perspectives on Literacy Research: Constructing Meaning through Collaborative Inquiry.* Cambridge University Press.

Marx, K. & Engels, F. (1991). *The German Ideology.* International Publishers.

Moll, L.C. (2013). *L.S. Vygotsky and Education.* Routledge. https:/doi.org/10.4324/9780203156773

Newman, F. (1998, October 30). *Therapeutics as a Way of Life* [transcript]. Annual lecture of the East Side Institute. https://eastsideinstitute.org/therapeutics-as-a-way-of-life/

Newman, F. (2010, March 28). *How to Talk.* East Side Institute. https://vimeo.com/29563016

Newman, F. (2010). *Let's Develop! A Guide to Continuous Personal Growth.* Castillo International, Inc.

Newman, F. & Holzman, L. (1993). *Lev Vygotsky: Revolutionary Scientist.* Routledge.

Newman, F. & Holzman, L. (1996). *Unscientific Psychology: A Cultural-Performatory Approach to Understanding Human Life.* Praeger.

Newman, F. & Holzman, L. (1997). *The End of Knowing: A new developmental way of learning.* Routledge.

O'Connor, J. & Lages, A. (2007). *How Coaching Works: The Essential Guide to the History and Practice of Effective Coaching.* A&C Black.

Vygotsky, L.S. (1978). *Mind in society: The development of higher psychological processes* (M. Cole, V. John-Steiner, S. Scribner, & E. Souberman, Eds.). Harvard University Press.

Vygotsky, L.S. (1987). *The collected works of L. S. Vygotsky, Volume 1.* Plenum Press.

Vygotsky, L.S. (2004). The collective as a factor in the development of the abnormal child. In R.W. Rieber & D.K. Robinson (Eds.), *The Essential Vygotsky* (pp. 201–219). Kluwer Academic/Plenum Publishers.

Wells, G. (2009). *The Zone of Proximal Development and its Implications for Teaching and Learning.* Cambridge University Press. https://doi.org/10.1017/CBO9780511605895.012

3

WHY GROUPS

In our country, we see a deeply dangerous turning away from public obligations that is the result of a dangerous turning inward to find sufficiency where it is finally not—only in the self.

A. Bartlett Giamatti (1990)[1]

The legacy of individualism is loneliness.

Terry Real (2022)

Historically, pandemics have forced humans to break with the past and imagine their world anew. This one is no different. It is a portal, a gateway between one world and the next.

We can choose to walk through it, dragging the carcasses of our prejudice and hatred, our avarice, our data banks and dead ideas, our dead rivers and smoky skies behind us. Or we can walk through lightly with little luggage, ready to imagine another world and ready to fight for it.

Arundhati Roy (2020)

For a brief moment in March of 2020, the world stopped. We sat together in global silence for two weeks as quarantines were enforced in almost every country in the world. What did we hear? Melodious birds we had never noticed before. The most delicate sound of the wind rustling through the trees. The sorrowful wail of an ambulance siren echoing on

DOI: 10.4324/9781003326465-5

an empty street. We heard the citizens of Italy on their balconies playing musical instruments at exactly the same time. In New York City, people hung out their windows at 5 o'clock every evening for weeks, banging pots in solidarity with frontline health workers.

People everywhere sought ways to connect in spite of being physically separated. It was an unprecedented moment which ignited an infinitude of creative acts to facilitate a shared sense of community—whether that be learning to do something new together as a family, delivering food for a neighbor with Covid or socially distanced outdoor group workouts. We were all in it together! At least, for a couple of weeks. Meanwhile lockdown dragged on for two more years (more or less depending on one's geography).

Social distancing and isolation magnified the already unfolding mental health crisis in the US. A 2021 Harvard survey found that 36% of respondents claimed to feel lonely "frequently" or "almost all the time or all the time" with that number jumping to nearly two out of three young adults aged 18–25 (Weissbourd et al., 2021, p. 1). While loneliness is broadly recognized as a public health (read: social, of the world) issue,[2] it is not generally seen as socially produced. By and large, loneliness is understood to be an internal subjective state, defined by an inability to form intimate connections and intense feelings of self-doubt and self-worth (Cigna, 2022), regardless of what is happening in the world around us—even a global pandemic! Might the unit of the "self" and the focus on individualism be the issue? And might the solution to loneliness lay outside of the individual?

In the classic *Bowling Alone* (2001) sociologist Robert Putnam postulated a correlation between the erosion of US social institutions since the mid-20th century and the concurrent increase in loneliness. The mass structures through which ordinary people used to connect for pleasure and solidarity—the bowling league, the fraternal lodge, church, unions, book clubs—are in rapid decline. Best-selling author Johann Hari writes in *Lost Connections*, "We are homesick even when we are at home" (2018, p. 97)—an apt description of the experience of feeling disconnected from all that is around us. To effectively address loneliness, John Cacioppo, a University of Chicago researcher and social neuroscientist told Hari that there had to be something more involved than adding other people to one's life. One has to feel, "you are sharing something with the other person, or the group, that is meaningful to *both* of you [emphasis in original]" (Hari, 2018, p. 100). The activity of creating meaning together is appreciated by both coaching and social therapeutics. We will speak more to this in the next chapter.

Perhaps in the collective creativity performed in the first weeks of Covid—amidst the uncertainty, fear, chaos, sickness and death—we felt more connected with each other than usual, in both a local and global way. But the rush of doing meaningful activities with and for each other at the beginning of the pandemic was left to fade, unsupported by American political leadership and our deeply embedded cultural insistence on individualism.

The Limits of Individualism (The Isolated Individual to Loneliness Pipeline)

The Western fixation on the individual has a long history. One way this gets expressed in contemporary times is through consumerist culture. Think of our highly individuated coffee orders, where we are asked to choose from dozens of add-ons. We are more likely to feel pleasure and satisfaction from things we buy than we are from relationships we form. Organized to be individual consumers of things, we can hardly see that we are producers and co-creators—of relationships, families, communities. This is a key driver of loneliness; we immediately disassociate (feel alienated) from what we have just done, felt and given towards a relationship. In late capitalist Americanized culture, we expect to get what we want emotionally, socially and sexually for our individual selves from other individual selves. When we do not get what we want, we turn to what we know how to do best—throwing it out. Living like this, as an individual separated out from the world, is a very painful way to exist. As Hari notes, "The primary cause of all this rising depression and anxiety is not in our heads. It is . . . largely in the world, and the way we are living in it" (2018, p. 14).

The more we feel alone, the greater the difficulty we face in seeing that we are all and always have been part of groups. If we are to consider our fundamental sociality, then we need to look at how deeply Western culture is organized around the primacy of the individual. Of course, individuals exist. But to reduce all the complex happenings of a day or a week, a year or a lifetime, to something happening solely *inside* us artificially truncates the richness of all that occurs around us, both in society and nature, in all of human history and all of natural history. If our emotional pain is socially and culturally produced, then must we not also consider that the cure is socially and culturally produced?

The primacy of the individual is now being challenged by different disciplines. Terry Real, popular author and family therapist, notes that neuroscientists are questioning "the wisdom of singling out the individual as the proper unit of study in human psychology" (2022, p. 36). We are excited by this development, as we are here arguing that the unit to be studied is the group, not the individual. Adam Grant, organizational psychologist at Wharton Business School, consults with top business leaders and is an advocate of team coaching. He too is concerned with the limitations of individualism. "Psychologists find that in cultures where people pursue happiness individually, they may actually become lonelier. But in cultures where they pursue happiness socially— through connecting, caring and contributing—people appear to be more likely to gain well-being" (Grant, 2021). Across the Blue Zones of the world—locations where people live the longest—two of the six universal qualities are social engagement and family, i.e., having active social support networks (Poulain, et al., 2004). Healthy relationships also fortify responses to trauma as well and become part of the cure to PTSD (Eubanks, 2022).

For David Brooks, public intellectual and *New York Times* Op-Ed columnist on culture and the social sciences, we are living in an era of hyper-individualism (2019, February 18). He founded Weave: The Social Fabric Project in 2018 whose manifesto declares, "We need to articulate a creed that puts relation, not the individual, at the center" (Weave, 2019). Brooks claims that the myth that an individual alone can make themselves happy or be self-sufficient is driving disconnection (2019, July 3, min. 1:45–2:45). University of Kansas professor of communication studies Jeffrey A. Hall has researched the impact of the contemporary shift to people spending less time with other people and more time attending to the self. Echoing Yale President Bart Giamatti's prescient warning to the class of '84 on the danger of shifting away from public obligations (see this chapter's epigraph), Hall found that "removing the routine obligations of social life drains presence, conversational practice, relational effort and friendship from all of us" (2022). Like losing muscle mass from skipping gym workouts, we lose our capacity to be social when we avoid interacting with others.

Coaching, by and large, holds to the individual model, in which co-creation is used as a tool to drive the client's internal process of surfacing the answer to an issue. It operates with the assumption that each person is their own individual, living their individual life. According to executive and life coaching authors Skiffington and Zeus, personal development "occurs within the context of self-knowledge and self-awareness . . . the coach, attempts to lead coachees to a deeper and rational understanding of their own personal truths and values" (2003, p. 34). We believe there is room in coaching—both in its roots and in its appetite for innovation—to offer models that move beyond the self. It might feel natural to look inward, but that does not mean that it is the only place we can look. However, looking anywhere else involves examining and questioning ways we have stayed invested in the individual model.

As we examined in the first chapter, coaching emerged out of the group work of *est* and other countercultural initiatives of the 1960s and 70s. It also emerged out of the Human Potential Movement (HPM), self-help and personal development trends of the times. The emerging demand for executive coaching created the market for individual work. As coaching expanded, it carried with it psychology's inward-looking constructs. For early coaching chronicler Vicky Brock, it was a "logical next step after group participation" (2014, p. 78). The client can look inside for self-knowledge and change how they think. They can change their individual story. One of coaching's main influences and founder of humanist psychology, Carl Rogers, asserted that what gets in the way of understanding ourselves is our social experiences—i.e., in interacting with other humans, we run the risk of losing, or never finding, ourselves (1961).

Even newer, more holistic approaches to well-being hold onto the individual, internal view of change. In coaching, psychotherapy and neuroscience involving trauma, somatics and psychedelics, great advances have been made to bridge the dualism of mind/body. There is broader mainstream understanding and acceptance today that mind/body is a unified whole. However, at the same time, those approaches rarely question the dualistic divide between inside and outside, self and other. The assumption that looking inward is the path to relieving our emotional pain is difficult to dislodge.

Human Sociality and Community

For us as practitioners, almost every client who walks through the door carries that same host of assumptions about themselves and the world based on a nearly impenetrable belief of the isolated individual. Our culture and our psychology drive the belief that we start out as individuals and then become acculturated to groups. As such, we do not see ourselves in relation to others, as social. There are, however, a few cultural exceptions where we do see groups: Music, sports and theater. In a marching band we expect to hear the total sound, not a particular instrument. In vocal harmonies, if the listener hears one particular voice, the performance is considered to fall short. As the saying goes, there is no "I" in team. The incredible feats of an individual player cannot be recounted without the team's efforts. In these cases, the unit is socially understood to be the group. It is theater that gave us the word "ensemble"—a seamless group performance. The phrase we use in English to capture this sort of group work is *the sum is greater than its parts*.

In the previous chapter, we shared how Lev Vygotsky saw child development as occurring first as a social activity, then on an individual level as the child adapts to social norms and the world around them. There is now a growing body of scientific research supporting the sociality of the human species, that we are "wired to connect" and that our "social behavior is a critical part of our adaptive toolkit. It allows us to come together and do things that we wouldn't be able to do on our own" (M. Platt, as quoted in Sukel, 2019). That is, in groups, we can perform ahead of ourselves. Or as Holzman puts it, "human development is not an individual accomplishment but a socio-cultural activity" (2015, p. 131). Studies are now showing that community-building is essential to social and emotional development (Weissbourd et al., 2021, p. 4). There is even a "community care" (as opposed to self-care) movement emerging within the nonprofit and social justice worlds (Dockray, 2019). The task of social therapeutic groups is to work together to create the possibility of human development. Along the way, clients create their sense of belonging and shared meaning.

By the 1990s, participants of the diverse therapeutic, cultural and political efforts led by Fred Newman[3]—shorthanded as The Development Community—took to exploring what it meant to share the responsibility of collectively creating the community itself. In a talk by Newman in 1990, later published as *Community as Heart in a Havenless World*, he said:

> I want to talk about community not as a haven, not a place where we can go and hide, but as an active principle, as a human, passionate, living environment which has the capacity to nourish those of us who are committed to engaging the cruelty of a havenless world. I want to talk about that kind of community . . . a community which takes responsibility for defining what community is (Newman, 1991, pp. 142, 145).

In social therapeutic Life Development Groups, the group takes responsibility for defining itself. The activity of creating, reshaping and rebuilding what the group is, week after week, builds community. Chapters 5 and 6 provide practical guidance to the practitioner on what that group activity looks like.

Many assume that seeing and working in groups requires giving up individuals and individuality. That is not the case. In our experience with both Life Development Groups and couples work, clients become *more of who they are* as they build the group. They discover how to articulate their wants, desires, reactions and emotions as part of a co-created play with others. When people work together creating their relationships, their communities, their families, their work teams—their groups—it is an antidote to the pervasive, lonely culture of individualism in the US and beyond. When people do this kind of couples or group work together in social therapeutics, it challenges—in practice—traditional ways of relating to ourselves and others as individuals with inner selves and inner problems (Holzman, 2015). Or, as our clients say of their experience in group sessions, we "get off the *me* [tread]mill and onto the *we* [tread]mill."

The Case for Heterogeneous Groups

If the unit is the group, then building the group involves using everything around us—our histories, our tragedies, our joys, our pains, our similarities, our differences, our conflicts, our families, our communities and the state of the world. Social therapeutic groups break with the most common model of group work—the assumption that participants must be "like" each other in order to get any help. Those groups are called homogeneous groups. Most groups today are based on sameness—whether that is in regard to identity (e.g., LGBTQ+), an emotional issue (e.g., depression), life experience (e.g., trauma survivor) or life goal (e.g., weight loss). The assumption is that with sameness comes understanding, and with understanding and being understood lies the path to recovery and normalcy.

There is a lot to unpack in that assumption. How does the cognitive act of understanding bring people together in a qualitative way? Might requiring sameness keep us at a distance from one another, less curious and more assumptive? How do we keep working out our relational/emotional muscles if we set identity-based boundaries restricting with whom we may converse? Some think the loss of everyday connection and conversation—including with people different than ourselves—increases our rigid assumptions of and subsequent disinterest in others (Grant, 2021; Hall, 2022). Our socially constructed identities overdetermine how we see ourselves, what we think we can do with others, who we think we can be in the world and how we are supposed to feel. In the unfinished work of social justice, there is a growing awareness that we must innovate *how* we come together, create together and build together in the organically heterogeneous groups in which we live, work and play. In our Life Development Groups, clients get challenged and challenge each other on "who they think they are." It is enormously valuable to hear how others experience us. It helps create the space for *becoming*. As we outlined in the previous chapter, transformation is better understood as the dialectical relationship between being and becoming.

Through the lens of Newman and Holzman's zpd, growth occurs when group members, with their differing levels of development, work together. This is a break from the idea that we must understand or know each other in order to move forward together. Instead, we must build together. Furthermore, if the focus is on the group rather than on a particular individual, then there is no longer a need to arrange groups based on a single interest. Everyone can build a group. The drive to understand through and coalesce around sameness gets in the way of seeing the activity of what people are doing together. In short, in heterogeneous groups it is more obvious that growth grows out of the activity of creating together with what there is.

An example of a social therapeutic Life Development Group session

A gay man asked the group for help on having a conversation with his partner of six months. They had gone out of town for a wedding. His boyfriend was away at a rehearsal for several hours and he (the group member) had sought out a casual sexual encounter. Should he tell his partner? The partner had reluctantly agreed to the arrangement and said he wanted to hear if/when there were encounters. However, the client was not sure his boyfriend really meant it. The client added that he was unsure about bringing this to group, as he was the only LGBTQ+ person in the eight-person group.

The group started out doing what we have all learned to do: Helping an individual solve their problem, to get it "right" or do it the "right" way. The group went on to give advice on what he should do, then slowed down and became more philosophical. "What do people in the group do when they desire different things than their partner (sexual or otherwise)," the coach asked. "I try to give voice to my needs," someone responded. Someone else shared their experience with monogamous and non-monogamous relationships and concluded that the intimacy created had way more to do with how partners spoke with each other and approached hard conversations than with setting rules for what types of behaviors were permitted. Another client raised the issue of possession in relationships. A woman added her experience of being treated possessively by her male partner and how hard and scary it was to leave the relationship.

The coach asked, "Can we converse with our partners, loved ones and dear friends in such a way to create a conversation, rather than speaking in a way designed for us to get our way or what we want? How do we do it here, in group?"

At the end of session, the client noted that he felt supported by the group and empowered to have a more open and connected conversation with his partner than he had considered on his own. He said he was glad that he was not leaving with a specific directive on what to do.

In the Life Development Group session above, the group both responded to the gay client and gave of themselves. In doing so, their differences from one another contributed to the conversation of the group. There was no need to identify (presume an understanding based on a category) with what someone else was saying. The philosophical questions from the coach helped to guide the conversation away from identity-based talk and toward more emotionally intimate conversation.

Social therapeutic practitioners offer short-term groups, but mostly their groups are ongoing. Many clients move out of crisis, begin developing emotionally (more on this in the next chapter) and decide to continue with group. They see the activity of building the group as a weekly opportunity for an emotional workout with others with whom they have built a sense of community. Rather than seeking tools to adapt better to society, social therapeutic clients seek to create new ways of being, seeing, doing and feeling together.

There are two other examples of heterogenous group work we have come across.[4] Interpersonal process group psychotherapy brings together people with diverse issues—grief, loneliness, etc. Clients are invited to include their emotional experiences in the moment as a way of understanding themselves better. This is a powerful advance and creates space to include how clients relate to each other in group, which can lead to important discoveries and growth. And at the same time, our sense is that the therapist remains the authority in group, adding explanations and causes to why a client might be the way they are, helping them to adapt to the world. The focus is to build up individuals, not necessarily the group. As a corollary, the invitation to the group to build itself is missing.

Corporate team coaching is growing rapidly, and again the business community is leading the way in innovating how people communicate and interact together in two important ways (see Rød & Fridjhon, 2020). First, a grouping of employees is assumed to be heterogeneous in demographic diversity, subject matter expertise and emotional development as well as leadership skills. In *The Wisdom of Crowds* (2005), James Surowiecki sought to understand the elements of high-achieving corporate teams and smart team decision-making. He found that diversity, independence and decentralization were key. Of course, Surowiecki's eye was turned towards discovering the best conditions for a specific outcome—achieving the company's strategic goals. Social therapeutics' eye is toward creating the conditions for the group to grow, without a predetermined outcome of what that might or should look like. In this way, social therapeutics is process-oriented, whereas corporate coaching is ultimately results-oriented. In the final chapter, we include a case study on social therapeutic team coaching.

Second, the *unit of team* is more commonly appreciated in corporate team coaching. Adam Grant advocates for companies to "start treating teams, not individuals, as the fundamental building blocks of the organization" (2019). To achieve mastery in team coaching according to the International Coaching Federation (ICF), the coach must relate to the client team as a unit (2020, p. 5). As for how to do that, we hope that this book offers innovative methodological guidance.

Seeing Groups (Everywhere)

As a social species, connected and interdependent—think: Robinson Crusoe's "no man is an island" or Tom Hanks in *Cast Away*—we are always in groups. Native American and Indigenous cultures have practiced a way of life in which it is understood that everything and everyone is connected. Geneticists are now discovering scientific proof of this ancient understanding embedded in our DNA (Dobbs, 2013). In Western culture, shifting to seeing that we are always in groups requires a challenging, but experientially learnable, shift of ontology. By experiential, we mean that the shift occurs through a doing-with-others (rather than through cognitive acts). By ontology, we intend a different "lens and mindset" through which to view the world around us. One example in human history of such an ontological shift occurred in the late Renaissance. In the early 1600s, Galileo published scientific evidence that the sun, rather than the earth, was at the center of the universe. This caused a huge upheaval in how people saw themselves in the world and in relation to God. The Catholic Church felt so threatened by this new way of seeing that they forced Galileo to retract his findings. As we know, that did not stop the shift to heliocentrism. Today we characterize that moment in human history as a scientific revolution. Humans created and disseminated a new lens—both scientific and cultural—through which to operate in the world.

Another kind of shift, this one in the 20th century, is that of social constructionism—the idea that we construct—socially—our understandings of how the world works, the norms of our society and who we are in it. We do this principally through creating narratives, mobilizing language and communication, inclusive of people's subjective experiences. Ken Gergen was an early proponent of and one of the pioneers of social constructionism. Chair of the Psychology Department at Swarthmore College when he published *The Saturated Self* (1991), Gergen postulated that what we can know in this post-modern world is created in relation to others also living in this moment. In other words, our understandings cannot be reduced to a single Truth; they change as the world changes.

Appreciating that we humans are the producers of world change and also the product of all of human history up until this moment, enables seeing groups. We live in society—with norms and rules that we are meant to follow—*and* history, made by humans who have again and again broken with these norms and rules to create something new. It is that capacity that we tap into in social therapeutic work: The capacity to create groups everywhere and to transform ourselves while doing so. Social therapeutics embraces the intentionality of creating a performance together by asking, "How do we want to do this?" Unfortunately, American capitalist culture (society) relates to us as consumers—of diagnoses, of products, of problems, of roles. It alienates us from our experiences and feelings as well as from others' experiences and feelings.

Taking the group with you

Sometimes the group will be working on something and a more experienced group member may say to another, "Take the group with you, when you're nervous and walking into a meeting." Usually there is someone in the group who objects to that metaphorical direction. They see it as ridiculous or as a weakness, saying something like, "Why would I take the group with me? I am an individual. What I do in group is separate from my life." Yet, when clients do take the group with them, they are embracing what they have created together. In holding onto individualism, that group member sees the group's work as a consumer, as someone whose role is to get as much out of the group as they can without giving much. To not take the group with them is a rejection of the group's offer, the coach and what everyone has built together.

Here is an example of what "taking the group" looks like.

A client does what she calls a "U-turn" in group. At first, she provides leadership to the group, saying something beyond herself, something bold and helpful to the group. Then, she has reactions to having done that and backtracks, takes it back and feels humiliated. This continues to be something the group engages with her on. Two months later, she reports to the group how getting closer to and building the group helped her through a recent struggle:

"I was in the mountains with Antonio (the person I have started seeing) and I felt shame and fear of failure many times (when I was cooking, when I was hiking, when I was doing anything I don't do on a normal basis). In those moments I reminded myself of what we all have built together in group and I felt so proud. I thought about: What would [group member] Michelle say right now? What would Roscoe say? Coach? How do I create a new performance in this moment? The group has helped me through the 'U-turns' that I'm inclined to make out of habit and reminded me that I have power and that I can be a leader in those moments. And everything turned out great! I'm grateful to be building our group with all of you and thank you for giving me that support."

This story exemplifies the social therapeutic process of "deconstructing the sense of self . . . and reconstructing the concept of social relationship." In doing so, people "exercise their collective power to create new emotional growth" (Newman & Holzman, 2004, p. 78).

It's All in the Activity!

Just as the knowledge that smoking or high sugar intake is bad for us is not enough to make us quit, it takes more than *knowing* the positive impact of sociality in order to effect it. In our cognitive-dominant world, our overthinking brains become obstacles to growth and development. In *The End of Knowing* (1997), Newman and Holzman entered the fray of the intellectual debates of the 1990s over whether, if and how science could continue and in what form. They dissect the modernist thirst for knowledge, tracing the history of science and its methodological error in expanding into social sciences, an area in which scientific objectivity is impossible. They offer social therapeutics as a positive way out of the modern fly bottle. They introduce *performed activity* as the path forward for the human race. We have to *do*, and *do with others*, for emotional growth to become possible. Relating to our doings as a performance, as we reviewed in the previous chapter, creates the possibility of doing something new, of becoming "a head taller" or other than who we are (our fixed role or identity). Newman and Holzman write:

> [It is a] story/myth that human life and growth require a way of knowing the world. It is this epistemic posture (considered by many to be as natural as our upright stance) more than any particular epistemological positions that fascinates and disturbs us. This book is part of our call for the *end of knowing* as the revolutionary, humane, and developmental move our species needs to make at this moment in history [emphasis in original] (1997, p. 7).

Of course, there are numerous wellness practices with widespread followings today that do not rely upon knowing, and instead sit in the moment and attend to the emergent. Coaching locates itself as part of this surge in non-cognitive-driven wellness practices. For example, a key posture of the coach is to "maintain presence," i.e., to stay in the moment with the client and be comfortable "working in a space of not knowing" (ICF, 2020, p. 14).

On our best days as social therapeutic coaches and therapists, we see, articulate and respond to human activity rather than responding to the particular facts, causes or explanations to which our clients are pointing. Is the group being judgmental? Distant? Conflicted? Loving? Curious? How is the group relating? In seeing and relating to the group rather than individuals, coaches shift from "me" to "we" environments, from interpreting to doing/responding, and from explaining to giving to the group. This is our attempt to put into writing a concretization of the ontological shift of social therapeutic method. Parts II–IV of this book attempt to show it. Hopefully the combined "talking about" and "showing" will make the practice of social therapeutics accessible.

In the building of the group, participants attend to what they are doing together. This creates space for collectively creating meaning and denies the individualistic pull to speak in, search for and identify a Truth or right answer. Holzman writes, "The [social therapeutic] methodology shifts the focus from cognition to the collaborative activity of creating something new together" (2020, p. 179). Social therapeutic clients relate to themselves and others as givers to the group, as giving the material from which the collaborative activity draws. This is another key element of seeing groups, to work with what is given as an offer to build with. Doing so functions as an inversion of our "getting" culture. Seeing groups is inseparable from seeing offers; building the group ("Yes, and-ing . . .," making offers) occurs without knowing beforehand what we are building together or where we are going.

Seeing the group rather than analyzing it

Ursula is a very successful professional. She is analytical, thoughtful and works with hundreds of people at her job. When she first joined the group, she would come prepared with questions for each group member, like she does with her work colleagues. It is part of her daily mindfulness routine to ponder others, to analyze their strengths and weaknesses and how she can best operate with them.

After a few weeks in group, she shared that she was learning to do something different—to experience the emotionality in the group, rather than analyze it. She saw that analyzing individuals in the group was a way of stepping out of the group rather than being in it. She was starting to see other areas of her life where she absenced herself from what was happening, rather than getting closer to others in the moment.

Beyond the Enlightenment

To become comfortable with performed activity (not knowing), we must engage with and dismantle the cognitive-dominant scaffolding we have inherited from the Enlightenment—the modernist philosophy/ methodology which positioned the individual as its central unit. We already mentioned Galileo's early 17th-century public demonstration that the sun, rather than the earth, anchors the universe. The advances in mathematics in 16th and 17th century Europe that enabled Galileo's discovery also ushered in the birth pangs of the modern scientific era. It was an era that chipped away at eradicating mystery, magic and God's omnipotence from everyday life, replacing them with an understanding of the natural world that could be measured, quantified, categorized and thereby *known*.

Incredible advances in human civilization have been produced through the scientific method. Here was a rational, objective system through which to study and discover the world. All of this seems natural to us. This is how we are taught science in school. Inquiries can be quantified, results predicted and categorized. Evidence and facts are used to prove or disprove a hypothesis. Causes and effects can be postulated and scientifically proven. Particular parts of a thing can be separated out for study. Whereas science replaced believing in God, today we relate to science as a God, an omnipotent force whose findings we unquestionably believe in.

The Enlightenment can be understood as the widespread cultural diffusion of the tools of scientific method. Starting in the 18th century, philosophers, intellectuals and the elite emphasized reason and individualism as a replacement for community and faith. It birthed a new political form: Democracy, based on the vote of the individual. It birthed a new economic form: Capitalism, based on the individual consumer. And as the Industrial Revolution unfolded, it birthed a new social form: Psychology, based on the behavior of the individual. Giving primacy to reason and rationalism drove a relentless pursuit of knowledge, justified imperialism and slavery on a scale never before seen in human history and drove the global expansion of capitalism. The results have been both extraordinarily productive and devastatingly horrific.

As we mentioned in Chapter 1, the discipline of psychology was born in the midst of this seismic shift, with a focus on individuals and individualism embedded within it from the start. From there, psychology embedded itself into mass culture. And here we are today believing that the individual is primary.

This is a simplistic history, of course. There are many fantastic sources on the birth of modern science, capitalism and the Enlightenment (Hobsbawm, 1962; 1975; Newman & Holzman, 1996; Wootton, 2015). Our goal here is to radically accept that we are all products of our times and carry with us the assumptions of the Enlightenment. Social therapeutics challenges the rational, scientific way of seeing and studying humans as individuals, as established by psychology and psychiatry, in favor of the fundamental *sociality of the human species*. We are a social species, rather than individuals contained within our own minds.

Two major premises of this book are that a) those modernist assumptions no longer help people to grow and develop, and b) it is possible to break out of them and create new ways to go forward. Indeed, we would argue that the conceptual revolution is already underway—we have shared in this and previous chapters statements from significant public intellectuals and leaders on how the scaffolding of modernism and the institutions built upon them are no longer functioning. On a cultural level, we must already be living in the midst of this shift into a new way of seeing for these insights to make mainstream headlines—even if we are not able to articulate exactly (read: know) what it is or how that is happening. Social therapeutics—with its unique root influences remixed and built upon by Newman and Holzman and informed by their community-building efforts—is a methodological articulation of a radical new approach to human development.

To go somewhere new, we must embrace individuals and individualism while also shifting to seeing and building groups. Newman and Holzman's articulation of being/becoming introduced in the last chapter is helpful here. In social therapeutics we relate to clients as socialized individuals who are building groups—the activity of which overthrows the assumptions of who we are as individuals. We are simultaneously doing both. We are products of our environment *and* creators of environments. It is that dialectical relationship that can hold the paradox of individual/group. Embracing that two things can be going on at the same time (both/and) opens the window to seeing what something/someone is and what they are becoming. It creates space for *possibility*, for new things to emerge *in relation to others*.

The Enlightenment framework cannot hold paradox. The Enlightenment was built upon the millennia-old Western philosophical idea of separating out particulars from the whole and then putting them back together as dualisms such as mind and body, inner and outer. However, whereas 20th-century social sciences like psychology moved more aggressively towards evidence-based models, the most advanced hard sciences, like quantum physics, were making discoveries that could only occur by giving up traditional scientific method. Holding paradoxes is grounded in a much newer form of science.

Quantum Physics and Relationality

Quantum physics was established in the 1920s when subatomic particles could be studied for the first time. Those particles did not adhere to the normal laws of physics. For example, particles could be both present and not present at the same time, in relation to other particles. The dualism of either/or was unhelpful to scientists as they sought to explain what they were seeing. With this, the foundations of modern science were immediately antiquated.

How can "A" and "not A" exist simultaneously? What does it mean to come into existence only in relation to the other? World-renowned theoretical physicist Carlo Rovelli beautifully articulates this contradictory unknowingness in regard to humans and our reality as we currently "know" it: "Properties are not determined until the moment of these interactions; they exist only in relation to something else. *Everything is what it is only with respect to something else* [emphasis added]" (2021, p. 199). We draw on Rovelli to deepen Newman and Holzman's articulation of being/becoming. It is in the moment in which we are relating with others that our "properties" emerge. As a social species we are always in relation to others. Thus, the answers to who we are/who we are becoming are not to be found within ourselves, but in our doings with others, especially the doing of our relationships.

Relationality in this sense is outward-facing and does not seek out a universal Truth or core essence. Rovelli illustrates this by debunking his long-held story of himself as a "solitary and rebellious 'I' . . . independent and totally free." He instead points to humans as a rippling network of networks; it is our *relational activity* that "make(s) up our 'I', as our society, our cultural, spiritual and political life" (2021, p. 200). Individuals are inseparable from the group and the world. *Our relational activity makes our world.* This is hard to see. Multinational corporations, media

Table 3.1 Differences between relationship-centered and client-centered approaches

Relationship-centered Approach	Client-centered Approach
The relationship is primary (client/coach; couple/coach; group including coach)	The client's individual identity is primary
Client and coach create/lead with what emotional development work to tackle	Client sets objectives of work
Client and coach relationship is key	Client's thoughts, actions and emotions are key
Coach asks, "What are we creating together when you say . . ."	Coach says, "I am here for you."
Coach asks, "What's important to you in saying this to me?" and follows the activity of creating the conversation together	Coach asks more questions on the content or how client might arrive at their desired goal, follows the content and client's individual emotional expression

giants, DSM-IV, political parties and the makers of personality and love categories are all deeply invested in having us believe that what makes our world are the descriptions and labels they have prepackaged for us, usually in the name of making a buck for themselves.

If what occurs is in relation to something/someone else, then humans become empowered to create meaning out of that relationality, a more connected alternative to the passive consumerism shaped by the types of entities just listed. If we are in relation to each other, and the meaning of those relations are constructed—built—by us in the moment, then we humans have the capacity to transform emotionally, socially, culturally, politically, etc.

Relational dialogue

The following interchanges attempt to put the spotlight squarely on what acts of relationality can look like in the coaching session. These will feel weird to the reader. Often it feels weird saying lines like these to a client. However, doing so breaks us out of the disassociation that occurs in our relationships. The examples below illustrate what simultaneously creating the conversation and the relationship (tool-and-result) might look like. The *how* of interpersonal interaction—how am I impacting on you/the group right now—is integral to social therapeutics. Seeing, embracing and expressing our relationality as it emerges in the moment is important material to be built with. In group work, either the coach or a group member might ask the questions we are about to present. For simplicity purposes, these are examples from individual and couples work. The questions pointing toward relationality are in bold.

Example #1

Client: "I can never make up my mind and procrastinate making decisions all the time."

Coach: **"What is it like to say that to me?"**

Client: "It's a relief. I don't usually talk about this with anyone."

Here, the emotionality came into existence in relationship to the coach, in the moment of the coach asking the question and the client responding to it. It was the activity of conversing together, rather than the client's internal wiring, that produced the emotionality. Once produced, it becomes material to build with.

Example #2

Partner 1:   "My partner shuts down when we have a fight. It drives me crazy. He won't say what he wants. He won't say what he feels."

Coach: **"Partner 2, what is it like for you to hear Partner 1's experience of you two having a fight?"**

Partner 2:   "I don't shut down."

Coach: "Well, I appreciate you giving that. I am actually asking a different question. When you hear Partner 1 describe their experience, what's that like for you?"

Partner 2:   "It's hard to hear."

Coach: "What's hard about it?"

Partner 2:   "I try so hard to be a good partner so that we don't have fights. I hate fighting. And I get frozen when Partner 1's blood starts to boil. I can tell she's pissed when I won't talk."

Coach: **"How is it for both of you to give your experiences of each other when you are having or about to have a fight?"**

These relational questions bring/keep the focus into the coaching room, on their activity in the moment (rather than explaining, labelling or describing situations in the past). Inviting clients to give what is going on for them in the moment in relation to the other is important for creating the emotional zpd. It opens the possibility of experiencing that what they give can be built with, created with, responded to.

Example #3

Client (speaking for 10 minutes):   ". . . My professors don't like me. I raise my hand and they don't call on me. The other students are so confident. I am always worried I am going to say something stupid."

Coach: **"Are you wondering what it's like for me to hear you giving all this?"**

Client (with an uncomfortable smile): "Yes."

Coach: "Oh, OK. Maybe you could ask me, 'What's it like for you to hear me saying all this?'"

Client: "What's it like for you to hear me say this?"

Coach (enthusiastically): "Thank you for asking! Before I answer you. **How was that for you to ask me that question?"**

Client: "Uncomfortable, weird, good. I have never asked that before. I don't usually think about the other person's experience when I am talking."

Coach: "What a wonderful discovery. I invite you to keep getting uncomfortable with all of this! I would like to answer your question of my experience of you talking about school: I experienced confusion, I didn't know where to focus. I had a hard time following you and wasn't sure where you wanted me to look. **How is that to hear from me?"**

Client: "It's hard to hear." (Extended pause.) "When I am unsure of what to do or what is expected of me, I just keep talking."

The coach takes the risk of being ridiculous in asking a question to the client's question (that the coach directed them to ask). The coach also gives something that is difficult to hear—that the client's internal loop is getting in the way of the two of them connecting and building together. The coach's performance is one of "Hello, we are here together, you can be an active participant in building our relationship. We impact on each other and we are allowed to invite and be curious about our responses to each other." Many clients have no idea that this is possible—thus, the encouragement to the client to actually speak aloud (perform) the new lines. The growth that emerges is experiential and highly impactful.

Relational awareness is the activity of attending to the relationship. How is our relationship doing? How is the group doing? What is it like to hear what Joanna gave to the group? How was it for you, Joanna, to give it? To hear the group's response? These are all questions that point people toward each other and the group, and away from what is happening in their heads. Clients quickly experience the relief of having tools to do something other than be stuck with the tape in their mind that loops with knowing certainty of what is really going on, what others are thinking, etc.

Taken as a whole, social therapeutics offers a practice that is group-focused, performance-based, focused on relational activity, non-knowing and attentive to the emergent. Social therapeutic practitioners lead their groups in "the activity of discovering a method of relating to emotional talk relationally rather than individualistically and as activistic rather than representational" (Holzman, 2017, p. 36). With this, we believe social therapeutics can solve the "conundrum" of group coaching work as articulated by Manfred F.R. Kets de Vries (2014), Distinguished Clinical Professor of Leadership Development and Organizational Change at INSEAD. Bringing Vygotsky back into the picture can help. Seeing the group is inseparable from the tool-and-result activity of creating the group. Building the group is a self-conscious, creative, relational activity. Here is how Newman put it in a supervisory session with practitioners:

> There is a recognizable activity called building the group. It's as much a building activity as building a bridge. You have to help a grouping of people do that together as the creating of the conditions for their emotional growth. That is a Vygotskian concept. The creating of the zpd is best understood as a developmental rejection of individuated growth. It is saying, in effect, that people do not grow individually. They grow as a social unit. And so in social therapy, we have to create the appropriate social unit for emotional growth (Holzman & Mendez, 2003, p. 70).

Much of this quote encapsulates what we have covered up to this point. The additional element, emotional growth and how to relate to emotional talk, is the final area we wish to explore in social therapeutics.

Exercises

1) Go through a day asking people you are close with, "What's it like for you to hear me say that?" and discover what it is like for you to do so. Notice if people's responses to you are any different, and if so, how.

2) Notice when you make dualistic separations: Mind/body; inside/ outside; thought/emotion. Try seeing (holding) both at the same time.

3) Try telling a story by using "we" as the regular pronoun, rather than "I" or "me."

Notes

1 Address to incoming class of 1984, Yale University (reproduced in Giamatti, 1990).

2 In 2020, 186,763 Americans died by suicide, alcohol and drug use (Trust for America's Health, 2022, p. 24). This accounts for 5.6% of total deaths and represents the 5th most common cause of death (Ahmad & Anderson, 2021).

3 For more on the breadth of Newman's work, visit www.frednewmanphd.com.

4 For an excellent source on group therapy overall, see Yalom (1985). See Agazarian (2018) for a psychotherapeutic understanding of the importance of attending to the group unit. See Rød & Fridjhon (2020) for systems-oriented couples work which also attends to the importance of the total relationship.

References

Agazarian, Y.M. (2018). *The Visible and Invisible Group*. Taylor & Francis.

Ahmad, F. B. & Anderson, R.N. (2021, March 31). The Leading Causes of Death in the US for 2020. *JAMA*, 325(18)1829–1830. https:/doi.org/10.1001/jama.2021.5469

Brock, V. (2014). *Sourcebook of Coaching History*. https://libraryofprofessionalcoaching. com/wp-app/wp-content/uploads/2022/01/SOCH-2nd-Edition-Free-2021-01-31-Secure-1.pdf

Brooks, D. (2019, February 18). A Nation of Weavers. *The New York Times*. https://www. nytimes.com/2019/02/18/opinion/culture-compassion.html

Brooks, D. (2019, July 3). The lies our culture tells us about what matters—and a better way to live. *TED*. Retrieved November 27, 2022 from: https://www.youtube.com/ watch?v=iB4MS1hsWXU&t=4s

Cigna. (2022). *The Loneliness Epidemic Persists: A Post-Pandemic Look at the State of Loneliness among U.S. Adults*. Retrieved December 27, 2022 from: https://newsroom.cigna. com/loneliness-epidemic-persists-post-pandemic-look

Dobbs, D. (2013, September 3). The Social Life of Genes. *Pacific Standard*. https://psmag. com/social-justice/the-social-life-of-genes-64616

Dockray, H. (2019, May 24). Self-care isn't enough. We need community care to thrive. *Mashable.com*. Retrieved January 15, 2022 from: https://mashable.com/article/community-care-versus-self-care

Eubanks, V. (2022, July 5). His PTSD, and My Struggle to Live With It. *The New York Times Magazine*. Retrieved July 27, 2022 from: https://www.nytimes. com/2022/07/05/magazine/ptsd-trauma.html

Gergen, K. (1991). *The Saturated Self: Dilemma of Identity in Contemporary Life*. Basic Books.

Giamatti, A.B. (1990). *A Free and Ordered Space: The Real World of the University*. W.W. Norton and Company.

Grant, A. (2019, May 2). *Mentors are Good. Coaches are Better*. LinkedIn. Retrieved August 2, 2022 from: https://www.linkedin.com/pulse/mentors-good-coaches-better-adam-grant/

Grant, A. (2021, July 10). There's a Specific Kind of Joy We've Been Missing. *The New York Times*. Retrieved July 10, 2021 from: https://www.nytimes.com/2021/07/10/opinion/sunday/covid-group-emotions-happiness.html

Hall, J.A. (2022, August 11). The Price We Pay for Being Less Social. *The Wall Street Journal*. https://www.wsj.com/articles/price-we-pay-for-being-less-social-1166006 8416?mod=Searchresults_pos1&page=1

Hari, J. (2018). *Lost Connections: Why You're Depressed and How to Find Hope*. Bloomsbury.

Hobsbawm, E. (1962). *The Age of Revolution: 1789–1848*. Vintage Books.

Hobsbawm, E. (1975). *The Age of Capital: 1848–1875*. Vintage Books.

Holzman, L. (2015). Relating to people as revolutionaries. In D. Loewenthal (Ed.), *Critical Psychotherapy, Psychoanalysis and Counselling: Implications for Practice* (pp.125–137). Palgrave MacMillan.

Holzman, L. (2017). *Vygotsky at Work and Play*. Routledge.

Holzman, L. (2020). Constructing Social Therapeutics. In S. McNamee, M. Gergen, C. Camargo-Borges & E. Rasera (Eds.), *The SAGE Handbook of Social Constructionist Practice* (pp. 171–182). SAGE Publications Ltd.

Holzman, L. & Mendez, R. (Eds.). (2003). *Psychological Investigations: A Clinician's Guide to Social Therapy*. Brunner-Routledge.

International Coaching Federation. (2020). *ICF Team Coaching Competencies: Moving Beyond One-to-One Coaching*. v 13.11. Retrieved December 27, 2022 from: https://coachingfederation.org/app/uploads/2021/01/Team-Coaching-Competencies-4.pdf

Kets de Vries, M.F.R. (2014, February). The Group Coaching Conundrum. *International Journal of Evidence Based Coaching and Mentoring*, 12(1), 79–91.

Newman, F. (1991). *The Myth of Psychology*. Castillo International.

Newman, F. & Holzman, L. (1996). *Unscientific Psychology: A Cultural-Performatory Approach to Understanding Human Life*. Praeger.

Newman, F. & Holzman, L. (1997). *The End of Knowing: A new developmental way of learning*. Routledge.

Newman, F. & Holzman, L. (2004). Power, Authority and Pointless Activity (The Developmental Discourse of Social Therapy). In T. Strong & D. Pare (Eds.), *Furthering Talk: Advances in Discursive Therapies* (pp. 73–86). Kluwer Academic/Plenum Publishers.

Poulain, M., Pes, G. M., Grasland, C., Carru, C., Ferrucci, L., Baggio, G., Franceschi, C. & Deiana, L. (2004). Identification of a geographic area characterized by extreme longevity in the Sardinia island: the AKEA study. *Experimental Gerontology*, 39(9), 1423–1429.

Putnam, R.D. (2001). *Bowling Alone: The Collapse and Revival of American Community*. Simon & Schuster Paperbacks.

Real, T. (2022). *Us: Getting Past You and Me to Build a More Loving Relationship*. Rodale.

Rød, A. & Fridjhon, M. (2020). *Creating Intelligent Teams: Leading with Relationship Systems Intelligence*. Independently published.

Rogers, C. (1961). *On Becoming a Person: A Therapist's View of Psychotherapy*. Houghton Mifflin.

Rovelli, C. (2021). *Helgoland: Making Sense of the Quantum Revolution.* Riverhead Books.

Roy, A. (2020, April 3). The Pandemic is a Portal. *Financial Times.* Retrieved June 6, 2021 from: https://www.ft.com/content/10d8f5e8-74eb-11ea-95fe-fcd274e920ca

Skiffington, S. & Zeus, P. (2003). *Behavioral coaching: How to build sustainable personal and organizational strength.* McGraw-Hill.

Sukel, K. (2019, November 13). *In Sync: How Humans are Hard-Wired for Social Relationships.* Dana Foundation Report from Neuroscience 2019. https://dana.org/article/in-sync-how-humans-are-hard-wired-for-social-relationships/

Surowiecki, J. (2005). *The Wisdom of Crowds.* Anchor Books.

Trust for America's Health. (2022). *Pain in the Nation: The Epidemics of Alcohol, Drug, and Suicide Deaths.* https://www.tfah.org/wp-content/uploads/2022/05/TFAH_2022_PainIntheNation_Fnl.pdf

Weave: The Social Fabric Project. (2019, February 13). *The Relationalist Manifesto.* https://www.aspeninstitute.org/wp-content/uploads/2019/02/Weave-Relationalist-Manifesto.pdf

Weissbourd, R., Batanova, M., Lovison, V., & Torres, E. (2021, February 9). Loneliness in America: How the Pandemic Has Deepened an Epidemic of Loneliness and What We Can Do About It. *Harvard Graduate School of Education & Making Caring Common Project.* Retrieved January 15, 2022 from: https://static1.squarespace.com/static/5b7c56e255b02c683659fe43/t/6021776bdd04957c4557c212/1612805995893/Loneliness+in+America+2021_02_08_FINAL.pdf

Wootton, D. (2015). *The Invention of Science: A New History of the Scientific Revolution.* Harper.

Yalom, Y. (1985). *Theory and Practice of Group Therapy.* Basic Books.

4

Seeing Emotional Growth as the Path to Transformation

While we may *misunderstand*, we do not *misexperience*.

Vine Deloria Jr.[1]

The way to solve the problem you see in life, is to live in a way that will make what is problematic disappear.

Ludwig Wittgenstein[2]

We just built the case for seeing groups; now we will tackle the challenge of seeing and creating emotional growth, the heart of social therapeutics. We are interested in the emotional growth of the group, or ensemble, because when the group develops, individuals grow. In our culture, there is little talk of emotional growth, certainly not as pertaining to creating groups. We believe that this has something to do with how emotions and emotionality are understood in our culture.

Seeing the "We" in Emotions

The dominant areas of psychology teach that emotions are an individual expression of something going on inside of us—usually in our brains, our ventral vagal system or with somatic work, inside our mind-body. These emotions have been caused by something—another person, generational trauma, an event, our genes or a broken neurotransmitter.

88

DOI: 10.4324/9781003326465-6

This understanding of emotions and emotionality is instrumentalist, or tool-for-result (see Chapter 2). For example, we generally think something along the lines of, "If I feel this way, then I should think about/tell myself something (tool) that will change how I am feeling (result)." Emotions are static things until moved by a cause, universally knowable, understandable and felt. If expressed properly, they can get us the results we want. What follows from this line of reasoning is that emotions can and should be identified and managed, so that they do not overtake us and make us act in socially inappropriate and unhealthy ways. This conceptual package functions within the "me" paradigm, where (individual, internal) processes, skill sets and mindsets are isolated into parts, known and changed or mastered. These assumptions are embedded in other "emotional" terms such as the following: Emotional recovery, emotional healing, emotional intelligence and emotional maturity.

Thankfully, discoveries in neuroscience are driving an expansion of understanding that emotions are not only biologically or physiologically driven, but also socially constructed. That is, that our interactions with the world play a role in the creation of emotions and the meaning we ascribe to them (Barrett, 2017). For example, during the first weeks of Covid, many experienced emotional distress as obviously generated by the world in lockdown, rather than by something inside of us. Another more ordinary example is the difference between saying, "My depression keeps me from going out and visiting friends" (an internal causal process) and "My partner yelled at me which triggered my depression which keeps me from going out and visiting friends." While still framed as an internal and individualistic experience, this second example acknowledges that how others operate does in fact have an impact on how we feel—and that that feeling might be unique to us. The word "depressed" might mean one thing to one person and something else to another which could be different again than the clinical definition of "depressed."

We would posit that the early coaches of the 1980s had some understanding of the social construction of emotionality. Recall that coaching grew out of the social movements that challenged how society was organized—politically, socially, sexually and emotionally. For Werner Erhard, his *est* seminars focused on participants taking responsibility for their actions and emotions. "Own it!" Erhard would say to the group. Coach U founder Thomas Leonard encouraged "overresponding" to big failure moments in one's life, a strategy that encompasses taking responsibility, being curious and exploring how it happened, getting vulnerable and looking at how one participated in creating the mess, working on it and then doing something different (1998, pp. 43–51). One implication of directing clients in this way is encouraging them to consider how one *chooses* to live in the world and interact with others when it comes to how one feels.

With all this said, the assumption remains that emotions are made and reside inside of us. Perhaps the world might impact on them, but they are still "ours." Without negating that we can experience emotions on an individual level, some public intellectuals are questioning that emotions get produced at an individual level and belong to each of us individually.

Thomas Hübl, renowned international facilitator, teacher and author, sees emotional pain as collective. He speaks specifically to trauma and locates traumatic experiences as part of the collective experience of the population (Hübel & Avritt, 2020; see also Menakem, 2017; van der Kolk, 2014). We find this perspective helpful in a general sense, in that it raises a challenge to *all* individual, private emotions. We agree with Hübl that what follows from identifying emotional pain as a collective experience is that the cure to emotional pain must also occur in collective—i.e., group—settings.

Another perspective on emotions leans toward relationality, along the lines of what we outlined in the last chapter. It comes from organizational psychologist and executive coach Adam Grant. In his opinion piece for *The New York Times*, he wrote, "Most people view emotions as existing primarily or even exclusively in their heads . . . But the reality is that emotions are inherently social: *They're woven through our interactions* . . . Peak happiness lies mostly in collective activity [emphasis added]" (2021). Here, the sociality of emotions feels closer to a social therapeutic understanding that the activity of creating shared meaning together is the pathway toward emotional growth. *How we relate* impacts how we feel and vice versa. The activity of meaning-making is created collectively and produces a felt emotional experience.

Thus, emotions and emotionality transform in working with the "we." They no longer reside in us; they are in the world, created socially. As such, both our emotional pain and our cure are social. They are neither products nor possessions of individuals. They are products of the shared relational activity of meaning-making. They are jointly created, in a specific moment and in a specific environment. We create emotions. In the "I" model, emotions are created for us.

Radical Acceptance

As co-creators of emotions, we are empowered to create an infinite number of them—not just a range of four or five and not just one at a time. As Newman liked to paraphrase from Shakespeare, "There are more emotions in Heaven and Earth, than are dreamt of in your psychology textbook."[3] That does not occur by magic, by conjuring up how one should feel or be. It comes from creating out of what there is. When emotions are created for us, it is easy to imagine that we should get rid of one and place another onto us. "Should" is a powerful word in pre-made emotionality.

For social therapeutics, there is no growth without accepting where you are at, without embracing what is coming up emotionally for you and without accepting where the relationship is at, or the world for that matter. If someone is feeling angry, they could choose to give that to the group to build with, rather than stay with the tape in their head that says, "I should not be feeling angry right now. I will go home and do exercises to not feel angry." The coach models this type of giving when they express their emotional subjectivity during a session. In coaching, we offer up our felt experience without holding onto it as a Truth. It becomes material to build with, to co-create with.

Having the experience that we can build with each other in the moment with where we are at in the moment is incredibly empowering. It is a radical acceptance of what there is to work with. Improvisation gives us the strongest look at this. The "Yes, and . . ." principle requires the performer to embrace and accept what their scene partner(s) is giving and add to it. Can we live a "Yes, and . . ." life offstage? Yes! Radical acceptance is a precondition and a result of creating the environment in which emotional growth becomes possible.

Radically accepting what someone has to give

Rebecca had been in a Life Development Group about three weeks and had hardly participated. One week, a leader in the group asked Rebecca why she was there and how come she did not speak much. Rebecca gave a short answer. Another group member asked the coach for help: "Coach, I think we need your help. Rebecca is here and we are glad she is here, but she isn't giving much to the group and I am getting reactive to that." The coach responded, "Maybe can we create a way to ask Rebecca what goes on for her while she's here in group." The group discussed this and decided to ask Rebecca that question, to which it became apparent that she was very actively listening to the group, and also that Rebecca is very shy and prefers to observe rather than get involved.

Several group members then turned to the coach for help on how to relate to Rebecca since she seemed to be saying her shyness would keep her from participating. The coach suggested the group find a way to developmentally create with Rebecca given who she is, a reluctant participant. After much back and forth, the group chose to invite Rebecca to interject at any point in the session, "I just wanted you all to know that I am feeling shy right now." Then, the group could decide in that moment whether to stop what it was doing and engage with Rebecca, or acknowledge that she was deciding to give what she could and continue on the work the group was engaged in.

If we are creators (of emotions), then when we speak in/give to the group what we say/give becomes material for group members to create with, to "Yes, and . . .," to complete and to play with (see Chapter 2). This is another path into seeing the activity of the group. This activity is a building/creating of the group, the unit of growth, grounded in awareness. Giving to the group what is going on for us in the moment constitutes a deprivatization of what we hold "inside."

In group, someone might say, "I have been feeling depressed." Another group member might ask, "What do you mean by 'depressed'?

What does that look like for you?" Yet another group member might say, "I would like to share my experience of you when you say you're depressed." The group's response is relational (see Chapter 3). People are caring and, at the same time, the material they are giving to help build the group challenges "the privatization of the emotional concern and the language that holds the privatization in place. Clients learn experientially that you can't only grow yourself, but you can grow in the process of participating in building the group" (Holzman & Mendez, 2003, pp. 64–65). We emphasize here the importance of seeing that giving to the group is growthful. Oftentimes in traditional group work, if other group members are allowed to respond to each other, it is in service of getting

Table 4.1 Current cultural/psychological and social therapeutic understandings of emotions

Current Cultural/Psychological	Social Therapeutic
Emotions live inside of us (where exactly?): • Brain • Generational trauma (whole body) • Genes	Emotions feel private but they are socially and relationally created; both emotional pain and the cure to emotional pain are social
We can control them inside of us before they get out: • Once they get out, we can be washed over by them • Emotions make us do things, we lose "rationality," they are bigger than us in the moment: ○ There is a cause to be known (we are not really angry for this moment, but from a past experience)	We can make decisions on how to perform in any given moment; we can recognize the emotion we are experiencing and choose to do something different
Emotions must be expressed in socially appropriate (normative) ways or else the individual has a problem that needs to be fixed: • Usually via cognitive-behavioral approaches	Emotions are offers: • To give to others • To create with
We can know our (emotional) Truth	We can play with and make new meanings with our emotions
	We can create new emotions with others

that "depressed" member to understand the better way or right way to be in the world. The goal of others' speaking is the improvement of that particular member. In social therapeutic groups, participants more commonly first experience growth through giving to the group those kinds of philosophical questions and relational remarks cited above. Later, they experience growth in giving their emotional pain to the group and being given to in turn by the group. Either way, the growth arises through that activity we call "building the group."

Emotional Growth

This brings us to emotional growth. Surprisingly, when we turned to an internet search to find how others in the helping professions characterize it, we found very little on the topic. Newman and Holzman use the term frequently. As social therapeutic practitioners, we know it when we see it in our groups, couples' relationships and clients. We will attempt to show the reader examples of it in the subsequent practical sections. What our research has yielded is that there is no existing definition of the term "emotional growth."

What does surface from an internet search is information about childhood social and emotional development—such as the theories of developmental psychologist Erik Erickson and others influenced by him. Thus, to the extent that emotional development exists in today's mainstream culture and lexicon, it applies primarily to children. These theories identify how parents play the leading role in teaching children socially acceptable norms of emotional expression, and what happens to children when the parents do not. These theories describe a progression of stages of development just as Piaget did in the case of childhood cognitive development (recall from Chapter 2 the methodological differences between Piaget and Vygotsky). Today, most academic research on the social and emotional development of children focuses on how to best support and succeed at learning in the school environment. This narrow view of emotional development obscures so much of our human capacity and creativity.

While not naming it emotional growth, coaching does nod towards it. Positive psychology, which has had a sizable impact on coaching (recall that it emerged out of the Human Potential Movement which we referenced in earlier chapters), acknowledges that growth can occur. There are some qualities that individuals can develop with the support of a mental wellness practitioner, such as openness to experiences, existential awareness, freedom of choice, creativity and constructive behavior.

Newman and Holzman have used the term "emotional development" as an expression of a relational process emerging from people exercising their collective power. That process includes a deconstruction of our assumptions on emotions and emotionality and the generative building activity of meaning-making (Newman & Holzman, 2004, p. 78). A takeaway from this would be that emotional development occurs through doing, rather than knowing; through a relaxing of the self, rather than a clinging to it; through an inviting of emotional co-creation with others.

Harlene Anderson is a keen observer of social therapeutics and herself a pioneer in family therapy and the Postmodern Collaborative Approach. In her forward to *Psychological Investigations*, Anderson observed that "helping to build the group is a precursor to emotional growth" (2003, p. xii). She brings to life from another angle the concept of the emotional zpd developed by Newman and Holzman when they carried Vygotsky's ideas into the therapeutic/emotional space (see Chapter 2 for more on Vygotsky). Emotional process or emotional processing in a relational, non-dualistic manner is a critical ingredient in emotional growth. Newman, speaking with practitioners-in-training, notes the connection between process and growth:

If flowers had to decide what they were going to look like as a function of growth, they would never grow. It isn't knowing what's going to come, it's knowing that you choose to participate in the process that you think increases the likelihood of this mysterious developmental phenomenon happening.

Development is mysterious, not in a way that makes it unscientific or religious but mysterious in the best sense of the word, in the sense that we fully engage in a process that we don't know the outcome of (Holzman & Mendez, 2003, p. 67).

One look at the emotional growth of the group

A client, Jorge, announces in group he is feeling panicked over a work deadline. Rather than the group relating to Jorge as having a problem (work) that could be/needs to be solved in order to make the panic stop, the group relates to the statement as an offer to be built with. Group members ask what panic looks like for Jorge and how he usually handles deadlines. Someone in group shares how they experience Jorge as a very calm person and are shocked to hear he can panic. Jorge begins to experience that he can feel panic while giving his panic to the group, while the group (including Jorge) creates with what he is giving. This activity opens up the possibility of Jorge and all the clients seeing more/other options of how to be (with others) while feeling panic, or any other feeling. It opens up that we can create other options, that we can make choices.

Human beings are choice-makers and decision-makers. We can feel one thing (like the desire to punch someone) and do something different (tell the person that we are angry, take a deep breath or go for a walk). We can seek out the offer in what someone is saying and add onto it. Much like Newman's articulation of listening as a creative act in Chapter 2, the group created with Jorge's panic without knowing where they were going. In the group's creation a new possibility emerges, for example, that Jorge can feel panicked and also decide to call a friend and ask for help. He can perform something other than who he thinks he is. This activity resizes our emotions; they become more ordinary (and less empowered to take over us) as we invite others to complete us. Recall the metaphor of "the workout" mentioned in the last chapter. Just as our bodies get stronger and able to do more when we invest in physical workouts, so too do our emotionality and emotional growth when we invest in regular deprivatized emotional workouts.

The group brings emotional growth into being as it creates and recreates itself, week after week. Group growth gets expressed in its ability to build with a broader set of issues/activities/experiences. Group growth looks like greater intimacy within the group and with the coach. The group can hear more and see more offers to build with. A group can grow to be more demanding of how people are in group (e.g., you cannot come here drunk; we want more from that person in this moment; we are no longer going to pursue that person who has rejected the group's help time after time). And a group can grow to express more—including the group's emotionality: Their love, joy, anger, disappointment, hurt.

Who decides that the group is growing, and how it has grown? The group, which includes the coach. How is that measured? However the group decides to measure it. Even growth and measurement can be performed as a shared meaning-making activity. This, of course, makes it difficult to establish a fixed definition of emotional growth. And perhaps that is why the term is barely searchable on the internet. Nonetheless, we have decided to craft some language around what emotional growth is, even though we see it as continuous tool-and-result activity and thus impossible to reduce to a neatly defined thing. Here is our non-definition of emotional growth:

> The process of seeing additional options of relating to the group/others and oneself; acting upon those additional options through performing ahead of oneself/doing a new performance; experiencing being where you are/the group is/the relationship is *and* someplace new at the same time; relating to feelings and emotions as part of, but not overdetermining of, one's experience, which can contribute to creating the environment for growth.

Just as quantum physics required a new method for seeing and understanding it, so too with emotional growth. And from our point of view, social therapeutics is the method for seeing, creating and practicing it. We will now add one more element to our non-definition above.

Practicing Emotional Growth

What are some of the ingredients of emotional growth? The major material of emotional growth is language, *how* we speak together. What are we doing when we are speaking? Is it behavior, i.e., using words to get a result? Or is it a creative activity? Just as people are creators of their lives, so too are they continuous creators of their conversations, experiences and relationships. If language is something we *do* with one another, then meaning is what we create together as we do it. One type of meaning we can create together is emotional meaning. And therein lies the space for growth (Newman & Holzman, 2014, pp. 155–157). Holzman characterizes this activity as "languaging" (2011). It encapsulates the activity of creating a conversation in which the very words we use can be deconstructed and a new shared meaning can be reconstructed.

To pursue languaging, we must introduce Ludwig Wittgenstein, whose work greatly influenced Newman and Holzman. Ludwig Wittgenstein was by many accounts the most influential philosopher of the 20th century (for more see Ray Monk's *Ludwig Wittgenstein: The Duty of Genius* (1990)). In his later writings, Wittgenstein sought to help us see language as an activity. The "natural" way of speaking gets us into muddles. It leaves us stuck in a fly bottle of Truth statements, static assumptions, labels and identities. There is no way around this everyday way of talking. We live and breathe it. It is embedded in our culture. The challenge is to reduce the power, the "hold," that these words and concepts have on us. Wittgenstein exposed and hoped to free us from the pathology embedded in our language, most especially our belief that we understand what the other is saying. In *Philosophical Investigations*, Wittgenstein devised endless language-games which illustrate how language holds us captive, how it traps us in particular ways of seeing and understanding. He rejected digging deeper for the Truth or right definition of a phrase, in favor of pointing to the unavoidable uncertainty and confusion embedded in communication. This kind of philosophizing was accessible. As Newman put it, "We can ask big questions about little things" that have the potential to shift how we see, understand and feel (1996, p. 34).

This activity is very present in social therapeutic Life Development Groups, where a healthy tension resides between the activity of building the group and the pull for participants to speak and feel in the individualistic ways they already know. Another way to understand what goes on in social therapeutic work is this: By opening up, by giving to the group the pictures in our heads of things we believe correspond to the words we use, we invite co-creation, joint meaning-making and even playfulness. Doing this activity makes visible that we are building together, creating a new kind of conversation that does not rely on either prescriptions or advice. We create the possibility of breaking out of our usual ways of talking and allowing for new things to emerge.

Here is where Vygotsky, Wittgenstein and the tools of theater come together. Holzman synthesizes it like this:

> Relating to therapeutic talk as performance, and to clients as an ensemble of performers who, along with the therapist, are staging a new conversation each session is meant as a rejection of truth (and its opposite, falsity) in favor of *socially completive activity* [emphasis in original] (Holzman, 2017, p. 41).

This quote encapsulates the totality of social therapeutic practice. Let's deconstruct it. Life Development Group is an ensemble performance. Experiencing oneself as an ensemble performer is emotional growth in our current socio-historical context. Group members and the coach create the play every week through talk, through emotional expression in relation to each other and the group. Just as no one in theater takes the scenes they perform or watch as Truth, so too in the social therapeutic group. "Staging a new conversation" is constant creating, constant meaning-making specific to the moment and conditions in which the group makes it. The group and coach are freed up from appealing to a Truth or ascertaining the Truth. What remains is activity—the building together in a social (i.e., group) context that allows for completion, for performing new lines in a dialogue, creating new scenes out of what has been given to the group and, importantly, philosophizing with a small "p." Learning to see that we are all members of an ensemble, of the multiple ensembles in our lives, opens up a whole new way of living, loving and relating to others.

Challenging Assumptions

> To scrutinize, actively and practically, our assumptions (that is, not just cognitively but emotionally, culturally and in every other way)—especially the ones that appear to go so deep they don't even look like assumptions at all—is very much a part of the developmental process (Newman, 1996, p. 115).

Newman took the group activity of language play very seriously. It is an important part of the process of growth and development. Through Wittgenstein, we are permissioned to look at language. Through Newman and Holzman's fusion of Wittgenstein and Vygotsky, we are permissioned to make new meanings together as we deconstruct/reject the representationalism embedded in language. This is very helpful for breaking out of our assumptions. The coach might question an assumption in a caring and curious way, as an activity of giving to the group: "What do you mean when you say you are an addict?" Asking this question in a group development context opens space for joint creation. It creates intimacy within the group as people get closer to one another in their experience. No longer does the group make assumptions that it knows what something means or what is going on. Clients find this of enormous value, especially around identity and labels (including diagnoses).

Group members grow to experience this type of talking as an invitation to engage in language play, to see from a different angle, rather than take it as a critique of doing something wrong in group. As the group grows, some members begin to imitate this way of talking, helping to create the environment in which new, developmental possibilities, new emotions and new ways of speaking can emerge.

For example, take "should" formulations. Someone in group may say, "I should be able to do this. I must be a real loser that I cannot." The coach or a group member might then ask, "I'm curious, how come you should be able to do that?" or "What about us and how we see you?"

Another example of making assumptions might be the quid pro quo of marriage. A spouse in couples session might express, "I'm frustrated. I cook my wife dinner all the time. Since she does not like to cook, she should do the laundry because that's something I do not like to do and it drives me crazy that she doesn't do it! I feel so taken advantage of!" The assumption that marriage should operate as an equal trading of responsibilities could be questioned by the coach: "How did that assumption get made? Was that handed down from society? Did you and your wife decide together that is how you want to organize your relationship?"

There are so many possibilities of how the group might challenge our subjective and emotional experiences when it is attending to the *how* of the dialogue. Here's another example. Steven comes into group and says he wants to work on the (behavioral) pattern he has had since childhood: "I am always trying to help others, but then I always end up feeling taken advantage of and very hurt. It's my pattern." These two sentences are filled with offers to build with. One offer is to deconstruct conceptually and play with the language used. Responses might include challenging how Steven knows it is a pattern, and what a pattern is anyway. Someone else might contribute what their patterns are. Now "patterning" is no longer Steven's individuated problem happening inside him; it becomes a language-game played with, performed by and belonging to the group. Another group member might question the assumption that patterns stay the same: "Are you saying that you are the same person now as you were twenty years ago when you are in this 'pattern'?" or "What kind of help do you give? Is that always the same too?" or even "How do you know you are being taken advantage of?"

All of this activity, this questioning, follows the spirit of Wittgenstein's language-games. In effect, Wittgenstein invites all people to philosophize in ordinary ways. He says,

> What I do is suggest, or even invent, other ways of looking. I suggest possibilities of which you had not previously thought. You thought there was one possibility, or two at most. But I made you think of others . . . Thus your mental cramp is relieved (Wittgenstein as quoted in Monk, 1990, p. 502).

In asking these kinds of questions—big questions about little things—the coach and group attend to the environment such that this philosophizing, questioning activity is neither a minimizing of someone's emotional pain nor a rejection of their experience. Instead, it embraces, shifts/loosens up and adds to their experience. In playing with language and examining our assumptions, participants create a new space for joint meaning-making. They create an environment in which it is possible for the group to grow.

Creating the Conditions

Building or creating the environment[4] for growth and development in social therapeutics includes both building with what there is—the specific people, the specific moment in history, the specific culture we live in—and building with what is coming into existence (Holzman, 2010, p. 35). Anderson sees social therapeutics in this way: "Building the group is creating the conditions and the performatory environment in which people can relate and converse in ways that are generative and invite emotional growth" (2003, p. xii). As we have noted, it is a continuous tool-and-result building activity; there is no stasis.

We see distinctions between "creating the conditions" and "creating the coaching container" that might make this social therapeutic practice more tangible. The coaching container in a group setting is commonly established by each individual stating their intention of what they want to get out of the session and/or the emotional boundaries they require for having a discussion. Once every person has spoken, it is assumed to be a safe space, until someone in the group says, "I do not feel safe." The container is related to as *a thing*, disassociated from the humans who just contributed to creating it. It becomes a spatio-temporal entity, to use as an evaluation of what was said before (people's intentions) and what is happening now (what they are doing). The container functions as a mediating force between individuals in the group.

Creating the environment in social therapeutics requires continuously building and attending to what the group needs, without having to know or define beforehand what that is. To the extent that intentionality gets expressed, it looks more like, "How do we want to do this together?" The act of creating the conditions is a group performance, a co-created speaking activity (à la Wittgenstein's language-games) that both constitutes and creates emotionality and emotional growth. Participants discover that they can create together and can do something different with all the emotions, conflicts and intimacy in the group.

Oftentimes, the coach will ask the group or couple, "Have we created the environment in which it's possible to have this conversation?" This is shorthand for inquiring of the group, "Do we have what we need for us to be able to hear each other, to be giving, to be philosophical in ways that can be built with by the group?" Clients often begin to imitate this line in group and make it their own in other areas of their life.

Not having the conditions

On the third session with their coach, a couple shared that they wanted to open up a sensitive topic: The wife's distrust of the husband's friendships with other women.

Wendy began describing how Nick's female friends would come to the house to hang out without her knowledge. Nick defensively explained that they were old friends from elementary school and there was nothing to worry about. Wendy countered with her deepened suspicions due to Nick always erasing messages on his phone. Nick pointed out that Wendy does the same. They continued to go back and forth in this manner.

The coach interrupted: "You are saying that you want to and are ready to have this conversation but I do not think we have the conditions for it. You are going back and forth just the way you do at home, as if I am not in the room having the conversation with you. I need more from you."

Wendy asked what the coach needed.

"I need you both to include my sensibility in the conversation. Your sensibility is to be debating, interrupting, challenging and bickering. You are creating an environment in which you cannot hear each other, let alone me. Is that what you want to be doing?"

Attending to building the environment creates space for others to join us in a new performance, both at the group and individual level. This creates the conditions for emotional growth. Tying this back into the opening of this chapter, the concept of emotional growth is nearly inconceivable when operating with the assumptions of private, internal emotionality, such as *my sadness lives inside of me*. When emotionality is seen as an internal state, what follows is a battle against it, or a fight to change it or even eradicate it. But making the problem vanish per Newman and Holzman via Wittgenstein, requires a social activity the meaning of which the participants construct in the moment and which belongs to the group rather than the individual.

As Newman put it, "people are helped much more—emotionally and developmentally—by giving than they are by getting. What I mean by giving is the active sharing of all your emotional 'possessions'—including, in the appropriate environments, our pathology, our pain and our humiliation" (2010, pp. 5–6). In group, this might look like a member feeling competitive with what someone is doing or saying, and yet deciding not to interrupt or talk about themselves, but rather giving their competitiveness to the group instead. For example, the member might say, "I have a hard time hearing John right now. All I can think about is how I get even more mad than he does." Or the member may decide to do something altogether different, like ask the coach what they are thinking (an act that is giving to the group by inviting the coach, presumably more developed around competitiveness, to share their response).

Developing this skill, this emotional elasticity, can provide numerous developmental benefits. Where we learn how to do this first is in a relational, group environment in which the focus of growth is on the group/the relationship. Through such experiences, we discover that it is possible to make different performance choices. In discovering the power and intimacy of creating with others, it grows our capacity to become other than who we think we are.

Seeing Transformation

What resonates with us in the word "transformation" is the implication of holistic, non-linear change. Some might hear it as a change "from" something "to" something else (with a measurable, modern starting point and ending point). But transformation in social therapeutics is a collective activity (Holzman, 2015). The group is continuously transforming without knowing how it will transform. In our role as social therapeutic coaches, we are usually more developed in seeing transformation, seeing what is new. When the conditions are present to be heard, the coach might give to the group or the couple how they see the transformation, the development of the group, couple or individual, while reminding everyone that together they created the transformation. We live in such an alienating world that we disassociate almost immediately from what we have made. When someone in group shares they are responding in a new way to their ex-girlfriend when she texts in the middle of the night, the group notices. The group shares the impact of hearing about this new performance and that it feels included in having helped to produce this new moment. The group appreciates that all the conversations about this relationship that have occurred over months have been part of the process of the client deciding to do a different performance in the middle of the night. It also appreciates that in making a different choice and then sharing that with the group, the client and group have together opened the possibility for even more transformation. And so on, and so on.

Transformation and growth can feel magical, spiritual. It is the experience of changing everything versus changing a particular thing. As we have shared, attempting to alter a particular behavior derives from seeing change as an internal, mentalistic process. Transformation involves a collective unit, something bigger than ourselves. Usually, the coach is the one who first shares how they see the growth of the group or the couple. Yet as clients come to "see the group" (i.e., experience their power in creating an environment for growth), they begin to give how they are experiencing the group's/couple's growth. A client might say, "Hey, before we were speedy and we didn't listen to each other. Now we are slower, more curious with each other. That feels more intimate. Our group has grown. It has transformed." The very act of giving the group's growth is inseparable from the individual's growth in being able to see it, as well as in their capacity to create environments for it.

Vygotsky wrote that a society addresses only those questions raised by history, that is, by the conditions specific to a moment in human history (Vygotsky quoted in Levitan, 1982, inside front cover). Today, history is raising the "we" questions. Seeing emotional growth as the path to transformation is an invitation to express our human capacity to change everything, including the world we live in.

Exercises

1) Try saying to someone you are close with, "I want to be emotionally closer with you" and notice what it is like for you to say that and to experience their response.

2) When you are feeling your usual way, try doing a new performance. For example, if you are stressed at dinnertime with your

family, try performing curiosity about someone else's day instead of focusing on your own.

3) Spend some time considering how your relationship with your partner or close friend/family member has transformed over time and share that with them. What kind of conversation follows from that?

Notes

1 Nabakov, 1999, p. xviii.
2 Wittgenstein, 1998, p. 31.
3 "There are more things in Heaven and Earth, Horatio, than are dreamt of in your philosophy" (Hamlet, Act I, Scene IV).
4 Social therapeutic practitioners and clients often use interchangeably the terms "building/creating the conditions" and "building/creating the environment."

References

Anderson, H. (2003). Forward. In L. Holzman & R. Mendez (Eds.), *Psychological Investigations: A Clinician's Guide to Social Therapy.* (pp. xi–xii). Brunner-Routledge.

Barrett, L.F. (2017). *How Emotions Are Made: The Secret Life of the Brain.* Houghton Mifflin Harcourt.

Grant, A. (2021, July 10). There's a Specific Kind of Joy We've Been Missing. *The New York Times.*

Holzman, L. (2010). Without Creating ZPDs There is No Creativity. In C. Connery, V. John-Steiner & A. Marjanovic-Shane (Eds.), *Vygotsky and Creativity: A Cultural-historical Approach to Play, Meaning Making, and the Arts* (pp. 27–40). Peter Lang Publishers.

Holzman, L. (2011, June 24). *Why languaging makes us special (for each other).* Loisholzman.org. https://loisholzman.org/2011/06/why-languaging-makes-us-special-for-each-other/

Holzman, L. (2015). Relating to people as revolutionaries. In Loewenthal, D. (Ed.), *Critical Psychotherapy, Psychoanalysis and Counselling: Implications for Practice* (pp.125–137). Palgrave MacMillan.

Holzman, L. (2017). *Vygotsky at Work and Play.* Routledge.

Holzman, L. & Mendez, R. (Eds.). (2003). *Psychological Investigations: A Clinician's Guide to Social Therapy.* Brunner-Routledge.

Hübel, T. & Avritt, J.J. (2020). *Healing Collective Trauma: A Process for Integrating Our Intergenerational and Cultural Wounds.* Sounds True.

Leonard, T.J. (1998). *The 28 Laws of Attraction: Stop Chasing Success and Let it Chase You.* Scribner.

Levitan, K. (1982). *One is not born a personality: profiles of Soviet education psychologists.* Progress Publishers.

Menakem, R. (2017). *My Grandmothers Hands: Racialized Trauma and the Pathway to Mending Our Hearts and Bodies.* Central Recovery Press.

Monk, R. (1990). *Ludwig Wittgenstein: The Duty of Genius.* Penguin Books.

Nabakov, P. (1999). *Native American Testimony: A Chronicle of Indian-White Relations from Prophecy to the Present, 1492–2000.* Penguin.

Newman, F. (1996). *Performance of a Lifetime: A Practical-Philosophical Guide to the Joyous Life*. Castillo International, Inc.

Newman, F. (2010). *Let's Develop! A Guide to Continuous Personal Growth*. Castillo International, Inc.

Newman, F. & Holzman, L. (1993, 2014). *Lev Vygotsky: Revolutionary Scientist*. Routledge.

Newman, F. & Holzman, L. (2004). Power, Authority and Pointless Activity (The Developmental Discourse of Social Therapy). In T. Strong & D. Pare (Eds.), *Furthering Talk: Advances in Discursive Therapies* (pp. 73–86). Kluwer Academic/Plenum Publishers.

van der Kolk, B.A. (2014). *The Body Keeps the Score: Brain, Mind, and Body in the Healing of Trauma*. Penguin Books.

Wittgenstein, L. (1988). *Wittgenstein's Lectures on Philosophical Psychology: 1946–1947*. United States: Harvester-Wheatsheaf.

Wittgenstein, L. (1998). *Culture and Value*. Blackwell.

Wittgenstein, L. (2001). *Philosophical Investigations*. Blackwell Publishers.

PART I
CONCLUSION

We began this book with an invitation to read it as a poem. To allow the reader to *experience* the words—to metabolize them, rather than cognitize them—as a tool-and-result activity that transports us someplace new. Now, we conclude this section by referring to the poem *Hymn for the Hurting* by Amanda Gorman (2022),[1] the youngest inaugural poet in US history. Her words speak to the totality of everything hurting—our hearts, our minds, our families, our communities, our country. Gorman encapsulates the tragic and blessed contradictions of our times with the poem's final two lines:

> But only when everything hurts
> May everything change.
>
> (Gorman, 2022)

In these pages we have attempted to share a toolkit for relationally and emotionally changing *everything*. Practicing a powerful and transformative method that builds with everyone and everything they give, social therapeutic coaches lead groups as diverse as a kaleidoscope of pedestrians walking down a city street. In Part I, we have tried to bring to a more practical level an approach to human development that is designed to be impossible to capture! Social therapeutics is continuous process, a

DOI: 10.4324/9781003326465-7

retooling of the totality of human life—the group, the relationship, the culture, history.[2] The labor of social therapeutics creates space for emotional growth, a fundamental activity required for these emotional times in which everything is hurting. Now more than ever, people are searching for more sophisticated (developed) forms of emotional life in order to experience connection and belonging, and to address persistent anxiety over the uncertain fate of our species.

We have shown how both social therapeutics and coaching grew out of a moment of mass experimentation in new ways of being and new forms of expression. What began as a reaction to existing social conditions and mainstream ideologies—in whose development psychology played a heavy role—forged its own path away from pathologizing human behavior. Coaching collected useful bits from several disciplines and has become a major force today, most especially in the corporate space, but also as a growing alternative to traditional psychotherapy. Business professionals experiencing improvement in their work performance and communication are seeking to carry that improvement into daily life. Thomas Leonard's vision is coming to fruition: "Coaching gives you the opportunity to design your life instead of letting it happen to you. In the future, I have a vision that millions of people will work with coaches not because they need one, but because they want one" (C. Richardson, personal communication, May 12, 2023).

Social therapeutics is a fusing of several 20th century discoveries: The breakthrough discoveries of child development by Lev Vygotsky, the philosophical investigations of language by Ludwig Wittgenstein, the unmooring of the tools of theater from the stage through the invention and mainstreaming of improv and the complete break with modern science that is quantum physics.

Fred Newman and Lois Holzman built with these elements to create an approach that shifts how we see, how we listen, how we feel and what we do. That shift is both small and big. Small in that we can all do it. We can each relate to the "we" rather than the "I." And big in that with masses of people doing so, we open up the possibility of shifting the world towards greater collaboration, creativity, inclusion and fairness.

As a practitioner, Newman passionately and brilliantly sought to help people exercise their collective power to create. The very thing that makes individual and species development possible is the exercising of power growthfully, i.e., in a generative, non-authoritarian way (Newman & Holzman, 2004; Holzman, 2015). The cries of ordinary people for fairness, growth and transformation are going unheard, even as the calls for individual, societal and global transformation by public figures are increasing. The demand of our moment is to create accessible tools that are radically different from what has come before.

Newman and Holzman insist, "We must find ways to work not for a new theory or a new paradigm but for a new world. *In developing this qualitative transformation, performed activity will be key* [emphasis added]" (1997, p. 163). To paraphrase Vine Deloria from Chapter 4's epigraph: If we can embrace, give and create with our experiences, we are freed from the need to understand them and (we would add) therefore be better equipped to perform them. And in performing them, we nurture the possibility of growth and transformation.

We now flip over the hourglass. The next chapters focus on the actual practice of social therapeutics. What follows are numerous examples of performed activity on the part of the coach, group members and couples. We hope the reader experiences how social therapeutics innovates and how coach and clients together create environments for performing, as Vygotsky would say, "a head taller."

Notes

1 The full poem is freely available here: https://www.nytimes.com/2022/05/27/opinion/amanda-gorman-uvalde-poem.html
2 This is in distinction from psychology's focus on the individual and individualized behavior, a concept which requires extracting out a small part of the totality of human life. Social therapeutics relates to totalities, rather than particulars.

References

Gorman, A. (2022, May 27). Hymn for the Hurting. *New York Times*. Lines 32–33. Retrieved May 27, 2022 from: https://www.nytimes.com/2022/05/27/opinion/amanda-gorman-uvalde-poem.html

Holzman, L. (2015). Relating to people as revolutionaries. In Loewenthal, D. (Ed.), *Critical Psychotherapy, Psychoanalysis and Counselling: Implications for Practice* (pp.125–137). Palgrave MacMillan.

Newman, F. & Holzman, L. (1997). *The End of Knowing: A new developmental way of learning*. Routledge.

Newman, F. & Holzman, L. (2004). Power, Authority and Pointless Activity (The Developmental Discourse of Social Therapy). In T. Strong & D. Pare (Eds.), *Furthering Talk: Advances in Discursive Therapies* (pp. 73–86). Kluwer Academic/Plenum Publishers.

PART II
COACH AS SOCIAL THERAPEUTIC GROUP LEADER

5

THE SOCIAL THERAPEUTIC GROUP LEADER

I have the experience when I work with people that I take them to places they have never been before. And my understanding of that—the place they've never been before—is *here* . . . [they] learn the simple yet extraordinarily complex activity of being where you are, learning to be who you are, learning to be what you are. Not from the vantage point of passively accepting all of that, but as a precondition for becoming *other than* all that . . . It is the necessary though not sufficient condition for growth and development [emphasis added].

Fred Newman (*Psychological Investigations*)[1]

This chapter illustrates some practical ways in which the social thera- peutic coach can lead group members to creating the conditions for their emotional growth. Fred Newman led thousands of social therapeutic group sessions over 40 years. His characterization of leading clients to "here" is neither an existential claim nor a mental trick. We have argued in the previous section that concepts bequeathed to us from the Enlight- enment and Western philosophy are no longer useful and have become obstacles that keep us from being "here." For Newman, those modern ways of thinking and speaking get us tripped up and keep us distant from one another. We are constantly thinking *about* someplace else we could or should be—whether that be a physical place (e.g., visiting family)

DOI: 10.4324/9781003326465-9

or a mental place (e.g., happier). Most people have one foot planted someplace else most of the time. Doing so alienates[2] us from where we are—here, together (Holzman & Mendez, 2003, pp. 72–73). The role of the social therapeutic coach is to continuously relate to the group where it is and to support group members—as who they are—in the activity of building it. That activity includes engaging with and challenging how we speak and the mental cramps we get trapped in. The emotional growth—the becoming, the performing something new—emerges out of the building activity.

Now that we are moving into practice, we will be sharing with the reader examples of language and "languaging"[3] that social therapeutic coaches and clients use. These are drawn from our group sessions. We offer them as directional suggestions, rather than as formulas to use to obtain certain results. The practice of social therapeutics is contextual and creative, and the method is holistically innovative. We therefore strongly urge a reading of the previous chapters to begin the immersion process into a new way of seeing, doing and feeling before diving in here. Throughout Part I, we have incorporated practical examples of the basics in social therapeutic coaching. Having some familiarity with them will aid practitioners in taking what we are giving here and making it their own.

Leading the Group

Leading is a word used often in social therapeutics. The coach "leads" the group. Members "provide leadership" to the group. What do we mean by leading? We can say with certainty what it is not: Knowing what we are doing! We say that to provoke and get a good laugh at ourselves as coaches. And we mean it. We cannot know. The work of building the group is not knowable, it is doable, see-able, create with-able, but not knowable. We intend leading as a bottom-up activity—empowering the group to create its own growth and that of its members, rather than a top-down declaration of what is really happening or what is "right." Both coaching and social therapeutics share a passionate insistence on co-creation and abandoning the all-knowing power of psychotherapy and psychiatry.[4]

Here are some characteristics of leading a social therapeutic Life Development Group: The coach has a responsibility to lead the group in seeing the group and hearing offers, which is inseparable from creating the group itself. Recall that the zpd is comprised of all participants at all levels of development.[5] As the group grows and stretches into new performances, there is more of a demand on the coach to grow in their leadership and relationship with the group, which impacts the group—and so on, and so on. Trust and intimacy emerge out of this continuous activity. Sometimes we refer to this as "leading from behind." That is, the coach does not get ahead of the group, but rather through listening and attending to the group's activity (rather than content), builds with what is present.

In other moments, leading can be directing, as in the coach offering a performance direction to the ensemble, like, "How about being more curious with each other?" When the coach or group member asks philosophical questions, that is leadership as well. It helps the group break out of inherited assumptions and ways of seeing.

Another aspect of leading is the vulnerability that comes with it. For example, the coach risks offering a direction to the group that the group might reject. (Of course, it is the group's prerogative to ignore the coach if it so chooses.) A related form of leading with vulnerability is when the coach asks for help from the group, sharing something the coach needs from it in order to help the group. We provide an example of this in the next chapter.

Finally, and importantly, leadership also involves locating the work of the group in the world, i.e., including that we are impacted on by the cultural, societal and political moment we are living in, including structural racism, polarization, an alienated consumeristic culture and extreme environmental degradation. The coach being grounded in history—embracing/acknowledging that we humans have both created and are shaped by our world—is an important element of leading the group.

While some of these formulations are certainly similar to coaching, taken together they offer a different performance of coach.[6] In our view, social therapeutics has a different practice of co-creation in its embrace of leading. A core assumption in coaching is that the coach is a partner to the client in manifesting what is "organic" to the client. The designation of "organic" becomes a place inside an individual separated out from the world and from their relationship with the coach. "Organic" operates on the dualisms of inside/outside, self/other. Dualism is part of the kit of "masters' tools"[7] that we have inherited from Western philosophy and the Enlightenment, which we challenge in Chapter 3. We are living in a time when it is becoming more obvious that we need new tools. Social therapeutics offers a new method with which to build those new tools.

As clients get a taste of development and begin to experience and learn how they are part of producing it, they are often eager for more. The forms of leadership expressed here can be learned in group by clients and applied outside of group in clients' lives. As a socio-cultural space (aka the zpd), group members will begin to babble, imitate and play with what the coach does.

Having a Co-Lead or Assistant Coach

We recommend that when running Life Development Groups you consider working with another coach in partnership. Many practitioners work solo. However, there are advantages to partnering with another professional. Each coach will bring different methodological strengths, which will make for a richer group experience. A lead coach receives support from the co-lead, which becomes especially important in moments when the coach is inviting the group to stretch. Two coaches can model what a developmental, intimate relationship looks like. They might have a back-and-forth conversation discussing how they are experiencing the group, or a direction for the group or what one coach is thinking in the moment. This illustrates ways of relating and speaking with each other that group members can pick up on and begin to imitate.

The value of having a co-lead

Group members are engaged in a conversation with Chen, who has been sharing the insecurity she feels about applying for a promotion at her company. Participants are speaking about how Chen's issue resonates with them, each person taking turns with their story.

Coach 1:   "How are we doing *as a group* in this work with Chen?"

The group momentarily acknowledges that the coach has spoken but continues on without addressing the question. This scene continues for another 15 minutes until the coach offers up a similar question, and again the group ignores it.

Coach 2 (to the group):   "I am curious about something. Coach 1 asked a question and I did not hear anyone respond to it. I am wondering what is going on for the group that no one responded."

Another possible direction is to speak directly to Coach 1.

Coach 2 (to Coach 1):   "I have a question for you, Coach 1. I noticed that twice you asked the group a question and both times the group didn't respond. I am curious how come you asked the question."

This sets up an interchange between the coaches, which may help the group better hear Coach 1. Or it could lead to a group discussion of how come it ignored Coach 1, or something else altogether. The main point is that the coaches are providing leadership in how they are relating to each other—in this case, performing curiosity. This could help the group shift its gaze to "look" toward more relational and growthful activities.

Launching a Life Development Group

The formation of social therapeutic Life Development Groups rests on three things:

- Bringing together people with differing issues they want to grow around and work on, with differing levels of emotional development (e.g., emotional honesty, vulnerability, creativity, caring and intimacy)[8]

- Relating to the group as a whole, rather than as an accumulation of individuals who happen to be sitting together in a room
- Continuously working to create an environment for growth

These characteristics of the Life Development Group distinguish it from other forms of group work which rely, to varying degrees, on the individual as the unit of change. A significant part of the social therapeutic coach's work is to lovingly and philosophically challenge the individualistic biases we all carry. Social therapeutic group leaders do not impose a fixed structure or rules onto the group. There is no agenda-setting, monitoring for equal speaking time among participants, teaching facts, giving exercises or discussing takeaways/lessons learned (except in the case of the group choosing to do those things). Instead, the group decides each week how to create itself, with the support and leadership of the coach. As groups discover this capacity to be generative, without establishing a right way or right place to get to, they discover their power. And if they can see themselves as co-creators in the group, they can carry that power into creating and co-creating their lives, communities, families, workplaces and world.

We unpacked the myth of the individual in Chapter 3. Here, in moving to practice examples, we want to bring in Newman's practical remarks on leading social therapeutic groups:

> [Individuals getting their fair share in group] is a fundamental issue, not just in [coaching] but in life. It raises the question of the existential character of relationships. Are relationships real things or are they reducible to the elements that make them up? I don't deny there are individuals but I take them to be secondary to relationships. As I see the world, it is filled with groups, relationships, combinations, and what people do as individuals is to be understood is terms of . . . our growth and development in a fundamentally relational world (Holzman & Mendez, 2003, p. 20).

In embracing the primacy of our relationality and sociality, the social therapeutic coach asks questions like, "How is the group doing?"

(i.e., What is the group's activity right now? Where is the group emotionally right now?) Is the group speedy? Conflicted? Playful? This helps to cultivate relational awareness in the group.

Supporting clients to give to and build the group turbocharges individual participants' emotional growth *and* the group's emotional growth. This is the exciting dialectical tool-and-result-ness of social therapeutics that we address methodologically in Part I (see especially Chapter 2).

Recruiting Clients to Group

The social therapeutic method of continuous life development lends itself to ongoing weekly participation in a group.[9] Clients come to see and appreciate their Life Development Group as where they go for emotional workouts with others, just as they might attend a regular spin class for physical workouts. It is not uncommon for group members to participate for years in a group. Their coach and group members are included in their life's journey of finding love, facing financial issues, having children, experiencing a traumatic event, building a career, having an illness or losing a loved one. Others stay until they are unstuck from the issue that brought them to coaching and then leave. Some return months or years later to reignite their emotional growth. And there are always those who decide group work is not for them.

Typically, a coach invites clients already involved in their practice to join a group.[10] The client-coach relationship remains very important to carry into the group environment. It is not unusual for a social therapeutic coach to work with a client in multiple settings. For example, a client might see the coach in individual sessions and in a group. A couple could work with the coach together, with each partner becoming a member of different groups. Usually clients move to only group work over time and pursue individual or couples sessions on an as-needed basis. The coach and client(s) make those decisions together.

One strategy for attracting new clients is to offer a short-term Life Development Group.[11] This clearly defined offer makes it easier for someone unfamiliar with or doubtful of group work to agree to participate. More often than not, these clients—new to the group experience—build an immediate sense of community with one another and express a desire to do another short-term cycle. Some might not continue, and new people might join. Several cycles might continue until the group decides it wants to meet in an ongoing fashion.

Starting the First Group

In a brand new coaching group, with most members unfamiliar with both the process and each other, the coach might begin with a general welcome and introduction, even before people get to know one another's names. Here are two different examples:

> Example 1. Welcome to our Life Development Group! The task we have in this group is to build an environment that helps the group to grow and transform. How we do that can be different from week to week. We bring to the group our questions, our experience, our pain, our sensitivity and our history. We create with what people give here. There is no blueprint for doing this; no rules of a right or wrong way. My job as the coach is to work on my relationship to the whole group to facilitate and support this creative endeavor. Let's start.
>
> Example 2. Welcome to group! My hope for this group is that it is something we create together. As the leader, I will support you all in the activity of building the group. Your job is to support me in doing that. We will creatively use everything people bring to group—your struggles, pain, history, philosophical questioning and sense of humor—in the process of building the group.

Often this type of introduction produces discomfort and/or confusion in clients. That is positive! The offer is for the coach and group to sit in the discomfort and build with what emerges. From its first moment, a social therapeutic group breaks out of the societal expectation that the group leader's role is to have the answers—answers to how to structure a group, deal with differences in the group, change someone's behavior or manage through uncertainty. A group member may respond to these opening lines by saying, "I don't know how to do that." To which the coach might say, "Yes, exactly! I don't either. Our task together is to do what we don't know how to do. That's how we grow. My job is to help the group to do that." Pointing to the group's responsibility to create itself offers something new, something other than the individuated expectations each participant brings, e.g., equal time, solving their problem, etc. Co-creation leads and drives the sessions.

Lois Holzman has characterized social therapeutics as a method of *non-knowing growing* (2018). The social therapeutic coach provides leadership by embracing the uncomfortableness that comes with saying, "I don't know." These three words give voice to the experience many have every day in trying to navigate contemporary society with its tottering institutions, rapid rate of change and increasingly isolated forms of life. Getting uncomfortable is a necessary pre-condition to growth. It points towards the need to *create* one's life and *make* new tools for living together, rather than to *adapt* to what is.

Another common client response to beginning the group is, "Can I talk about my problem?" The coach might reply, "Yes, and our task is to discover together how to talk and how to listen together in such a way that what you give becomes material for the whole group to grow." Or, "Yes. Are you open to the group helping you give it in a way that connects with and builds the group?" What starts as a tool-*for*-result request (can I get my problem solved?) becomes a tool-*and*-result practice of method (let's build something with the "problem").[12]

Raising the activity of *how* from the beginning is another way to challenge participants' understanding of growth. It highlights the primacy of relationality—how members are relating to each other, the group and the coach—over the specific content spoken by group members. With the issue of *not-knowing* and *how* on the table from the first moment together, group members get the sense that they are somewhere different, doing something different.

Improv Games

Some social therapeutic coaches prefer to initiate a new group with an improv-type game and then move to the welcome statement explored above. This is especially the case for groups over video call, where feeling connected to faces in boxes on a screen might seem challenging. Other people might call these games ice-breakers, but that is not their purpose. Social therapeutics relates to the entirety of a session as improvisational. So, rather than a stand-alone, separated out activity, improv games immediately invite participants into a shared experience of being bounced out of their comfort zones. Play of this sort can expedite active listening and risk-taking, with low-risk content. In addition, games are fun, often bringing laughter into the group and creating a shared relational experience from the beginning. The best improv exercises are physical and/or nonsensical in nature, which subverts the natural pull for individuals to talk about themselves in an individuated way. A quick search on the internet and YouTube for improv games for adults will result in many good options.

For other practitioners, improv games may dampen the creation of the radical group-focused atmosphere that comes with the coach opening the group with lines like the ones we outlined above. By asking from the first moment, "How do we do this together?" the coach immediately invites clients to lead in creating and taking ownership of the group.

Bringing Someone New into an Ongoing Group

Anytime someone joins the group it becomes a brand new ensemble. As the reader might guess by now, there is no set way to bring someone into group. The coach welcomes the new member at the beginning of group, but there is no protocol on what happens next. The group responds to this new circumstance however it responds. Usually, if the client has been a silent observer, the coach would make a point of asking them toward the end of the session, "Charles, what has this been like for you?"

The coach works to relate to the changed configuration as a *new group*. The new person brings in new emotionality, questions and leadership that can be valuable for reorganizing the group anew. In addition, by creating space for the client to choose how to be in their first session, the coach learns something of what they might bring to the group. Will they refer to their relationship with the coach? Are they skilled active listeners? Challengers? Question askers?

A new person came into group and immediately shared who she was and a little of what she wanted to work on. She kindly asked if people could tell her why they we were there. People went around the room introducing themselves and discovered that they mostly had no idea of each other's motivation for joining group, even though many had been in group together a long time. "We should introduce ourselves to each other every week!" commented one member, acknowledging that doing so gave participants a fresh appreciation and understanding of one another.

New members often assume that they are joining a "fixed" group that they need to learn to "fit into." Ongoing group members often make this assumption as well! They assume a new person needs to adapt to the group as it already exists, with its (insider) language, patterns and hierarchies. The coach looks for opportunities to challenge this belief and to support those group members who also do so.

When a Client Leaves a Group

Emotionally, relationally and socially, leaving the group can be difficult for people. Usually a client speaks with the coach beforehand and then comes to group to share their decision to leave. The coach or a group member might ask whether the client is set in their decision, or if they are open to having a conversation about this decision. In this way, the topic of "leaving the group" becomes an offer to be built with by the group as much as any other offer. The decision or change in decision (sometimes, in response to the group's work, the client makes a new decision to stay on) by the individual becomes a shared process with the possibility for intimacy and expressions of wanting, anger, disappointment and other emotions.

The group may respond in a variety of ways: Expressing love and excitement for the client's growth, or disappointment mixed with support. The group might engage in philosophical questioning and discover that the person is leaving in reaction to the intimacy of the group, or a feeling of responsibility for the lives of others in the group. Sometimes the group tries to convince the person to stay. While reinforcing that the participant has a right to make their choice, the coach may also express their support or disagreement with the client's decision. The coach might say, "I support your decision *and* I think staying in group and working on this issue would be growthful for you and the group. I would love to do that with you now, or sometime in the future."

Method Moments

We offer here some common scenarios that occur in Life Development Groups and how a coach might decide to relate and respond to them social therapeutically. We begin with typical group patterns and how the coach might attend to the ever-present tension between the "me" and the "we" in building the group. The challenge for the coach is to introduce questions which help clients to notice the "individuated speak" and reorganize it *collectively*. Posing questions to the group reintroduces process and repositions the group: "What's it like for the group to be doing this together?"; "How do we want to respond to Terrence's asking for help?"; "How can we talk together in a way that might have an impact on the whole group?"; "How does the group feel about getting closer to Maria and the issue she is raising?"; "Arnold, what do you need from us so you can be here *with* us, rather than ranting *at* us?" In these questions, the coach looks to address an individual in group by way of speaking to the group.

Breaking Out of Problem-solving

When confronted with a problem in our pragmatic American culture, we draw the conclusion that there must be a way to solve it. This works well when a car breaks down, or when we run out of frozen peas, but does not work so well when it comes to emotional growth. Newman puts it like this: "What's critical for development . . . is *how* we go about seeking answers, rather than the what of the answers we come up with, if any [emphasis in original]" (1996, p. 115). For the International Coaching Federation, to be certified as a master coach, "There [must be] no evidence of 'fixing' a problem or the client" (ICF, 2017, p. 8).

That said, most clients want and expect to get help for themselves and their problem. Most people bring into group the learning acquisition model we are all taught—that of collecting and sharing information in service of solving a problem or trying to be helpful. A group member may suggest a solution to the problem, and another member might then recommend a different solution. A competition could develop on who has the better solution. The client with the "problem" is expected to evaluate each suggestion and provide explanation for whether it would work or not. Offering explanations, identifying causes, seeking solutions to problems, competing with group members (or the coach) to say the smartest thing—these ways of speaking tend to keep clients individuated and, while caring in intent, more distant from each other. While coming from a place of wanting to help, there is little emotional risk-taking, vulnerability or relationality.[13]

The task for the coach remains the work of practicing the social therapeutic method, asking, "Is this what we want to be doing with Marta?"; "How is the group finding this conversation?"; "How is the group doing talking in this way?" This is the kind of moment where the coach might also give their subjective experience: "I see that the group is trying to be caring of Marta, and, I feel uncomfortable relating to all of what she has given to us as a problem that must be solved."

Some coaches may wait for the group to fail/get stuck/ask for help before speaking. And of course, the group has the right to continue problem-solving even after the coach speaks. By exploring and deconstructing together the activity of solving problems, the group becomes more aware of itself and its power to transform.

When the Group "Fails"

As with everything else we have discussed in this chapter, "failure" is material to be built with by the group. This runs up against the societal notion that failing is to be avoided at all costs. There are many ways coaches and/or clients might experience a group session failing. Clients may think the coach does not "do enough" or they may feel unsupported in the risks they are taking. A client may leave the room/virtual room in a visible huff and other members might feel badly about it. The group might spend 90 minutes giving updates on their lives, uninterested in putting something on the table for the group to work on or asking the coach for help. All these scenarios do occur.

In social therapeutic group coaching, failure can be developmental and create space for discovery. The coach looks to lead the group away from the individualistic notion that a particular person caused a mess in the group, and towards the group's participation in the totality of what got created. The coach might wonder, "Was the group being protective of Natalie? Did that keep us from getting closer to each other, to me and to Natalie?" Philosophical issues can be raised with the group, for example, "What does failure mean?"; "Can the group be radically accepting of its failure?"; or "Is the group interested in challenging the concept of failure?" The coach might take responsibility and share with the group, "I didn't support the group enough in that difficult moment." Finally, the coach can never know the importance or impact of any particular session. An incredibly intimate group may follow one week after a group the coach thought went terribly.

The Power of Silence

While most practitioners are trained to sit in silence with a client, it can feel really uncomfortable sitting in silence with eight clients (who do not know what they are doing and are really hoping the coach does). The coach might feel a strong desire to set an intention or a direction, say something smart or ask a question. However, allowing the group to sit in the uncertainty of silence returns the focus to the group's generative capacity. Usually, at some point, someone will make an offer that the group can create with. This is another example of the group experiencing both its capacity and its responsibility to figure out how to build together given everything that is going/has gone on, including silence.

As we shared in Chapter 4, emotional growth emerges in the spaces in between. Sometimes a group's silence may be awkward and unexpected new things grow out of it. Sometimes silence can be profoundly connected and intimate, with the group taking in the beauty of what they have just created together.

Clients Who Drive Group-oriented Conversation

As the group grows, leadership emerges within the group—that is, some clients develop the ability to see and speak on behalf of the group. They begin to ask group-focused questions or make comments that express the group's activity. They speak to relationships in the group and the group's history as well as to their relationship with the coach. They might ask the coach for help on what is happening in the group—i.e., ask the coach a question, or address/build on something the coach had said earlier that the group did not pick up on.

Here is an example of what that might look like: A group member, Jennifer, has asked for help and group members engage in a lengthy discussion focused on giving advice to her. A more group-oriented participant, Adeola, might jump in and say to the group, "I feel like the group is trying to get to the bottom of Jennifer's problem and fix it. And I am not sure we want to be doing that. I am pretty sure I do not." Or Adeola might turn to the coach and say, "Coach, I need help. I am having reactions to how people are relating to Jennifer. It feels like we are trying to fix her. Is there some other way we could be responding to her? A way that includes the group, rather than each of us as individuals giving her advice which she rejects?"

The coach is listening and looking for this type of participation; it is giving to the group and it is an offer to build with. The coach might decide to acknowledge and support Adeola in the moment by saying something like, "I appreciate what you are saying Adeola. What do others think of what Adeola just said?" and see where the group goes. The coach might experience that the group left Adeola's offer untouched and after some time might say to the group, "I'm still back with what Adeola said earlier about the group being less than intimate with Jennifer in how we are talking with her. Is the group interested in pursuing what Adeola had to say?" Notice how the coach chooses to build with Adeola's offer in way that includes the group. The coach does not declare the right answer, nor what the group should do.

The way to "see" the group is to engage in the activity of building the group. The coach looks to support those who do. Just as importantly, the coach looks to invite those clients who express conflict over doing so, thereby socializing those conflicts with the group. Giving those concerns and questions also helps to create the group.

> Tim asks for help on his marriage and the group does not seem to respond. The coach makes an offer: "I would be interested in inviting Tim to give more to the group around the abusive troubles he experiences in his relationship. This may involve me and all of us becoming closer emotionally to him. Where is the group at around doing that?" One response comes from Janie, "I am not sure I can do that emotionally. It is heavy. It brings up

horrible memories of my previous relationship. It is very emotional for me." Group members further explore their fears and emotions around abusive relationships as well as around getting closer to Tim, someone who has been standoffish in group. The coach, looking to build with everything people give—including, and especially, conflictness—responds, "I am so glad you all are giving this to us. Where is the group at now? Do we have the conditions to do this together with Tim?" (For more on creating the conditions and creating the container, see pp. 102–104.)

When One Member Dominates

A frequent assumption about the unstructured group experience is that one or two people will dominate the conversation, leading to a negative experience for other group members. Social therapeutic groups are not immune to this dynamic. The challenge is for the coach to avoid shutting down the speaker(s) while also supporting the choices of all group members determining how they want to participate. What is the coach noticing in the group as this type of situation unfolds? Do participants seem interested or bored? Are they watching passively or listening actively?

Sometimes participants will relate to a member who is speaking "too-much" as an irritant who shuts down the group. In our view, "dominant member" is a term that focuses on the actions of the individual rather than the group process that produced one or two people speaking.

In this sort of situation, the coach might check in with the group by saying, "How are we doing with this conversation?" Or even ask another group member directly, "Luis, how do you think we are doing?" as a way of inviting leadership from other participants who are more developed in their group sensibility, i.e., someone who is able to give their experience of the group in that moment. The coach could build with that response and ask further questions that explore looking at how the group got here, like, "Are people having emotional responses to the conversation, or a different opinion or understanding?"; "What kept members from interjecting and sharing their experience of one or two people doing all the talking?"; and "Did they consider asking the coach for help to reorganize what was happening?"

These kinds of questions attend to the activity—including the emotional labor—of the group. They open up the discussion towards a shared sense of ownership in building the group. The group could discover its capacity to express agency and thereby its power, rather than feeling victimized by others or by the situation. In other words, the group could decide to do another performance instead of sitting back and waiting for the domination to end. The leadership the coach provides encourages and challenges the group to create an environment in which members are *actively choosing* how they are participating.

Client Fragility

Another way an individual might "dominate" is to organize the group around their identity as a fragile person—e.g., they need to be related to in certain ways or else they will fall apart, get triggered, shut down or blow up. The social therapeutic Life Development Group is a wonderful environment in which to explore the relationality of "being fragile." This book offers numerous examples of the group *building with* what the individual is bringing, rather than *taking care of* that person.

The fragile client sends the message, "You have to be careful with me." The group (and the coach) might get protective of that person and avoid being "uncareful." Or the group may respond by saying it does not want to feel hamstrung or have to walk on eggshells with this person.

One area that might get explored is the gap between how the fragile client sees themselves and how the group experiences them.[14] The client might say, "I am always scared that people are rejecting me or angry at me." The coach or a group member might ask, "What about with us? Do you experience the group as rejecting and angry at you?" or someone might point out, "My experience of you here in group is that you are often rejecting of us." For the coach, the key in leading the discussion is to focus on the activity "in the room," to keep engaging how people are in group with each other (here), rather than slipping into descriptive examples of what happens at home, at work or at Sunday dinner (there). As we lay out in Part I, describing things (one's own fragility, in this case) is often a less relational, more individualized act, more prone to requiring "correct" facts, causes and explanations, which leads down a cognitive road rather than a developmental one.

It is often most powerful in these instances that the group, rather than the coach, gives its experience of that person. It is more hearable, less likely to be taken as an authoritative proclamation of who the person really is. It also experientially undercuts the client's identification with their feelings as the primary understanding of who they are (see Chapter 4), as now they have others' relational experiences of them to consider.

Working with a Silent Client

A common assumption in group work is that it is a problem when members do not speak. Judgments and assumptions include that there is something wrong with the client or that they cannot get help unless they do speak. However, engaging people in the activity of creating the group, of giving to others, is vastly different than getting someone to speak for speaking's sake. In Life Development Groups, a client's silence is not automatically equated with problematic disengagement.

> A man did not speak in group for one year, even though he was encouraged by the coach and group. He had joined the group to stop being a shy truck driver and become more relational with people. One day, after 18 months in group, he announced to the group that he was leaving his job as a driver to start law school. Furthermore, he shared that he had built relationships with his work colleagues and they had celebrated his big news by organizing numerous send-off parties for him. He was no longer the reserved, isolated person who had come into group. He attributed his growth to being in group. Then he gave his experience of his emotional/relational growth, including the transformation in how he was relating to people and the new ways people were experiencing him.

As with everything regarding the social therapeutic method, the coach sees the silent client through the lens of activity. Attending group week after week is an act of participation and choice; so too is active listening. Developing connections with other group members in the waiting room before and after group is part of building the group's sense of community. In Life Development Groups, it is not uncommon for participants to meet up outside of sessions and build friendships. Someone who does not speak in group may be sharing outside of group their experience and ways the group impacts on them.

The client and coach relationship remains important. This includes the history of what they have built together (this presumes there has been/ is individual work) and the developmental issues/challenges identified by client and coach. There might be some scenarios in which the coach senses that a quiet group member may have a unique take on the group's activity that could be helpful to the group. The coach could directly invite their contribution with an open question, like "Hanniyah, what are you thinking?" or a more pointed question: "Hanniyah, this is a topic that hits close to home for you, I am wondering what this discussion is like for you."

In this chapter we have attempted to bring to life the role and activities of a social therapeutic Life Development Group coach. We have offered possible "lines" to perform in differing scenes such that a coach may begin to babble and experience seeing and leading the group. In the next chapter we will show extended moments from groups—client and coach activity—that include commentary on various elements of the social therapeutic method.

Notes

1 We are indebted to Lois Holzman and Rafael Mendez, editors of *Psychological Investigations* (2003), whose writing has influenced the structure of this chapter. Newman's quote here is pp. 72–73.
2 By "alienation," we intend the Marxian understanding of how we separate ourselves from our own process of production, losing our capacity to see who we are as creators of our lives.
3 See p. 98 on languaging and the section *Practicing Emotional Growth* in Chapter 4.
4 "Coach is comfortable not knowing as one of the best states to expand awareness in" (ICF, 2017, p. 3).
5 For more on "seeing the group" please review Chapter 3. For more on hearing, building with and making offers see p. 168 and the section on improv, pp. 51–53. For more on the zpd, see pp. 43–44.
6 See tables on pp. 54 and 80 which illustrate relevant differences between social therapeutics, coaching and therapy.
7 See Introduction, especially p. 2.
8 See our case for heterogeneous groups on pp. 69–72.
9 Most social therapeutic coaches prefer 90-minute sessions.
10 Most clients come to social therapeutics for reasons similar to seeking coaching or therapy—relationship issues, feeling lonely, desiring skills to advance a career, improve one's social life or navigate a life transition or loss, etc.

11 These typically run for four to eight weeks, with four to ten participants. Groups can be started with three people.
12 For more on tool-for-result vs. tool-and-result, see pp. 56–57.
13 See pp. 79–84 for more on relationality in social therapeutics.
14 In social therapeutics the "gap" is relational, between people, to be created with and by everyone without knowing where that activity will lead. In traditional coaching, the "gap" is individualized, known and to be closed. It is the space between where the individual is today and where they want to be in the future.

References

Holzman, L. (2018). *The Overweight Brain: How our obsession with knowing keeps us from getting smart enough to make a better world.* East Side Institute Press.
Holzman, L. & Mendez, R. (Eds.). (2003). *Psychological Investigations: A Clinician's Guide to Social Therapy.* Brunner-Routledge.
International Coaching Federation. (2017). *ICF Core Competencies Rating Levels.* Retrieved March 2022 from: https://coachingfederation.org/app/uploads/2017/12/ICF_Competencies_Level_Table_wNote.pdf
Newman, F. (1996). *Performance of a Lifetime: A Practical-Philosophical Guide to the Joyous Life.* Castillo International, Inc.

6

GROUP COACHING NUTS AND BOLTS

What follows in this chapter are numerous snapshots of social therapeutic Life Development Group sessions derived from our practices and shaped into illustrating a methodological moment. The examples become more complex as the chapter progresses. While in the previous chapter we speak directly to the coach and give examples of how a coach might respond, here we attempt to spotlight moments of method in action, in the ongoing group process. This is enormously challenging. The writing of these scenes becomes de facto a distortion of "what really happened." Nonetheless, we hope that the reader will see something different than they are used to, will experience a shift in understanding or will be surprised by seeing a new possibility. Practicing social therapeutics is neither impossible nor easy. It is experiential, non-cognitive and holistic. We have created thematic sections beginning with the activity of asking for help—seen in social therapeutics as a proactive, relational offer with which to be built. Then, we move to multiple group scenes in which emotionality sits at the core of the group's work. Hopefully the reader will experience what the sharing of, and building with, emotionality/emotions can look like. We conclude with a series of group discussions in which participants make new meaning out of the material provided by group members.

DOI: 10.4324/9781003326465-10

The reader will experience examples of seeing the group, performance direction, individual growth as part of group growth, language games, the creation of the emotional zpd and the group and individuals performing ahead of themselves. Amidst this group activity is the coach's leadership guiding—but not dictating—the group in building environments for growth. We name and attempt to connect those elements to chapters or sections in Part I in which we have laid out the concepts of social therapeutics. Other foundational elements, like radical acceptance,[1] are not illustrated here, as they have been discussed and examples provided earlier on. We again encourage the reader to move back and forth through the book several times for a holistic experience of social therapeutics.

NOTE: For reading clarity we use the gender-neutral pronoun "they" to represent the coach or an individual (unnamed) group member and "it" to represent the group.

Asking for Help

In social therapeutics, asking for help is a developmental activity. It is a relational process that involves building with others. It breaks with the individualistic notion of "figuring it out ourselves" and invites others in to co-create with our thoughts and feelings. It is performatory in two ways: First, most find it uncomfortable to ask for help, so the asking itself can be performing "a head taller"[2] of what the individual usually does. Second, other group members might offer comments, responses or philosophical questions which the individual had not considered and could not have come up with[3] on their own. These elements taken together open the possibility of stretching and "doing a new performance," of creating more connection and intimacy—in other words, the possibility of emotional growth.

Even for a long-running group, or an experienced group member, it can be difficult to say, "Group, I want to ask for your help." For new groups it is both a hard and an unknown experience. (This is where the individual work the coach has done with the client before joining group can be helpful. It can be in an individual session that the coach encourages the client to bring something up in group and ask the group for help.) Here are some moments of the coach leading in the activity of asking for help.

Asking the Group for Help

Depending on whether the group is in person or online, the start of group might differ. In person, the participants might be chatting amongst themselves in a waiting area and then enter the coaching space together. There is a sort of natural distinction between pre-group and the start of group. Over video call, that distinction disappears as each participant sits in their own waiting space and joins the group at the discretion of the coach.

In any event, the coach usually "officially" begins an ongoing group with something like, "How are you?" or "Hi. Let's start. Does anyone have a developmental challenge they want to bring to the group?" or "Welcome. Who has something they would like to ask the group for help with?" Sometimes someone comes in ready to ask for help, sometimes not. It is not unusual for there to be an uncomfortable silence at the beginning of the group. Here is a scene from a four-week Life Development Group.

The coach opens the group, which is meeting for the third time, and participants remain quiet for a long period. "Hmmm. You are all here, you have decided to be here tonight. What's going on that you are silent?"

"I find that question of 'what help do you want from the group' difficult to answer. It makes me anxious," a group member offers.

The coach responds, "I hear you. It's not a usual question we ask each other. What is difficult for you and others in asking for help from the group?"

Various group members respond: "I don't like asking anyone for anything"; "It's too exposing"; "I am afraid the group won't want to help me"; "You all will judge me"; "I am conflicted about it. I love the group, we have come up with other ways to be and speak that I would never have come up with on my own. But, if I'm honest, I like deciding all by myself. I don't want to have to justify what I do to anyone."

This opens a conversation about what people mean by "help" and what clients ask of others in their lives. It emerges that clients feel comfortable asking others for help cleaning the kitchen or picking up something at the store, but not at all comfortable asking for emotional support during a tough day or for help to stop eating junk food or to get over a reaction they are having to a colleague or to make a decision—small or life-changing.

Nearly everyone provides reasons they do not think to ask for help from others with those kinds of issues. In addition, several clients express frustration that their loved ones do not just automatically know to help in those scenarios.

The coach asks, "OK, I hear the group saying there are degrees of comfort in asking for help and degrees of frustration when our unspoken needs to do not get met. This brings me back to the question: What is it about asking for help, and I mean specifically asking for help here in group, from us, from me, that keeps you from asking?"

After some back and forth, a client takes the risk, "This group session is so interesting to me. I do want to ask for help with some relationship challenges. I guess that previously I have not spoken up and asked directly. Can I talk about what is going on?"

Commentary

This scene shows how the coach can lead on an issue—clients asking for help—which is integral to building the group. Perhaps a more traditional approach would be for the coach to explain to the group why asking for help is important—a cognitive way of imparting information that sets the coach up as knowing the "right" way to do social therapeutics. This disempowers clients by relating to them as passive learners (or consumers of the right way) and obscures their role as active participants in building the group.

Instead, the coach invites the group to co-create by moving "around and about" asking for help—interrogating what it means to people, when they do it or not, what goes on for them in asking or not asking for help, etc. This activity aids in creating an environment in which a client could step forward and ask for help from the group. A possible alternate scenario would have unfolded if someone had turned to the coach and asked, "Why do you keep asking us this question of 'Do we have something for which we could ask the group's help?'" That would have been an invitation to the coach to give more. In that case, the coach might have shared how they see asking for help as a developmental activity. The conversation would have proceeded differently, though hopefully in a way that was just as co-created, non-outcome driven and philosophically/linguistically playful.

The Client Who Does Not Want Help

Over two months, a client has given updates to the group of an upsetting work situation with an abusive manager. A successful businessman, Hasan has continuously told the group he is grateful that he has a place to express his feelings. At first the group wanted to help him leave his job, but he did not seem interested. The group has typically expressed concern for Hasan and has listened to his updates on how badly he has been treated at work. In this session, the group grows in how it relates to Hasan.

"How is the group doing with how Hasan is talking with us?" the coach asked after a particularly intense back and forth with the group trying to help Hasan and Hasan rejecting the group's offers.

Group members responded with, "I get frustrated that he seems to say the same things in here"; "Honestly, it doesn't seem like Hasan wants the group's help"; "Coach, what are you seeing?"

The coach replied, "Yes, I would agree. I experience Hasan as rejecting of the group. He wants to say what he has to say, but isn't particularly open to inviting the group to build with it."

Another group member added, "Yes, I care about Hasan, but when he talks in here about work, it feels very controlled and controlling of us." Hasan did not have much of a response to this and the group moved on.

Two weeks later, Hasan again began discussing his terrible manager and what was happening to him at work. A group leader, Cristina interjected, "Hasan, I hear you describing this awful week at work, but I don't hear you asking us for help. Are you wanting help from the group?"

Hasan said yes, but his activity and what he was saying demonstrated no.

The coach turned to the group, "OK, so what does the group want to do when Hasan doesn't want to do what we are doing, which is listening for offers with which to build the group?"

Cristina said, "I don't want to do this anymore with Hasan. I want him to grow, to get out of these situations where he is passive. I would rather we work with someone who wants help tonight."

The group built with Cristina's comment and decided that next time it would be much more proactive in asking Hasan straight-up what he wants help with from the group.

A month later Hasan opened the group: "I have been thinking about the group and what you all have been saying to me on how I do not ask for help here. My wife told me last night that she was tired of hearing me complain about work. So, I guess I am hearing from everywhere that I am bothering people when I bring up my boss. I do not know what to do. Can the group help me with that?"

The group celebrated Hasan asking for help! And began working with him on what to do when he does not know what to do.

Commentary

The coach did not bring their experience of how Hasan was rejecting of the group until the group had worked with him for some time and the coach had the sense that it (the group) might be able to hear what they (the coach) had to say. The question the coach decided to posit to the group was a "how" question (How is the group doing with how Hasan is talking with us?) that pointed toward Hasan's activity of relating to the group as a receptacle for his bad experiences at work. Group members gave their experience of Hasan *in group*, i.e., relationally, and went through a process of deciding together how it wanted to respond. In this case, it expressed its power to reshape the group's activity (rather than passively hold space for Hassan's work problems) by focusing on people who wanted help from the group.

That Hasan came to group acknowledging that he heard the group and its demand on him to be less controlling with the group, and give the group something to build with, was developmental for him and the group. Hasan allowed the group to impact him. The group discovered that it could voice demands on group members from the posture of "taking the side of the group."[4] It heard Hasan's offer of not knowing how to ask for help (exposing not knowing to the group is very different than rejecting what the group is giving) and built with that.

The Client Asks the Coach for Help

Jane has been working in group on how quick she is to judge people—what they say, what they wear, what car they drive. The coach and group have pointed out how her judgmental mindset keeps her stuck in her head and distant from whomever she is with. Jane was invited by the group to ask the coach for help the next time she found herself judging the group/group members.

Jane speaks to the coach shyly, saying, "I need your help right now. I am feeling really judgmental of Lauren."

The coach responds, "OK. Say more."

"She is talking with us like she is so smart and we are just a bunch of dummies! I do not want to just sit here stewing about it!"

"OK, can you say what you are saying *and* connect it with what the group is doing?"

Hesitantly, Jane begins speaking. "Lauren, I really feel . . ."

The coach jumps in: "Can you say it to the group, rather than to Lauren?"

"Group, we are working on family stuff tonight and I find the conversation intense. Then Lauren swoops in and talks like she has it all together in her life. It drives me crazy."

"Thank you for giving that to the group. How was that to say to us?" the coach inquires.

"Uncomfortable! I feel like I have no idea what I am saying or how it sounds."

The coach offers to Jane: "Maybe you could ask the group."

"Group, how does what I just said sound?"

The group shares how much it appreciates Jane trying this new performance of not staying in her head. It felt her be more present and connected with the group in how she said what was going on for her. Lauren gave that she found Jane's comment hard to hear and that she is coming to see how invested she is in "looking good" to others.

Commentary

A prerequisite for this interchange between coach and client is that they have built a relationship where the client trusts they can ask the coach for help. Another prerequisite is the group creating the conditions for this to occur—being willing to support and build with Jane's attempt at a new performance in group (rather than correcting or judging her).

The coach directs Jane in a "Yes, and . . ." way by suggesting she perform/give to the group and then add what's going on for her. The focus does not rest on whether Jane is right about Lauren, but rather on radically accepting Jane's offer, in the context of her working on giving her judgmentalness to the group. What followed was relational. There was no attempt to resolve or rationalize a conflict.

By asking the coach for help, Jane invited the coach to give more to the group, by way of helping her. The coach was able to support Jane to do and say things that changed where she was standing—from outside of the group (and in her head) judging it, to inside the group (outside her head) participating in what the group was doing. The group is learning that asking for help from the coach enhances what the group can do together and fosters its growth.

The Coach Asks the Group for Help

This virtual group has been meeting for a while. The coach has noticed a change. Some participants are joining late, another one tends to turn off their camera and yet another does not show and does not let the coach know they will not be attending. This has been bothering the coach, who is noticing they feel irritated and disrespected. The coach decides to ask the group for help on this.

"Hello everyone. I would like to start the group tonight by asking for your help. I have been noticing that people are appearing late into group or disappearing off video. I experience that as disruptive to building the group together and it certainly makes it harder for me to lead the group. I want to ask for your help by coming on time, letting me know if you are not coming and staying on camera for the full session."

A group leader asks what about the group's behavior is making it harder for the coach to lead group. This allows the coach to give more on their experience, which is heard by the group as an offer to respond to and build with. Group members share crazy work schedules, horrible traffic or children's sports practice as reasons why they arrived late or left early. Someone else takes the risk to say that the comings and goings of other members during sessions are frustrating: "I show up every week on time ready to work! I really want everyone to be here."

This opens up a conversation on prioritizing group. For example, the group explores how to speak with managers about having an important weekly commitment, setting up carpools for children's soccer practice or making sure someone can be in a private room where they will not be disturbed.

The coach shares their appreciation for the conversation and the renewed commitment to showing up to group.

Commentary

This is an example of the coach giving their subjectivity to the group in a way that tried not to be moralistic or authoritarian. In asking for what they needed from the group, the coach took the risk of getting closer to people's commitment (or lack thereof) to coming to group. The coach did not know how group members would respond. Some made a point of being supportive of the coach, another provided leadership to the group by raising that they expect everyone to attend on time and regularly, others raised the actual challenges they face in attending. The group's response was to take the coach seriously and explore what they needed in order to join and stay present for the entire session.

The Group Deciding What to Do

In any given week, group members may be more interested in checking in with others rather than bringing something to work on. The social therapeutic coach is attuned to if and how the group is noticing what it is doing and if it wants to do something different.

Three different people pursue Deidre about a conversation that occurred in group a few weeks prior regarding her struggle to have more work-life balance. The first group member asks Deidre how she has been doing since the work she did in group. Deidre responds plainly, not offering much. Another participant asks her another question about work and then another about how she is feeling about work.

After the third question Deidre replies, "Well, I feel a little put on the spot, but I can share something," and went on to talk about her workday and the challenges she deals with.

Then there is a pause.

Roberta turns to John and says, "I am interested in how you are doing around losing your job. You seemed good last week and I want to check in if that's still true and if you are making progress in your search."

"Thanks for checking," John answers and proceeds to give an update.

Another group member interrupts John and adds, "Also when we finish, I want to check in with Amelia. She has missed a few sessions and I think it would be good to hear from her."

At this point Sam interjects, "OK . . . I think I am getting irritated. I don't know what is going on for the group that we keep moving around from person to person."

The coach supports Sam, saying, "I appreciate your saying this. It seems like the group has not yet landed on what it wants to do this evening."

The group begins discussing how to determine who to work with and what to work on in the group.

Commentary

There were several moments in this group session in which the coach (and likely the reader) was wondering what the group was doing. It felt less connected, less intimate. A challenge for the coach is to allow the group to do what it does. One week a group might do check-ins, the next week it might work intensely with someone, another week it might philosophize together and yet another session might include a disagreement within the group or between the group and the coach. In this session, when Jacob raised his concerns with the group's activity—jumping from person to person—the coach related to his comment as an offer to build upon. The experience of the group making a decision together turned out to be developmental. Ultimately the group decided that it wanted to work with a person who was asking for help from the group.

Supporting the Creation of the Emotional Zone of Proximal Development[5]

A client, Fernando, asks the group for help. He has just returned from a visit with his aging parents, who live far away from him, and it was bringing up a lot of stuff.

Fernando shares how frustrating it is having elderly parents who do not ask for help and do not want to take care of themselves. He expresses his fear of them dying, as well as his upset over their disconnection from one another and increasing dysfunction. Fernando is teary-eyed as he gives this to the group.

The group asks some questions and tries to come up with suggestions for what to do. There is back and forth on whether Fernando's father is experiencing Alzheimer's.

The coach is listening closely for an offer that might invite the group's emotionality and says, "This is so difficult. I feel very emotional listening to Fernando being open and giving with us. I also hear a hint of us getting into labeling or pathologizing the cognitive state of his father. I understand the pull to accurately define a loved one's cognitive decline, though I am not sure what is important about us identifying his father's true state. I am more interested in where the group is at emotionally around your experience of Fernando talking with us like this."

One group member shares that they felt touched that Fernando got choked up: "I don't think he has ever cried in group before. I am glad he is letting us be with him like this. I feel closer to him. He is being more human." Another member builds on that and adds, "Yeah, I like getting to know emotional Fernando. I was really irritated by you a few weeks ago, Fernando. You were patronizing to the group and would not get your hands dirty [be vulnerable] with us as we worked." A third member, Paola, disagrees, "Actually, that group was all over the place in that session and I thought Fernando was just as patronizing as others."

The coach experiences the intimacy of the first two comments and notices a defensiveness and distance in Paola's comment. Given the history with this particular group, the coach decides to jump in with a question: "Paola, I am wondering if you are feeling protective of Fernando."

"Well, Fernando is really sensitive, that's why he's always intellectualizing. I don't want him to feel criticized by the group."

"Oh, that's helpful. You're protecting him from getting criticized?" the coach asks.

"Yeah, probably."

Another group member says, "Actually Paola, I experience you protecting members of the group often. It's almost as if you want to put the brakes on group when it gets too intimate for you."

"Honestly," Fernando chimes in, "I was grateful for Paola's comment. I was feeling really uncomfortable with people's responses to the coach's question of what it's like to be with me tonight. It's like people were accepting of me being emotional. I am realizing how much work I do to *not* be emotional."

This opens up a conversation in which group members share ways they choose to be or not to be emotional and with whom. Several contribute their fears of being emotional. Others express ways that taking the risk to share what's going on emotionally had generated more intimacy in group and in their relationships.

Commentary

There are many things going on in this scene. Fernando gave to the group something going on in his life and the group built with it. What began as an individual being teary-eyed over a family visit became an emotional zpd, i.e., an environment in which it was possible for group members—with varying emotional abilities—to give how they are emotional with others in group and in their lives. Another way to put it is that Fernando's initial sharing of an individual thing about him (that was his, that he possessed) became an experience belonging to everyone in the group. The sense of community people experience in the activity of building group together is why clients return week after week, even after they are no longer feeling stuck or in acute emotional pain.

Something else developmental was occurring. People were giving their experiences of Fernando in group (sensitive, patronizing, intellectual). This generated other points of view of who Fernando is (not emotional) and is becoming (able to express emotionality), that he could not possibly have seen or appreciated on his own. That relationality created the possibility for Fernando to see how he is with others in a new way. Seeing in a new way opens the door to acting on new possibilities/doing a new performance.

The coach here worked to relate to the group as the unit of development and stay in a generative, not-knowing process. The coach could have gotten into whether Fernando really is sensitive, or was feeling criticized, by asking Fernando and the group more about it. Those directions could have produced intimate and developmental group work as well. Given how the group was going back and forth on a descriptive fact (Fernando's father having dementia or not), the coach chose to build with the relational offer of how Paola was responding to the group's conversation. Note the relationality that is baked into the dialogue. This group has already learned to give what it is like to be in relation with others in the group—i.e., how participants and the coach impact on each other and see each other.

Deprivatizing Emotional Pain

We speak extensively in Chapters 3 and 4 on the individualism-to-loneliness pipeline and the socio-cultural understanding of emotions that keeps us trapped in our pain. What follows here are several examples of how Life Development Groups relate to and build with emotionality and emotional identities in the group. The activity includes challenging assumptions, curiosity, radical acceptance, creating new language and making new meaning together. When the coach and group perform these activities, the issue that the client brings in as their own "thing" becomes reshaped and liberated from their head. The experience of others creating with our pain can turbocharge emotional growth.

Depression as a Doing

In an ongoing group, a regular member who is prone to bouts of depression gave to the group that she was feeling unable to do anything.

Jennifer expresses gratitude that the group is virtual, because otherwise she may not have been able to get out of the house to a group meeting space: "I am having really bad depression," she says, "I barely get out of bed most of the time."

The coach responds, "I am thankful that you made it here to be with us. I appreciate the hard time you are having. May I invite the group to explore the meaning of depression with you?" Jennifer agrees.

"I am curious what you mean by 'having' a bad depression?" the coach continues.

"Well, I am not sure the best way to say it. I have had this depression most of my life. They say it is genetic and biological."

"When you say you have it, where is it? Is it somewhere in the brain?" the coach guesses.

"I think so, though sometimes it feels like it is in my heart, or feels like dead weight I carry on my back."

"What is that like?" a group member asks.

"The weight keeps me from doing stuff."

"Hmm. Maybe we can play with how you do depression," the coach offers. "Group, maybe we can help Jennifer play with that."

The group begins to explore how Jennifer "does" depression, asking questions like: "How are you in bed when you are depressed?"; "Do you just lie there?"; "Do you sit up in bed?"; "Are you able to look out the window?"; "What would it be like to do that?"; "Can you stretch while lying in bed?"; "Does being in bed get tiresome?" Out of this conversation, Jennifer says that she is finding it helpful to look at depression as a doing rather than as a feeling. She is seeing possibilities of existence beyond her usually limited ways: "I felt a nudge unstuck."

Commentary

Wittgenstein's language-games[6] come into play here, where the focus is on the activity of speaking rather than the assumed Truth-referential meaning of the words (i.e., assuming everyone understands/knows the same meaning of the word depression). The shift from "having" depression to "doing" depression repositioned where Jennifer and group were standing. Shifting where we stand changes how we see. The coach and group play an immeasurable role in presenting other ways of seeing. In Part I we presented Newman and Holzman's case that we need others to help us see who we are and who we are becoming—that relationality is an activity, a doing. It removes the illusion that there can be objectivity or "knowing the Truth." This group scene exemplifies the relationality of the group members through playing with the client's use of depression language.

Taking the Group with You

"I had the group with me" is a phrase that members of advanced groups might say as they recount to the group something developmental that occurred during the week, outside of group, that the group had helped to create. Here is a look at one way that gets produced.

Week One

Megan comes to group complaining that her ex-boyfriend, still part of her circle of friends, reached out to spend time together, yet again. And once again, her hopes got dashed when she discovered that he had no interest in getting back romantically with her.

One group member questions how come Megan keeps putting herself in a situation where she would continue to get hurt. Another member shares how frustrated they feel to hear Megan tell the same story over and over of her interactions with her ex. The group reminds Megan of the numerous times she and her ex have fought so aggressively and loudly that friends and neighbors had to step in. Megan was participating in escalating situations that might someday get her physically hurt. Another group member shares that she feels scared by Megan's anger.

At first, Megan keeps complaining. However, as she continues speaking, the group hears something new in how she is talking. Megan is giving the group how she is feeling—angry and humiliated. Another group member notes how they feel closer to Megan as she gives what is going on for her emotionally. Other members share ways they like and admire Megan for taking the risk to give this to group; still others give things they do when they are feeling angry or humiliated.

The coach wonders aloud to the group, "Is it possible that Megan is letting herself be given to and loved by the group? Afterall, the group has created an environment in which members can caringly share their responses to her. That is a loving activity—could Megan have that?" The coach adds, "Letting ourselves be loved by others, receiving love, is often harder than loving."

Another group member, Zachary, picks up on this and becomes more lovingly demanding of Megan: "I'll tell you something. I'm pissed at you and I love you. I do not want you to interact with him anymore, anywhere. It's not good for you. So stop it! The next time you see him, think of me and the group and just get out of there."

The coach builds on this, asking, "What about 'having the group' with you in these moments? You are letting us be loving of you here in group, what about carrying our love for you into other places in your life?"

Megan replies coolly, "I might, but it's unlikely."

The group is not open to pursuing the coach's offer of taking the group with one "out into the world." Members say things like, "I don't think about the group during the week"; "I come in here trying to talk about my loneliness and how badly dating prospects treat me and you, coach, keep telling me to focus on the group!"; "Why would I think about group when I'm in the middle of a family situation?!?"

This had the coach thinking throughout the week: "The group seemed rejecting of what I was giving. How is it that they see themselves as individuals getting (validation, sympathy) from others in the group even though what they are doing is the relational activity that builds the group and helps them grow? What does the group want from me? What do they want to build with each other?"

Week Two

Right out of the gate Zachary follows up: "OK Megan, I want to know if I'm going to have to get lovingly angry with you. Did you engage with your ex this past week?" Megan replies that she ran into her ex twice that week and walked right out instead of engaging. The group celebrates this new development and its part in helping it happen.

The group moves on. Another member, Laquan, shares that he had met an interesting woman and asked her out but now, just before the date, he is paralyzed with self-doubt and feelings of unworthiness. The group works with Laquan. Some take risks by sharing when they get paralyzed or their experience of first dates. The group collectively explores how to be relational when you are nervous and worried of what your date might be thinking of you. It comes up with a performance direction for Laquan— "Give her a little something of how you're doing in the moment of the date"—and some lines to say like, "I'm enjoying hanging out with you"; "I'm thinking I would like to do this again. Would you like that?"

By the end of the session Laquan says, "I am definitely taking the group with me on this date! I will think of you all and your support of me when I start doubting myself with this woman."

Commentary

This extended scene offers ways that social therapeutic group work deprivatizes emotions and emotionality. Both Megan and Laquan took the risk to expose their humiliation, fear and anger. The group made loving demands of each of them to stretch and try a new performance. In this example we wanted to spotlight how groups build intimacy, create emotional connection and foster a sense of community. It is important to hear the group's responses to both Megan and Laquan as giving, as (mostly) loving demands of them, rather than an order or a self-righteous declaration.[7]

As practitioners, we all experience the unknowability of the impact of our work. What seems unhearable one week becomes embraced by the group the next! In this case, the coach decided to offer two developmental stretches based on what was emerging in the group process in week one. The first was introducing the experience of letting oneself feel loved by others (this "stretch" of deprivatizing emotional pain involves allowing others to love you—even while you feel unlovable). The second stretch was the choice to stay connected (unalienated) throughout the week with what the group had created together (deprivatized emotional intimacy, loving demands, performance directions), i.e., taking the group with you. This offer was built with the following week, in a different conversation on a different topic. This encapsulates the magic and the power of development in social therapeutic group work.

Dealing with Loss

In Chapter 3, we introduced the concept of living in both society and history[8]— that we as humans both follow society's scripts and we create new ones. The issue of death gets raised in this group session and the coach brings their understanding of society/history to the discussion.

Larry starts group by sharing that he has just lost a significant friend: "The group is important to me and I want you to know about him. But I am not sure I want to take attention away from the group." One group member wonders what Larry meant by "take away from the group." Another member builds with this and says, "You are an important person in this group and don't often give us much of your emotionality. We would love to know you better and who this person is to you."

It is an intimate conversation with the group. Larry shares his special history with his friend who has passed. Even though the man was not a regular presence in his life, Larry has been feeling a deep sadness and tearing up during the week. Others in group share their experiences of loss and what it means to them. "Well, we all have to learn to live with the loss and keep living our lives," one participant remarks.

The coach responds to the general tone of the conversation, which the last speaker had captured and says, "This question is meant to be provocative. I hear the group saying that you have to 'deal with' the loss. What have you 'lost' when a person is no longer physically on this planet?"

The group responds to the question with quizzical looks. A few members try to answer: "Loss is when something or someone isn't there anymore"; "I have experienced a lot of loss, my parents died when I was pretty young." Then Matthew shares, "I lost my mother and I have not gotten over it."

The coach asks what it is that Matthew has not gotten over with his mother. Matthew responds, "I am still furious at her. For how she left and how she treated me my whole life."

The coach responds with care, "I hear that and know that about you. And, you are telling us that she really has not left your life. You are still relating to her. From a societal point of view, yes, she is dead. She no longer pays the cable bill or calls you on your birthday. However, if we look at the process of human history—where social processes come and go, where they continually transform and new developments are created—everything is a continuous process that is reinvested into new, remixed entities. Loss, from a historical perspective, is where these experiences are continually developing and transforming. Loss can be redeveloped to create something new and life-giving."

"Are you suggesting I could redevelop my relationship with my mother, without her consent?!" Matthew asks. The group chuckles.

"Yes, you could. And we could do that with you if you would like to do that with us. I would like to do that with you," the coach replies.

Other group members respond, "I am intrigued. I'm not sure I totally understand, but I like the idea that there's more to loss than a big hole"; "I am feeling relieved by what the coach is saying. As we spoke about Harry's friend, I felt like I was being introduced to this interesting person for the first time." The group discusses the experience of getting to know the special people who have been/are part of participants' lives. People discover that they are feeling more emotionally present with the group.

The coach adds, "Yes, we have created an environment in which we could bring those we have 'lost' here into group with us. We are not relating to them as 'lost.' We are including them and your relationship with them here."

Commentary

Western culture shapes how we respond to death, endings, mourning and loss.[9] An underlying assumption of this culture is the dualism that something either exists, or it does not. In this scene, the coach looked for an opportunity to introduce another way to see death and loss—embracing the contradiction that a dead person is both not there and there. In Matthew's case, the coach encouraged him to embrace that his mother has died, but that she is still "there" because he remains in (an angry) relationship with her. The coach offered the client the possibility of transforming that angry relationship. Also embedded in this conversation is the deprivatizing of the emotionality of loss. The group performed grieving together as they built with Harry's offer.

Fighting in Group

This ongoing group has nine participants. Ilana and Mary can get rather tense with each other at times. In this session, they begin yelling at each other, each accusing the other of cutting them off and being nasty on a personal level.

There is a long silence after the yelling dies down.

The coach breaks the silence and inquires, "Where is the group at with Ilana and Mary's exchange?"

Ilana jumps in before other group members can respond, "I don't like talking about this as though it is just me and Mary going through this. I need us to talk about it like the group is collectively creating this fight."

This provokes another participant: "I see what you're saying, but honestly you two do this all the time in here and you should do a separate session together to fix your fighting and then come back to group." Mary concedes, "I need to be better at having more finesse in responding to Ilana instead of coming in hot and reacting to her." Someone else, picking up on the coach's question, points out, "Mary, you are taking it to be as if it's just you that's the issue. I think the coach is trying to get at something else. Coach, why were you inquiring about where the group is at?"

The coach responds, "Thank you for asking. I have the experience of the group hanging back and leaving Mary and Ilana alone with 'their' mess. It is the group's right to choose to do that. However, I would like to understand better why the group sees itself as separated out from the fight."

A group member replies, "Well, when I walk down the street and see a couple fighting—yelling and being physically intimidating—I put my head down and get out of there." Another member says, "I like to watch. If I am to be honest, it feels safer. I can evaluate the fight—who's right, who's wrong, how I would do it differently."

Ilana, repeating a version of what she had said earlier, remarks to the group, "I know I can find Mary provocative at times and I lose it. But I need help from the group in those moments. If the group is holding back, then you're leaving us alone and I do not appreciate that."

"I find what you and everyone are saying helpful," says the coach. "You see, we—the group—are in the fight, whether we want to be or not. The fight is happening here. This is the group we build together, week after week. So do we want to look at ways we participate in the fight?"

A discussion ensues in which the group decides to break into the conversation the next time Mary and Ilana start getting into it. And how they decide to break in is relational and developmental. Rather than simply telling the women to stop fighting, the group decides that it will, in the future, put the demand on Ilana and Mary to ask the group and the coach for help. The responsibility shifts away from the individuals and the assumption that those individuals should "fix" themselves before speaking to each other in group. The group steps up to take responsibility for all that is happening in the group, including those moments when two particular people converse like they are the only two people in the room.

Commentary

The coach focused on the activity of the group and spoke with the group by acknowledging everything going on, including tension, fighting and hanging back. The coach's question of "Where is the group at?" was built upon by a group member who asked the coach for more. This is an example of a group member providing leadership by supporting the coach. The request for more allowed the coach to give more, in a way that might not have been heard by the group earlier on. This was part of creating the environment in which the group could do something different, i.e., transform the group and how people were relating in it.

The reader will see here several instances of the coach leading the group, the characteristics of which we fleshed out in the previous chapter. The coach gave their subjective experience of the group "hanging back," of distancing itself from the mess of the fight. The coach invited the group to give more philosophically/emotionally around the activity of hanging back when they said, "I would like to understand better how come the group sees itself as separated out from the fight." This was directed at the group, including Mary and Ilana who also responded. The coach also gave their advanced skill of seeing groups by locating the issue at hand as happening in the group: "The fight is happening here. This is the group we build together, week after week. So do we want to look at ways we participate in the fight?" The coach followed this with the invitation for the group to look at its fight-participating activity together. This completes the shift away from looking at Mary and Ilana as members who should fix their relationship (outside of group) and toward the group building with everything, including fighting.

Creating Meaning Together

The human capacity to create meaning is unique to our species, as far as we know. Playing language-games in the Wittgensteinian sense deconstructs what we usually take to be a known entity. Moving away from defining, knowing, explaining, identifying and searching for causes in our conversations, makes room for ordinary human creativity. These examples illustrate the playful, creative culture of Life Development Groups.

Emotionality, Values and Loneliness

In this session, the coach locates the group's philosophizing on loneliness within the context of living in a lonely world.

"What kind of lonely are you?" one group member asks another. This spurs a creative conversation in the group: "I'm a frustrated lonely. I want to have a romantic relationship and it just never seems to work out"; "I am future lonely, my kids have told me they are not going to have kids, I will not get to be a grandma"; "I am a social lonely. I go out but never feel connected to people"; "I am a married lonely. My wife and I do not talk below the surface."

With appreciation for the group's creative honesty, the coach remarks playfully, "Excellent! We have such a breadth of loneliness expertise tonight!" The coach then asks how it was to hear the variety of loneliness, careful not relate to them as fixed labels, but rather as meanings emerging as the group builds its conversation.

Various group members respond and the coach follows with a question, "What do you *do* with your loneliness?"

"What do you mean, what do we *do* with it? It's just there weighing me down in a fog around my head and chest," someone responds.

"Well," the coach continues, "do you drink? Yell at your dog or TV? Shut down, close the curtains and stay inside?"

Some group members say they would do something that gives them pleasure, like visiting a garden. Others turn to taking a CBD gummy, or really getting into how messed up they are for feeling lonely.

The coach decides to respond by challenging our most common assumptions about emotions: "I do not think loneliness is inside of us. I do not think that we did something to cause it. I do not think it's an individual state. We no longer have the social infrastructure of community and connectedness. Our culture insists that we are on our own, battling the world to get what we want. We get related to as consumers of things, but not producers of anything in our lives. No wonder we feel lonely! We disassociate from what we just created with others—a nice conversation, a successful project, a lovely dinner, this group session—and move onto the next thing. Our society is lonely!"

A group member notes how much she appreciates the group's conversations and how she feels connected to others in the group. Another group member suggests creating a group chat in which any group member could text when they are feeling lonely. The group is enthusiastic about this idea. The coach supports it wholeheartedly: "Here in social therapeutic Life Development Group, we create it week after week. Part of my job is to help us see and have that we build this, it's ours."

Commentary

This scene is designed to show one way a coach might bring in their values, their worldview, to group. Once again, shifting where someone is standing might alter how they see. Standing in the "I am an individual who is less than other people because I am lonely" place, the world looks one way. Shifting to "I am a lonely person in a lonely world" could open up new possibilities, including possibilities of connection and growth. In this case, the group decided to stay connected with each other in between sessions.

Dealing with Diagnosis

In our work as coaches, we are very clear. We do not diagnose. We have not been trained to diagnose. That is the domain of professional licensed psychologists and psychiatrists. It would be an unethical breach to identify and apply a diagnostic label of mental illness to a client. And beyond professional ethics, some—including the founders of social therapeutics—have warned of the undevelopmental societal consequences of the mass proliferation of diagnoses (Newman & Gergen, 1999; Newman & Holzman, 1996; Morss, 1996).

Yet, given the way many diagnostic terms have been infused into everyday life, clients may come to a coach requesting a diagnosis that matches the distress they are experiencing. They might be seeking relief by gaining knowledge of "what's wrong with them."

As co-creators and co-meaning-makers with clients, coaches can relate to the client's request as an offer to build with, and to move "around and about" the "problem" such that it "vanishes"—a philosophical/relational activity we explored in Chapter 4. Here is one look at how social therapeutic coaches might approach dealing with diagnosis.

This group of six members has been meeting for nearly two years. A new member, Edwin, joined about four weeks prior to this specific group session.

In those weeks, as Edwin shared hard things going on in his life, he expressed certainty on what others thought of him—his roommate, his cousin, his new employer. According to Edwin, those people always knew that he was inferior, a fraud, a bad person, that he and he alone had "fucked up."

As the group got to know Edwin, it started to challenge his assessment of other people's impression of himself. For example, a group member would ask, "How do you know your roommate thinks you're a loser?" And Edwin would definitively explain, "Because I accidentally ate a piece of his pizza" or "Because he dissed me the other day."

This week, the coach asks Edwin, "Do you think we think you are a loser?" There is a pause, followed by Edwin essentially saying yes: "Everyone in the group has a much better life than me. He's a doctor, she's an accountant, he's in a relationship, she's in school and knows what she wants to do, her acting career is taking off . . ."

The group very lovingly responds by sharing their diverse family, life and job struggles and their emotional pain. Their responses seem to have little impact on Edwin. He seems stuck on another moment during which he felt slighted by someone. Then he says, immersed in his self-destructive thoughts, "I want a diagnosis. Coach, can you give me a diagnosis?"

"I'm sorry Edwin, not only am I not allowed to give you a diagnosis, but I wouldn't give you one even if I could."

Edwin looks crestfallen.

"However, if you are open to it, together we could come up with a name for your 'condition,'" the coach adds.

Edwin nods affirmatively.

"How do we do that?" someone asks.

Someone else offers to the group, "Well, Edwin is always so sure of what someone else is thinking about him."

"Yeah, it's like he's convinced he's a mind reader," another group member confirms.

"What about Super Mind Reader Syndrome? SMRS," another group member suggests.

The group cracks up. Then someone reminds the group that Edwin's mindreading of group members is often way off from the member's experience. Mind reader might be an overstatement!

Another group member offers, "How about *Wannabe* Psychic Syndrome?"

Everyone loves it. Edwin laughs, "Yeah! That's it. That's my diagnosis. And, after I get psychic on people, I often get really worked up and lose it so bad I cannot hear anything anyone says. So, I would like to add, Wannabe Psychic Syndrome *with Total Meltdown Dysfunction*."

The group joyously and playfully repeats his new label and agrees it is a great fit for Edwin.

Commentary

This experience had a huge impact on Edwin and the group. He became much more aware of those wannabe psychic moments and worked to not go with the assumptions he usually makes about others. The group experienced its power to create meaning together and grew its capacity to challenge and support Edwin to do something different with the group in those moments.

Important note: When the coach (but any client could as well) brought the conversation back into the "room" ("Do you think we think you're a loser?"), a connected and intimate dialogue ensued, which in turn created the conditions for Edwin to ask the group for what he wanted (a name for what's wrong with him). That was a huge emotional risk for Edwin. With the coach's leadership, the group responded to him philosophically, playfully and lovingly. They created a meaning-making activity together as part and parcel of radically accepting Edwin and where he is at developmentally.

A couple months later, during a group session in which everyone was giving their growth and appreciating other's emotional growth, Edwin gave how much more grounded he had become and less reactive to the people in his life: Bosses, his roommate, a woman he was dating. Edwin said to the group, "I think I'm ready for another diagnosis." The group enthusiastically concurred.

Notes

1 See pp. 91–94.
2 See Lev Vygotsky and child development (pp. 42–45).
3 See Ludwig Wittgenstein and language as activity (pp. 97–101).
4 In couple's work we often say, "taking the side of the relationship." For more on social therapeutic couples coaching see Chapters 7 and 8.

5 See pp. 42–45 for more on the zpd and the emotional zpd.
6 See pp. 97–101.
7 People speaking in order-giving and self-righteous ways can happen, of course. The group would choose if and how to engage that. For our purposes, we hear them here as loving demands.
8 See p. 73.
9 There are many other cultural, intellectual, spiritual and religious traditions that respond to death and loss as a continuation and natural part of life.

References

Morss, J. (1996). *Growing Critical: Alternatives to Developmental Psychology*. Routledge.
Newman, F. & Gergen, K. (1999). Diagnosis: The Human Cost Of The Rage To Order. In L. Holzman (Ed.), *Psychology: A Postmodern Culture of the Mind* (pp. 73–86).
Newman, F. & Holzman, L. (1996). *Unscientific Psychology: A Cultural-Performatory Approach to Understanding Human Life*. Praeger.

PART III
THE SOCIAL THERAPEUTIC COUPLES COACH

7

SOCIAL THERAPEUTIC COUPLES COACHING

Marriage is one of the most powerful institutions in the world. Even as it transforms and evolves, it continues to have a hold over us—whether as a form of life we want to emulate, or one we want to reform or rebel against. For all the diversity in today's romantic arrangements, the heterogeneous married couple remains the societal norm and overdetermines how we think about partnerships.[1]

Social therapeutics carries its method into couples work by relating to the couple as a group. The relationship—the sum greater than the individuals who make it up—is the unit of growth. A practitioner introduces in a consultation call, "My job is to help you both identify what the relationship needs, and then to support you and us to create that together." This comes from the understanding that the relationship has been co-created by its participants. Perhaps the relationship needs more patience, more intimacy, better listening, harder conversations or forgiveness. Clients may be looking for a relationship tune-up or deciding whether to stay together or separate. There can be years of hurt and pain built into the couple's dynamic. Often one spouse is looking to point the finger at the other as the cause of the relationship troubles. However, that kind of accusation is akin to pointing to a house, zeroing in on one brick and saying, "You see, he laid *that* brick. That's a crooked brick! That is the problem with this house!"

DOI: 10.4324/9781003326465-12

The coach is continuously pointing toward ways both have created the tensions, failures, joys, hurts, frustrations, growth and curiosities in their marriage. This does not imply "equal blame." In social therapeutic couples work, we try to help couples get out of blame, judgment and measurement mode and into a build-with-everything-there-is mode, including all the horrible, messy stuff. A social therapeutic coach might say, "If there is a side to be taken, I intend to take the relationship's side. In bringing me into your relationship, we open the possibility of performing it in a new way. I say *performing* in the sense of breaking out of your tired scripts that you have been repeating for a long time and are telling me you want to get beyond. We will create new lines and new scenes together."

Couples work is different than group work. For one thing, it is easier to get swept up into the content. A couple is more likely to pull the coach in by asking them to take sides, judge who is "right," and/or identify which partner is more hurt, more injured or more entitled to righteous indignation. It is easier to lose sight of the activity[2] that is occurring and what is emerging in the session. Another issue is that marriage, romantic relationships and love come with deep societal expectations, pre-formed roles, rules, traditions and customs. So, while we have deconstructed individualism in Chapter 3, here we feel it important to look at the hegemonic cultural expressions of coupledom and provide tools to coaches for this specific type of work. As part of that exploration, we take a quick look at the history of couples work and the emerging area of couples/relationship coaching, as well as the resources available to couples coaches today.

A Brief History of Helping Couples

What is known colloquially today as "couples counseling" or "couples therapy" first emerged in the mid-20th century as an extension of the family therapy movement, whose work focused on defining the "ideal family" and stages of family development. A belief in eugenics—the "science" of identifying and managing "deviants"—held influence at the time[3] (though there were progressive attempts at family work growing out of the Settlement Movement[4]). The purpose of couples work was to save the marriage and keep families together at all costs.

By the late 1950s and early 60s pioneers like Nathan Ackerman, a psychoanalyst, borrowed from systems theory in biology to designate the couple (and the family) as its own living system in which one small change could impact the whole system. Following this, new schools of family and couples therapeutic work emerged within systems theory (Bateson et al., 1956; Boyd-Franklin, 2003; Haley, 1963; Satir, 1967; Watzlawick et al., 1974). This was an early flirtation with seeing the couple (and the family) as a group. However, the approach tended to rely on the therapist knowingly seeing the system and then strategically intervening into the relationship. The client still lacked the agency to transform themself or the system itself. Today innovations in team coaching are emerging which position the participants to co-create and transform the system (see Rød & Fridjhon, 2020).

With the rise of the women's and gay liberation movements in the 1960s and 70s, the systems, roles and assumptions of marriage and romantic relationships came under fire. All kinds of people were challenging the status quo. Women pushed against the traditional dynamics of power and intimacy in relationships with men, calling for more equality in the home and greater emotional connection. The gay and lesbian communities were experimenting with alternative partnership forms. Both movements along with the counterculture were breaking apart sexual taboos and opening up new forms of sexual expression. The heterosexual model of a white middle-class married-for-life couple with 2.2 children, a house and a garage was coming apart at the seams.

The 1990s brought the birth of positive psychology with Martin Seligman's evidence-based research, offering practitioners a pathway for focusing on human strengths and learnable skills to help people be their best selves. Grounded in a present- and future-focused practice, tenets of positive psychology were readily incorporated into coaching. As one coaching founder Thomas Leonard told *Newsweek* in 1996, "We're not selling coaching services; we're selling a partnership in someone's life" (Newsweek Staff, 1996).

And, as coaching grew, new specializations got established. The Relationship Coaching Institute formed in 1997 to train relationship coaches. Founder David Steele, a former psychotherapist, believed that the principles of coaching were more effective than traditional psychotherapy in helping people to achieve their goals in dating and coupling. He and his wife Darlene went on to author *Radical Marriage: Your Relationship as Your Greatest Adventure* (Steele & Steele, 2014).

Relationship coaches have another resource in Yossi Ives and Elaine Cox's *Relationship Coaching: The Theory and Practice of Coaching with Singles, Couples and Parents* (2015). Ives and Cox identify the unique strengths of coaching for achieving more satisfying partnerships and better communication: "It is not the role of the coach to advise the client on his or her goal, but it is appropriate to share ideas around development and learning and propose new perspectives for the client's consideration" (Ibid., p. 2). This holds to co-creation—part of coaching's self-conscious break with traditional therapy, which relies on advice-giving or explanation by a knowing practitioner. Ives and Cox offer a developmental approach, leveraging coaching to boost clients' capacity to form enriching relationships (Ibid., p. 5). We feel close to their position that "coaches do not necessarily need to know what is wrong with the relationship in order to help to strengthen it . . . The coach can trust in a constructivist, goal-focused approach where new aspirations are discussed and described and the method of achievement is brought into focus" (Ibid., p. 105).

Among the skills and approaches they survey, Ives and Cox include a quote by social constructionist John Shotter on the importance of "the relationship" as a unit to be attended to in couples work. We want to include it here and add that Shotter had a close professional relationship with Newman and Holzman, the founders of social therapeutics.[5]

[When] two or more forms of life "rub together" . . . in their meetings, they always create a third or a collective form of life within which (a) they all sense themselves as participating, and which (b) has a life of its own, with its own voice, and its own way of "pointing" towards the future (Shotter, 2009, p. 26).

The role of the social therapeutic couples coach is to continuously ask questions from the perspective of what would be helpful and growthful for the relationship. This involves each person fully embracing that they have participated day after day, year after year in producing the current state of the relationship. Each partner is also making a choice to take emotional risks in the spirit of their and the relationship's growth.

While coaching resources for couples/relationship coaches are scarce, resources for couples themselves are in abundance. Clients often come into coaching armed with information—what their love language is, a certain type of communication style, their individual diagnostic labels and other identities. We will say more about how a social therapeutic coach might respond to and build with these types of characterizations later in this chapter. For now, we would like to call out a few of the relationship resources clients may have already turned to before coming to a coach for help.

In 2002, Terry Real founded the Relational Life Institute. An internationally recognized family therapist and bestselling author, Real made his mark by focusing on men and depression. He carried that into couples work by helping men become more emotionally present and vulnerable. Because they are not typically socialized to express emotions, men have been less equipped for the shift led by women towards more emotionally intimate and satisfying relationships. Without the tools to do anything different, men end up choosing to remain attached to what they know— traditional family and relationship structures. As Real astutely points out, "The great story of the 20th century is that women have changed dramatically. Have men? Not so much" (Real, 2018, min: 6:22–6:27). Most recently, Real has focused on the relationship as the unit of growth. In *Us: Getting Past* You and Me *to Build a More Loving Relationship* (Real, 2022), he includes a chapter entitled "The Myth of the Individual" and pushes on the importance of the "we."[6]

Esther Perel and Orna Guralnik of Showtime's *Couples Therapy* are very talented, high-profile therapists with a large following. It is wonderful to watch them work with couples and give of their expertise. Clearly, it is no longer shameful for a couple to seek help to improve their relationship, nor for singles to get guidance on how to build intimacy with potential partners. Today both coaches and therapists rely on various tools and approaches which have allowed for an expansion of specializations within couples work, including sexuality (Nelson, 2008), trauma (Real, 2022), attachment (Heller, 2019; Johnson, 2008), radical honesty (Steele & Steele, 2014) and infidelity (Perel, 2017).

In the late 1990s, John and Julie Gottman decided to study approximately 2000 couples to learn the traits that made for successful long-term relationships. John published their findings and offered practical tools to couples in *The Seven Principles for Making Marriage Work* (Gottman &

Silver, 1999). A popular resource for couples today, The Gottman Institute offers skills trainings and scripts that couples can learn to help them traverse through conflicts, explore greater connectivity, repair damages in the relationship and deepen their friendship.

The Gottmans are onto something in the creation of new scripts. The relationship arena is more explicitly scripted by societal mores. Our interactions are socially learned, even though we are taught to believe they are natural. The institution of marriage lends itself to the mechanics of theater and theatrics (as does the family, though that institution is outside of the scope of this book). Many plays, films and novels explore endless dynamics of marriage and relationships. It is somewhat easier, we think, to see partnerships within the metaphor of performance—scripted or improvisational. The reader will experience that metaphor more in this chapter.

Our choice of the word "ensemble" in couples work comes from the desire to point to the "groupness" of the couple—and the couple plus coach—and to remind the reader that, while we might unselfconsciously follow prewritten scripts of what it means to be a good husband, wife, girlfriend or boyfriend, we could also decide to create new ones. We have the capacity to decide how we want to do our romantic relationships (and other relationships). Couples often find relief in discovering they can relate to their "scenes" together as that of creating the next line in the continuously lived play entitled, *Our Relationship*.

The Performance of a Relationship

Many things follow from tapping the metaphor of performance in couples work. In session, the coach is relating to "the ensemble" which includes both the couple and the coach, who is being invited into the totality of the couple's relationship—the good stuff and the messy, hurtful stuff. Building on our discussion of language as a doing—an activity—in Chapter 4, the couples coach plays a critical role in listening for and questioning the ways in which couples speak with each other that makes it harder to connect. Most clients will begin describing what happened, explaining why it happened and who caused it to happen. The coach, introducing performance and giving clients a performance direction to try out, can experientially shift people into new ways of talking and being together. *Performed conversation* is another tool available to the coach. Suddenly, without thinking about it, partners are standing in a new place and performing other than their usual script. The role of improv games and play take on another dimension in couples work. Here, a coach might not only offer a game or two at the beginning of working together, but also suggest a game customized to a developmental issue at hand. We have already provided an example of this—a "Yes, and . . ." exercise played by a couple engaged in deciding on a vacation together (see pp. 52–53). Being uncomfortable together, bouncing out of time-worn ways of relating to each other can be helpful for couples. We now offer some practical illustrations in couples work of social therapeutic concepts and tools presented in Part I.

Building the Ensemble

From the first conversation, the coach can convey something like, "I am glad we are working together. My job is to help the relationship to grow. In attending to the relationship, we are creating an ensemble performance together. In theater, the line one actor says is inseparable from the totality of the play. In relating to your relationship—your lives together—as an ensemble performance, we are on our way to creating the conditions in which it becomes possible for you both to create new lines and new scenes. How does that sound to you?"

Couples usually come to coaching seeing each individual's contributions or lack thereof: "He only washes the dishes and never changes a diaper"; "She only complains"; "He never says how he feels"; "She always spends more than our budget." This list of misdeeds overlooks the flow and synergy of how one contribution may influence and beget another in an ensemble fashion. Blame, judgments and explanations of causality often get in the way of seeing how the scene was jointly created. Both partners participated in creating the mess—just as they jointly produced the positives in the relationship. Rarely do couples experience that their contributions—a well-cooked meal, raising children, saving money for a family vacation—are part of an ensemble performance.

"How can we advance our shared performance?" the coach might inquire. This is the next line in the performed conversation, done by everyone together in the play which might be called, *Our Couples Coaching Session.*

Hearing the Offer

In improv, a performer is listening for something their scene partner says that can be built with. This is called an "offer." One performer in the improv scene wipes imaginary liquid from their head, looks up and says, "Oh man, why does it have to rain on the day I wear my suede jacket!" Their scene partner opens up an imaginary umbrella and places it over their partner's head as they exclaim, "Here, I will protect you with my superpowered antidiluvial hovering device!"

This act of *yes, and-ing* . . . is harder to do in real life when couples might be so angry or hurt that they cannot hear each other or the coach. The coach might ask a client, "What offer did you hear in what your partner just said?" This question encourages slowing down to listen and respond in a way that builds connection rather than ignoring or dismissing their partner. It also reminds everyone that they are creating a scene together; what they do and say has an impact on others. A coach might share what they are hearing as an offer to build with and see if that lands with the clients. Finally, as clients gain experience with listening for offers to build with, they may turn to the coach and say something like, "Help me out coach—I am not hearing an offer in what my partner is saying. Do you hear an offer? I don't know how to build with what they are saying." Of course, the concept of "offer" is intended as a neutral entity. In social therapeutics, what gets built with it can be beautiful or messy, easy or difficult, etc.

Encouraging Imitation

After a period of the coach relating to the relationship and speaking to the couple as a "we"/"us," a client might begin to pick that up and imitate[7] the language and posture. That is great! "Let's talk about how *we* are feeling about this challenge. How are we doing as an ensemble, as a couple?" a client might say in session. As mentioned previously in social therapeutic group coaching, it is important for the coach to support a client who focuses on creating the ensemble. "I am noticing and appreciating how you are speaking in the 'we.' What's that like for you?"

Another way the coach can encourage imitation is when a couple comes to see that one of them handles a type of interaction better than the other: "How about imitating your partner's performance in those moments, rather than doing what you usually do?" Here, the coach relates to all of what is present in the scene as material for everyone to make use of. If someone is good at something, imitate what they do in that situation. All of this occurs in the spirit of taking the side of the relationship. If the coach senses that a client is imitating in order to be the coach's favorite or to compete with their spouse, it would be important for the coach to check that out. They might ask the client, "What's important to you that you are saying this right now?" Asking a curious question allows the coach to relationally discover if the client is indeed being competitive or if something else is going on.

Giving Somebody a Line

If the scene includes all of what is present for everyone to make use of, then what people say and give belongs to the group. The social therapeutic coach, a member of the group, can "cheat" for someone and help them with the next line in the scene. This is the kind of scenario in which the coach actively plays a director-type role. Oftentimes clients have no idea that it is possible to say hard things in a nonjudgmental, nonreactive, more ordinary way. In this sense, the coach offers a real-time custom-designed stretch into a new performance, creating new kinds of conversations on the spot that tend to be more hearable, more intimate and more open. (And, over time, the client might grow to be able to cheat for their partner as well.) However, the conditions for performing "cheating" are not always there. A client might not "feel like" uttering a new line, preferring instead to get satisfaction from unleashing their fury or shutting down emotionally. It is very hard to break out of what we know how to do in those moments and very difficult to see new possibilities by oneself.

The coach might offer, "Can I help you with a line here to say to your partner?" If they agree, the coach may offer lines like, "I am glad you asked"; "I would like to get better at this"; "I do agree with you"; "I would like to talk. Though I shut down when you yell and that makes it hard for me"; "I apologize for this terrible behavior and hurt it has caused you"; "I would like you and I to work on this together." The client then delivers the line out loud and the scene continues. The coach will want to circle back with the clients on their experiences and discoveries of trying new lines with each other and the coach. Adding this relational activity builds the tool-and-result-ness of the scene, enabling an enhanced embodiment of the discovery experience—that the couple *can* and *can choose to* create new lines together. This differs from a more traditional cognitive means of learning, knowing and then applying certain lines (tool-for-result) to a situation in order to obtain a specific outcome. As the clients grow, they may become aware that they are stuck or shut down and may turn to the coach to ask, "Coach, can you help me with a line here? I would like to respond differently than I usually do but I don't know how to."

Getting Started

Unlike group coaching, in which the coach typically invites a client to join group, in couples work it is often the couple that reaches out to the coach for help.[8] Partners usually seek the expertise of the coach to teach them how to better communicate, how to operate in a healthier way or how to decide whether to stay together or separate. They carry with them the expectations of what a relationship should look like, societally-driven ideas of how it should be "fixed" and premade tools to do the job. However, social therapeutic couples coaches relate to their clients as toolmakers rather than tool users—as creators of their relationship—which immediately challenges those expectations.

Bringing a Partner in to Work

When the coach decides with an individual client to bring the partner in to do couples work, there can be the assumption that the coach will side with the individual client and immediately be more challenging of their partner. However, in taking the side of the relationship, the coach works with what is there—and what is there includes the history of the coach engaging developmentally with and putting demands on the individual client. The coach might want to share with the client, "I may be more demanding of you in the beginning of our couples work than on your partner." Doing so can help orient the partner to the experience of social therapeutic work and create the conditions for building their relationship with the coach.

The Couple and Coach Relationship

In social therapeutics, the unit is the group. The unique form this takes in couples work is that the group is made up of the couple *and* the coach, a three-person group. From the beginning, this challenges the expecta-tions of clients who tend to want an outside mediator to fix the other spouse or fix the relationship. Instead, the coach is asking to be invited into the couple's relationship, into their lives. In doing so they together create an emotional closeness where the couple trusts the coach will not judge or take sides. They also together create an environment of presence, openness and emotional transparency in which the coach can give their subjective experience of the work. This can include giving the pain and hurt (and intimacy and joy) the coach witnesses in the relationship and the coach's desire to impact on (or celebrate) that. It could also include the coach's reactions to being ignored (couples will tend to debate or con-verse as though there is no one there) or not included in decisions that may impact the relationship or the clients' work with the coach.

In the first session and throughout the work together, the coach might say something like, "How would you like to do this together?" or "What are you wanting from me in this first session together?" Sometimes cou-ples come in wanting to get right to focusing on "the problem," while others want to give the relationship's history.

Another valuable question to include in the first session is, "How do you feel about working *with me*?" This reinforces that the couple and coach are building a relationship together. It opens the possibility of the couple asking the coach questions about themself. We welcome this as part of including the coach's subjectivity and history in the relationship. For example, it may be important for the clients to ask the coach to share any particular belief system or personal or political reasons for doing work with partners. Importantly, it acknowledges any obvious differences of race, class, sexual orientation, religion, gender, ability, etc. with the cli-ents. The coach could go further and ask, "How do you feel working with me, a ___ person?" Finally, it acknowledges that the totality of the work together will include and build with everyone's differences.

Clients want to feel seen, respected and safe. This kind of question acknowledges the obvious and invites the client's honest response. It is a way of saying, "OK, we have these socially constructed identities that impact how we move through society and how we feel in the world—let's not ignore that. As we work to take the side of the relationship and focus on your emotional growth, I want to honor all of who you are and what you bring to our work, including being a ___ person." All of the above "lines" carry with them the offer to the couple to build their relationship with the coach such that it allows for honest, direct and meaningful communication. This creates an environment in which the coach can experience the couple more fully.

Taking the Side of the Relationship

We want to say more on what the practice of taking the side of the relationship looks like. Clients tend to do what they know how to do, which is to speak on behalf of their own interests. "You hurt me when you do . . ."; "He acts like a jerk all the time and he needs to change"; "She never wants to have sex"; "I am ready to leave this marriage, I can't take their defensiveness anymore"; "It's only fair that I get what I want, after all I do for her." These kinds of statements embody the activity of the spouse organizing the coach to take their position. They are looking for the coach to turn to their partner and say, "Yes, as a matter of a fact, you are a jerk and need to change!" It can be challenging to resist getting taken in by either the rightness of the statement or by the need to address/fix the content of what is getting raised. How can the coach respond without taking a side, or critiquing the client? How does the coach speak on behalf of what would be developmental and growthful for the relationship? It might be that asking the partner the content question—e.g., "Why don't you want to have sex?"; "How come you are defensive?"; "What do you want?"; "Do you understand why your partner thinks you are acting like a jerk?"—can be done as part of taking the side of the relationship, but very often it might not be. There may be more to discover before opening up and responding to the content.

In these moments, the coach might ask the couple, "Who is speaking on the side of the relationship right now?" or "It appears you are on your side, in your role, and your partner is on their own side. But nobody is speaking for the relationship or what the relationship needs and how to grow it." This will often draw puzzled looks. Everyone has been taught to speak and see in "I" terms rather than "we" terms. The uncomfortableness of the question is to be built with. "What's uncomfortable/confusing for you around that question?" the coach might ask. This acknowledges the significant difference between how the clients and coach see what they are all doing together. Experiencing that difference lays the basis for exploration and for asking the coach, "How do we create a 'we' environment?" This is the beginning of the couple experiencing how to relate to the totality of the relationship.

In another context, e.g., immediately after a blowup in the session, or a breakthrough in the session, the coach can introduce the "we" by asking, "Are you both open to taking a look at how you just created this scene together?" Another example might be when partners compete on who is the better parent. They might perform that bickering in front of the coach unselfconsciously or as part of proving to the coach that they are the partner who does it right. The coach could give their subjective experience: "I am sensing that you are each competing for and invested in being the better parent. Is that the case?" If that lands with the clients, the coach might continue, "Where is your relationship as you act this way?"

There are cases in which a partner (or both, or at different moments, each partner) actively obstructs the seeing and building of the relationship. In that case, the coach will want to engage that person directly. This could be perceived as taking sides. It is important to convey, "I am experiencing you as not wanting to or not being interested in or not being able to explore the 'we' right now. I am saying this not to lay blame on you, not to say that you are the cause of all the relational difficulties. However, I need to know where you are at with working on *the relationship* that you and your partner have created together. That is how I can help you and your marriage."

Hopefully the reader can see the value and connection of staying in the process with seeing the group (the relationship). Building the group is continuous process, continuously hearing offers and creating something with them. As couples develop this skill, they develop more tools to get out of the jams, judgments and blame that keep relationships stuck.

Incorporating the Tools Clients Bring with Them

Some clients may come to couples work armed with assessment tools, experience with Gottman exercises or results from relationship quizzes. The coach can relate to these as an opportunity to get to know the clients better. The coach can be curious and ask, "What have you found helpful about these tools?"; "How does having a 'quality time' love language show up for you in the relationship?"; "How do you draw on Gottman's work when you are having a hard moment?" Social therapeutics is sensitive to the ways labels overdetermine us. Just as societal scripts direct us towards certain behaviors and roles, so too can quiz results and relationship categories take on a meta-Truth that forces us to fit into existing labels, rather than create/decide for ourselves who we are and what we want. The lines above allow the coach to meet the clients where they are at, without relating to the labels as "Truths" about the person. Rather, they become useful elements in a toolbox that can provide clients valuable skills to practice. They can be related to as offers to be created with.

Sexuality, Trauma and Abuse

In this chapter, we have decided not to address certain issues and their particularities in couples work, such as sexuality, trauma and abuse. A main reason is that there are many fantastic coaches and practitioners specialized and doing good work in these areas. In addition, some of these challenges may require psychotherapeutic support. Our vision here is to introduce readers to the core concepts of the method of social therapeutics and its practice in the group and couples context generally. We felt that diving into these complex topics were outside the scope of this book. We hope that the reader is gaining enough of a foundation in relationality, "looking at" activity over content, creating the zpd, giving and building with emotions, playing with language and creating meaning, doing new performances and "having the group with you" such that they see ways of carrying social therapeutics into these areas. For example, one spouse pushing the other away is an activity that can be noticed and worked on social therapeutically. Knowing the cause of the pushing away is not required in order to help clients to grow. Something from the client's past may emerge during a session and the group may make meaning with it. However, providing an explanation to accompany the newly created meaning is not only unnecessary, but also can shut down "collective processing"—the sitting with the activity everyone just did together.

In our culture, these issues (and many others) trigger feelings of shame, humiliation, self-doubt, self-harm, disconnection and more. Our broadest methodological statement here is for the coach to radically accept and build with these expressions as they emerge, checking in with the group/couple to see if the conditions have been built to go further.

Our developmental social therapeutic perspective is similar to others, along the lines of, "What you had to do to survive (as a kid, as a wife, as a solider, etc.) worked for getting you out of that situation, but it seems like those tools are no longer serving you now. Are you open to discovering new ways to be with us (in group/couples) and in other places in your life, while you are experiencing the pain? That pain will never go away, *and* there is so much more you can build and create in your life. I want to help you do that and in doing so it will resize that pain. Is that something you would like to do?" Many clients are relieved to learn that their lives do not have to "get resolved."

Of course, there are instances where a coach must adhere to the industry's ethical guidelines and refer the client to a licensed mental health practitioner.

Method Moments

Many aspects of social therapeutic method in practice were explored in Part II; here, we add some elements that weigh more heavily in couples work.

Relationality and Breaking Out of Knowing What the Other Will Say

We have previously shared some basic examples of relationality (see pp. 81–83). When it comes to couples work, the questions, "What is it like to hear your partner say *x*" and "What is it like to say *x* to your partner?" cannot be asked too many times. Couples often interrupt each other in session with, "I know what he is going to say" and then prove they are correct by saying it. How can a coach address someone who does the talking for their partner? This is an important leadership moment for the coach to reestablish that they are part of the couple's relationship: "It is important to me, as the coach, that I hear what he thinks. Without that I can't help you both. *Can you help me* create space so that I can get to know both of you?"

Other facets of relationality might appear more mundane, though from a methodological perspective are just as important. Take this question from the coach: "Do you think about how your partner is experiencing your complaint (about house chores)?" This reminds the partner that what and how they do and say things impacts. Are they curious to hear how it impacts? It breaks with the abstraction of declaring something as right or good because that is how it should be!

Couples always have differences. They could be related to class or race, communication styles or spouses' relationship to money. Acknowledging and exploring them is part of radically accepting[9] the other, a necessary precondition for growth and transformation. The coach can ask questions such as: "What kind of conversations do you have regarding your differences?" or "How do you feel about looking at the way your differences impact on the pain and challenges in your relationship?"

If Not Compromise, What?

A common motivation for couples seeking relationship help is the desire to gain clarity on what they believe they should find—compromise. Compromise implies that there must be something in the middle, between the distance of the partners, that everyone can agree on. Here's a simplistic example: I want to eat chicken, my partner wants to cook hamburgers. I reason that since we have eaten more chicken recently, it is only fair that dinner tonight is hamburgers. However, soon it will be my turn again to have my needs met.

The underlying assumption is that each individual can and should make concessions in order to resolve differences. This works reasonably well when people are negotiating disputes over property, money and territory—with the emphasis on *reasonably*. Individuals will cognitively consider the best and worst options (game theory) and come up with the solution that best rationalizes their needs. We are taught that one might have to negate one's needs today in order to get something for themself down the road.

Social therapeutic couples coaches might respond to the discord of what to eat for dinner by suggesting, "What else is there that you both like to eat?" Perhaps they could happily agree to order in pad thai instead. The coach could also offer something like, "Can you both find a way to give to the relationship?" Being giving might look like one spouse saying, "You know what, you're stressed out, honey—let's grill those burgers. I want your belly to be happy." Or being giving could also look like the couple deciding on the latest mushroom burger they have been wanting to try. These are both "we" decisions.

Compromise implies stasis—a state in which people and relationships stay the same and things must be balanced out for fairness. Measuring becomes the medium for evaluating compromise. These abstractions take a step away from the actual people involved and the capacity they have to give to the relationship. Put another way, compromise relies on "No, but . . ." and "Yes, but . . ." dialogue.[10]

In *yes, and-ing* . . . our partner—whether over a dinner choice or an old relationship wound—we keep creating in the spirit of giving to the relationship. And in continuously creating and giving, we open the possibility of having more in our lives. The zero-sum game approach to relationships tends to be a developmental nonstarter. All of this said, there may be non-negotiable positions held by one or the other partner, which the couple and coach would need to decide how to respond to.

The Shoulds

Our society bombards us with 3000 "shoulds" before we get out bed every morning: "I should be better at this"; "He should be doing that." These imperatives derive as much of their weight from liberal as religious ideals. The self-improvement and wellness industries thrive off of "shoulds." They often overdetermine how couples are together. The alternative is to be continuously deciding how they want to be together.

Here are a few examples of how coaches might respond to should-ing during a session. To a client who says, "I feel like I have to provide for my wife," the coach might respond with, "Is that what both of you want? Are you repeating a moral stance, a personal decision or a shared decision?" Or the coach might inquire, "What do you mean by should? Where does should come from? What do you draw from when you say should?" when a client declares, "He should just know to close the windows when we leave the house. I should not have to tell him to do it every time!"

A client might say in a couples session, "Elizabeth told me I had to go to her company party even though I really dislike these gatherings. And if I do go, I want payback in some other form." The coach is looking to point toward the relationship, "Let's talk about what you both would want from *each other at the party*" or "How come this issue is important to Elizabeth and how we can create a performance of you both going to the company party together?" With "the shoulds" comes the feelings of obligation and resentment. In creating a joint performance direction for the party, the couple attends to their relationship while they are out in the world. Elizabeth might feel more supported and her partner might feel less alone.

Breaking Out of Gender and Other Roles

While what we are about to write might sound cliché, and while younger generations of men may be more open to taking on roles that have historically been "women's work" (read: stay-at-home dads), we feel it important to add this section to recognize the deeply embedded gender roles couples often contend with. Our culture plays its part in shaping who we are, including our emotional capacities. We all have societally shaped underdevelopments.[11]

There is emotional work involved in building and maintaining any type of relationship. Women and men are socialized differently around emotionality and intimacy and this plays out in particular ways in romantic relationships. Men are encouraged to brush off and wall off their hurt, while women are generally given more opportunities to acknowledge their hurt, sadness and emotional upset. As we mentioned earlier, Terry Real has specifically identified the challenge that heterosexual couples experience in our post-feminist world, where women experience greater equality and have developed greater economic independence (2018). Men's loneliness and their difficulty in making and sustaining friendships has become a public discussion (Mansour et al., 2021; Pearson, 2022; The Economist Staff, 2022; Weiss, 2021). We must also consider the acculturation of men to being providers and that the pressures that come with that role ward off vulnerable emotions. Often, experiences of anxiety, pain, helplessness and shame are masked by anger and rage, leading to a masked depression. In couples work, men's underdevelopment shows up in their defensiveness and instinct to compete. The coach looks for moments to help men connect with what is going on for them emotionally, to experience giving it and creating with it. In addition, men learn to slow down, listen and discover *that* they can create with what their spouse is trying to say.

In working with women, it is important to address women's impotence. Often it looks like this: They are underdeveloped in asking for what they want or pushing for what the relationship needs. Women can hold a self-righteous rage at their spouses that, while perhaps justified, ends up protecting their partner from growth and participates in keeping the relationship stuck where it is. The work is to support women to develop more powerful and relational performances that go beyond reacting to the experience of being held back or not listened to.

These underdevelopments play out as well for those who choose alternative relationships and gender identities; we are all impacted by the social scripts and gender expectations that shape how we understand relationship language. However, by standing outside the societal institution of heterosexual marriage with its weightiest scripts and role expectations, nontraditional relationships tend to hold more space for self-consciously creating the relationship.

Making Demands on the Client

Making demands is part of the social therapeutic lexicon. Especially in partners work, where we are up against institutionalized scripts, it can be hard for a client to hear a demand the coach or partner makes of them. Sometimes the coach finds themself in a position where they need more from the client to support developing the ensemble. Sometimes the client is disruptive or is showing up to session having smoked or drunk enough to affect their ability to engage and listen. Sometimes a partner may want to leave coaching after some improvements to the relationship, while the coach feels the couple still has much more to gain by continuing with sessions. These are all examples in which the power in transforming what is happening occurs when the coach speaks to their subjective experience, rather than provides an analysis or cognitive explanation. There are loving ways to say to a client, "I really want to work with you. And, if you want to work with me, I need you to take care of this issue/do something different when we are here together." The coach can even include some of their personal history/experience around the issue (drinking, disruptiveness, defensiveness or refusal to listen) and add, "I want you to know this about me so we can create the conditions to work together. Can you help me with this?"

Asking the client whether they can work with the coach on this is important. Having a feel for the client's substantive response to the demand, as well as their conflicts around changing those performances while in session, is an important part of creating the conditions required to help them. There are ways to set up prearranged rules and structures for working together. However, there is power in a relationship that is not mediated by a structure. Using structure—whether implementing a rule, an expectation, a "should" or a description of a dysfunction—is more likely to engender a rebellious reaction. The coach can offer the client the opportunity to make a relational choice by saying something like: "I want to work with you. I respect you and I need your help for us to do this together. When you are loud, insulting, not listening or disruptive, I can't do it. What are you hearing in what I am saying right now?"

Avoiding Morality

When it comes to hurtful things people in relationships do to each other—cheat, lie, be abusive—it is nearly impossible to avoid speaking in moral terms (see Perel, 2017). The very words we speak have morality baked into them and can be weighted with judgments and accusations, e.g., infidelity, lying, deception, abuse. If a coach has a judgment of a client's actions, it can be important to give it as part of continuing to build the coaching relationship. "I am having a hard time learning that you came home at five in the morning after a drunken one-night stand. It makes me furious that you made a choice that was so hurtful to your spouse. Of all the hurtful things couples do, this one infuriates me." *Pause.* "How is that to hear me say to you both?" That can open up the conversation. When couples engage in morality talk, it contributes to an environment in which it becomes difficult to discuss the experiences that brought about the behavior as well as the experience of/impact of what has occurred. And in keeping it closed and undiscussable, it covers over that these acts occur every day of the week. While they are painful, they are not unique.

In an environment where the clients are able to hear, the coach might say something like, "I hear your pain about this, and what has happened/ is happening is not unusual. It is actually pretty ordinary. Are you want-ing to have your relationship driven by judgmentalism and morality, or would you like to learn the impact you have on one another and how to create something different together?" If they are wanting the latter, part of that process will include having some hard conversations through which the couple can build up their emotional muscles and grow as a couple and individually. Through that work, the "what he (or she) did" and the "what is wrong with the other" becomes theirs together. They discover they can attend to "the relationship" and move beyond the perceived roles of immoral individual and victimized individual.

Notes

1 For our purposes, we will focus on romantic partnerships of all gender types. In addition, as numbers of single adults grow, we have seen an increase in friends seeking "couples" help.
2 See Chapter 3, pp. 75–77.
3 Eugenics has gone down in history as a tool for racism and genocide by providing "scientific" cover for the superiority of the white and Aryan race.
4 The Settlement Movement played a significant role internationally in establishing the field of social work. Interestingly, Chicagoan settlement activist Viola Spolin went on to found improv, an important element of social therapeutics.
5 Shotter's and Holzman and Newman's essays sit side by side in *Discursive Perspectives in Therapeutic Practice* (2012) edited by Andy Lock and Tom Strong. Newman passed away in 2011, Shotter in 2016.
6 See Chapter 3 in this book for more on the limits of individualism and developing the capacity to see groups/relationships. See "The Man-Woman Thing" (Chapter 4) in *Let's Develop!* (Newman, 2010) for Newman's understanding of the role of feminism in social therapeutics.
7 For more on imitation and completion, see pp. 43; 47–51.
8 There are also instances in which a coach might want to suggest to a group participant or individual client that couples work could be beneficial. It is not unusual in social therapeutics that couples or short-term individual work occurs contemporaneously with group work for a period.
9 For more on radical acceptance, see pp. 91–94.
10 See pp. 51–53; 59 on *yes, and-ing* including the exercises.
11 Social therapeutics acknowledges that the modern industrial culture we humans have created has left us stunted, alienated from what we create—including alienated from our emotions. Social therapeutics also strongly holds to our human capacity to create, grow and transform ourselves, our relationships and our world. Our underdevelopments are part of accepting where we are now—individually as well as societally and culturally—as a precursor to growth.

References

Ackerman, N. W. (1958). *The Psychodynamics of Family Life*. Aronson.
Bateson, G., Jackson, D.D., Haley, J. & Weakland, J. (1956). Toward a Theory of Schizophrenia. *Behavioral Science: Journal for the Society for General Systems Research*, 1(4), 251–264. https://doi.org/10.1002/bs.3830010402
Boyd-Franklin, N. (2003). *Black Families in Therapy: Understanding the African American Experience*. The Guilford Press.
Gottman, J. & Silver, N. (1999). *The Seven Principles for Making Marriage Work*. Harmony Books.

Haley, J. (1963). *Strategies of Psychotherapy*. Grune & Stratton.

Heller, D. P. (2019). *The Power of Attachment: How to Create Deep and Lasting Intimate Relationships*. Sounds True.

Ives, Y. & Cox, C. (2015). *Relationship Coaching: The theory and practice of coaching with singles, couples and parents*. Routledge.

Johnson, S. (2008). *Hold Me Tight: Seven Conversations for a Lifetime of Love*. Little, Brown.

Lock, A. & Strong, T. (Eds.). (2012). *Discursive Perspectives in Therapeutic Practice*. Oxford University Press.

Mansour, K.A., Greenwood, C.J., Biden, E.J., Francis, L.M., Olsson, C.A. & Macdonald, J.A. (2021, December 8). Pre-pandemic Predictors of Loneliness in Adult Men During COVID-19. *Frontiers in Psychiatry*, 12. https://doi.org/10.3389/fpsyt.2021.775588

Nelson, T. (2008). *Getting the Sex you Want: Shed Your Inhibitions and Reach New Heights of Passion Together*. Quiver Books.

Newman, F. (2010). *Let's Develop! A Guide to Continuous Personal Growth*. Castillo International, Inc.

Newsweek Staff. (1996, February 4). Need a Life? Get a Coach. *Newsweek*. https://www.newsweek.com/need-life-get-coach-179824

Pearson, C. (2022, November 28). Why Is It So Hard for Men to Make Close Friends? *New York Times*.

Perel, E. (2017). *The State of Affairs: Rethinking Infidelity*. HarperCollins.

Real, T. (2018, November 9). The Masculinity Paradox panel in *Therapeutic Perspective on the Core Challenges of Masculinity*. https://www.youtube.com/watch?v=y2Y85jzdbFc

Real, T. (2022). *Us: Getting Past You and Me to Build a More Loving Relationship*. Rodale.

Rød, A. & Fridjhon, M. (2020). *Creating Intelligent Teams: Leading with Relationship Systems Intelligence*. Independently published.

Satir, V. (1967). *Conjoint Family Therapy: A Guide to Theory and Technique*. Science & Behavior Books.

Shotter, J. (2009). Listening in a Way that Recognizes/Realizes the World of 'the Other'. *The International Journal of Listening*, 23(1), 21–43.

Steele, D. & Steele, D. (2014). *Radical Marriage: Your Relationship as Your Greatest Adventure*. RCN Press.

The Economist staff. (2022, January 1). Why men are lonelier in America than elsewhere. *The Economist*. https://www.economist.com/united-states/2022/01/01/why-men-are-lonelier-in-america-than-elsewhere

Watzlawick, P., Weakland, J.H. & Fisch, R. (1974). *Change; Principles of Problem Formation and Problem Resolution*. Norton.

Weiss, A. (2021, November 21). The Devastating Toll of Men's Loneliness. *Psychology Today*. https://www.psychologytoday.com/us/blog/fear-intimacy/202111/the-devastating-toll-mens-loneliness

8

COUPLES COACHING
NUTS AND BOLTS

Examples in this chapter showcase social therapeutic couples coaching work, with a focus on what the relationship needs. The coach's eye rests on supporting the couple to see themselves as a "we" working to grow the relationship, and to discover what might follow from that. Seeing the "we" is often challenging for clients. The reader will notice that in these nuts-and-bolts selections, there is little engagement on identifying a problem to be solved. Similar to the group work featured in Chapter 6, these examples reflect an amalgamation of our work with couples over the years to highlight a specific social therapeutic point.

Each of the three sections of this chapter point toward the performatory aspects of social therapeutics. (Performatory in the sense of our capacity to perform "a head taller" and to tap into the performance tools of theater and improv. We feel that the term "performative" fits better into a more traditional measurement and goal-oriented framework.) In Hearing the Offer we draw from improv to keep building the conversation, without knowing where it will go—without the client investing in getting what they want. This is a performance of being on the side of the relationship. The second section, Imitation, illustrates ways the coach can empower clients to feel permissioned to break out of well-worn scripts, expectations, blaming and judgments of each other. In the final section, Doing New Performances, we show how the coach and couple build

DOI: 10.4324/9781003326465-13

their relationship in support of the couple doing something new together. Again, by tapping into the language of theater, the activity becomes more accessible to clients, and they experience their own agency in creating and shaping their relationship.

One additional note: With the size of the group reduced to three people, for simplicity's sake, we have refrained from attributing quotes to a speaker when the context makes clear who is communicating.

Hearing the Offer

The coach is always listening for what can be built with. Sometimes offers are easy to spot: "I want to live with you." Sometimes they are not as shiny: "I don't know if I can do this relationship anymore." The following are scenes in which the coach helps the couple to see that they are creating their conversation and their relationship. The coach's leadership, active listening and seeing the relationship/group are all integral in the social therapeutic practice of hearing offers.

Making Meaning versus Problem-solving

Often couples come to a coach seeking a solution to a problem they have already identified. In this case, this couple has been fighting over how the husband is always away working, leaving the wife to feel unsupported in running the house and parenting. This is their first session with the coach. The coach challenges the couple's problem/solution paradigm and offers a new way to connect.

As Linda is lamenting her husband's extended absences from the family, RJ interrupts, "That is not my fault. You know that my job takes me all over the country."

The coach learns that RJ is an assistant strategist for the city's football team. He travels to observe and analyze how other teams play in order to inform his team's game strategy.

RJ adds, "I love my job. My whole life has been about sports. This is a dream job for me."

"And it takes him away from the house all the time. I know that he loves this. I love sports too. But I did not realize the work would be 24/7. He comes home and then watches more sports. When we are together, he is preoccupied. He is OK with the kids, but I feel he is just waiting for them to grow a little so he can coach them. When I try to tell him this, we end up bickering a lot."

"I hear you saying you want more time together, Linda," the coach offers.

"Yes! We used to laugh. We were very affectionate. I miss that. Plus, I am a pretty emotional person. RJ, not so much."

RJ responds, "Well, I am not sure what to do. I do have to be away a lot. And I am a pretty analytical guy."

The coach sees an opportunity: "RJ, what's it like for you to hear that Linda misses you and the ways you have enjoyed being with each other?"

"Like I said, I can't help being away."

"Yes, I hear that, though I don't know that your being away is on the table right now. I want to invite to you consider my question. How do you feel hearing that Linda misses you?"

"I don't know what to say. I don't understand what she is asking."

"That's helpful. Let's try this: Are you interested in hearing how I am hearing you and Linda speak?" RJ replies affirmatively and the coach continues, "I am hearing Linda speaking a different language than the one you are familiar with, and clearly a master at. What she is giving originates in a different sport—a sport of emotionality and relationality. Can I help you master a new sport?"

"I had not thought of it that way. How can I do that?"

"Well, to start, there is no problem. You are not the problem. You do have a job to do; there is no need to justify that. Linda seems to understand that. What you might try is responding back to her experience that she misses you. Give that a try."

"Yeah, I miss the fun we had together and our affection for each other. I miss that too."

Linda responds with a smile, "I like this new sport. How do we keep training in it, coach?!"

Commentary

The coach, focusing on the emotional impact of how they were speaking with each other, tried a couple of different ways to help RJ hear

Linda. Building with what was going on in the scene, the coach decided to play/improvise with the sport metaphor. It became the offer to build with. "Master a new sport" took on a specific shared meaning for RJ, Linda and the coach in that conversation and helped to create the environment in which it became possible for RJ to give an honest, present emotional response to his wife and the coach.

The coach's eye was on relationality—i.e., helping Linda and RJ relate to each other and the coach in the moment, giving what they are feeling/what is going on for them. Here, the coach invites the husband to grow into a new performance, developing new muscles in a new sport. Wittgensteinian language-games[1] helped to reorganize the tension in the relationship.

The coach might have felt the pull to explain to the couple: How each of them speaks in a different a language, why their differences get them tripped up in their communications and how to think differently about interacting before they do. In Chapter 3, we explore how rational concepts like explanation may be limiting humanity's capacity to create connection, community and intimacy in today's social, emotional and cultural environment.

Relationality as a Pathway to Hearing Offers

This couple has been married ten years. Both are first-generation Americans. The wife, Sofia, has recently had an emotional affair with a work colleague, which ended when he moved onto another job. Shortly thereafter she broke her leg, which required her husband, Kenji, to play a very active caretaker role. Both have family obligations that take up a lot of their time outside work, as well as busy jobs. They sought help from the coach on if and how to repair the relationship. This is their eighth session.

Kenji opens up how angry he has been feeling in the relationship. Rather than going straight to waiting for his wife's response, he turns to the coach and asks, "What are you hearing?"

"I appreciate your asking me this question. I hear you asking me how I experience you sharing your anger." The coach takes a breath and continues, "Sofia, before you respond to the content of what Kenji is saying, how is it for you to hear Kenji give his anger? He's an expert at bottling up his emotions. This is the first time, at least with me here, that he's unbottling. He's doing something new."

Here, the coach builds with Kenji's invitation to slow the conversation down by completing[2] him—saying what he has just said in a different way—in an attempt to make it more hearable to his wife. The coach then invites Sofia "to look" and respond to the fact that her husband had just performed differently (in relation to her and the coach). He gives what is going on for him, rather than keeping it to himself (private). The coach's comment is also a reflecting back to the couple that new things, new ways of speaking together and expressing emotions are happening and can continue to occur.

Sofia seems nonplussed. "I have heard it before," she replies, and then goes on to identify the moment she believes his anger began. The couple goes back and forth on which particular thing caused their problems. The coach reminds them that reducing their relationship to one moment obscures that they have created their relationship this way over many years. Throughout their marriage they have avoided having hard conversations—about their lack of emotional and sexual intimacy, their families not getting along, feeling insecure and how they would care for one another's chronic illnesses. They have not yet invested in developing the tools for doing those kinds of conversations. Do they want to do so now?

Kenji takes another risk: "Is love enough? I love you, and I am deeply unhappy in this marriage. I don't know what to do."

Sofia responds, "I think we are good for each other. I don't know if marriages go in and out of working." The coach invites Sofia to add to what she is saying by including what it was like to hear her husband say, "I love you and I am deeply unhappy." She says, "I have fear and doubt when he says that." The coach goes with what she's giving: "Let me not assume. What is the fear and what is the doubt?" Sofia replies, "That he has already decided to break up our marriage."

"Well, why don't you ask him?" She does.

The coach again encourages the couple to respond to each other in the moment with what they are giving. This very present relationality supports Sofia to take the risk and say the unsayable—the question that would have otherwise been hovering in her mind by itself. In giving it to the group (couple and coach), it becomes an offer to build with.

Kenji replies, "I don't want it the way it is now."

Again, the coach looks to support continuing the conversation. First the coach checks in with the husband: "I hear you saying you want an overhaul of the relationship. A total change in how the relationship is organized. That you need you and Sofia to work through the hard issues you spoke of just now." Kenji confirms.

"OK Sofia, the offer on the table is, 'I don't want it the way it is now.' There are range of ways you could respond in addition to saying that it's the little things that make the relationship special. Add something that lets Kenji know you heard him. You might not like what he said. You might agree with him, or you might not agree with him, but you heard him. You could say, 'I really appreciate that you are opening this up, even though I find this terrifying' or 'That's hard to hear. But honestly, I don't either' or 'I don't think I see it the same way as you, but I want us to keep talking' or 'I don't know how to overthrow our relationship, but I am open to keep working at it.'"

Commentary

In this case, both partners used their relationship with the coach to ask for help and to create a slow, more intimate conversation. The coach kept pointing to what they have and have not created in the relationship, avoiding the search and debate for a cause of their problems. Additionally, the coach assisted Sofia in including her emotional, present responses to what her husband was raising. Both took risks to be vulnerable and honest. The coach helped the couple to stretch beyond themselves by pointing out offers to build with and completing them by giving an array of possible lines for Sofia, one of which might have been close to how she was feeling.

The Coach Asks for Support

This couple has a history of being aggressive with each other and provoking abusive fights. Both are successful professionals with a young child and have been married for 11 years. The first session focused on what the couple wanted to accomplish with the coach. This is the second session in which they are sharing some of their history.

"We were in this small college town, connecting around our intellectual interests and ambitions. We kept discovering how alike we were," Micah reports.

Olivia adds, "We had similar politics, and that really created a bond for us."

They continue reminiscing over their early love story. "We were so in sync that after just eight months together we made the impulsive decision to move to a different state where I could complete my training," Olivia adds.

"I am experiencing the love and sweetness of that time," the coach shares.

"Then things started to change. About four years into the relationship, right around when we married, I had another great career opportunity in a different city. Micah did not want to move again and we started really fighting. I was devastated that he wouldn't support me."

"We came back from our honeymoon and you wanted to pick up and leave—again!"

"You shut me down and my hopes for a career. I thought that was important for both of us."

"That's not fair. I was just trying to tell you that I was disappointed. I did not say you could not take the job."

The back and forth continues on who is right.

Aware of the escalating bickering, the coach jumps in, "This argument from seven years ago is still very immediate for you both. I do not think we can solve it. Both of you are right. What do we want to do now, here, the three of us?"

The couple ignores the coach and continues their argument for some time. The coach stays attentive for any offer from the couple to include the coach in the conversation. It never arrives. Finally, the coach interjects, "I cannot hear a thing you are saying anymore! It is important for me to listen, and I am no longer able to. I cannot follow what you both are saying. Can you help me?"

The couple pauses, looks at one another and says, "Well, this is what it is like for us all the time. What do we do now?"

Commentary

This couple had come to the coach for help in their marriage and yet the way they were relating with each other and the coach made it seem like they preferred doing what they know how to do—bicker. They did not express any interest in getting help. Micah and Olivia had built up a nearly impenetrable script of resentment toward each other, which they were performing for the coach in the session.

When the coach said, "I cannot hear you!" that was an offer. It was a reminder to Micah and Olivia that they were not the only players in this scene; there was also the actual, material presence of the coach. What did they want to do with that? Did they want to continue with the scene as they know how to execute it, or bring in the other scene partner and be curious on how that might transform the play?

The couple asking, "What do we do?" was the response to the coach's offer. This helped to create a different environment. One in which, with the coach's support, Olivia and Micah could begin to hear each other and the coach. Over time, they grew to be able to open up the deep pain and hurtful behavior that had become the drivers of their endless fights.

Imitation

As babies, we imitate those around us without hesitation. We do not worry that we do not know how to do something. We are encouraged to make the sounds and gestures of others as part of the journey of growing up. We speak to this at length in Chapter 2. In these examples, we encourage couples to imitate the coach in performing new lines with their partner as a developmental activity. In imitation, we are freed up from having to *know* what we are doing or what will happen, creating space for something new to emerge.

Either/Or; Both, And

Mark and Francesca, an interracial couple in their 30s, both work in the entertainment industry. They have just started seeing the coach, whom they sought

out to partner with as they began a journey of ethical non-monogamy. They
married young and, until recently, were each other's only sexual partner.

Mark kicks off the session sharing how an artistic project he just completed was his best work ever. It was a piece which intimately expresses the growth/evolution of his and Francesca's relationship and yet his wife Francesca does not appreciate it. They have been arguing all week because the star of the piece is a woman he has a crush on. Francesca, a performer herself, is not the star and has long been aware of Mark's crush.

Francesca has reactions to this characterization of "what happened." She starts to fill in some of the details, including the content of conversations they have been having all week, their emotions and their history with the other woman—with whom they are both friends. She expresses irritation that Mark never includes the broader context and that she always has to fill in for him.

The coach suggests and everyone agrees that Mark do a "take two" of his opening comments to include some of the new facts and experiences added by Francesca. In his second take, he focuses the story exclusively on how Francesca felt.

"How did those two versions land for you both?" asks the coach.

"The first was how I felt, and the second focused on how she felt," Mark reports.

"That is very helpful! How come the takes are *either* 'your side/about you' *or* 'her side/about her'? I hear you saying Mark that your experience is that *either* you get to feel good about your film *or* you have to feel badly/guilty—like Francesca might take your excellent artistic work away from you."

Pointing out and embracing our limiting tendency to speak/see/live/react in terms of "either/or" creates some new space. It opens up the conversation. Francesca gives more: "This is the first time I was not involved in his creative work. It's the first time he got help from others to do parts of the production that he is less skilled in—which is great—and it's also the best work he's ever done. That's hard for me *and* I'm happy for him. We have always taken credit for each other's success." Mark adds, "During the pandemic we were doing everything together, and now we are starting to do things separately again. It's hard for me to hear Francesca's hurt around something I am so proud of."

"How about we do a take three?"

The coach continues, "Either/or gets us so tripped up and stuck. What about a 'both, and' take where you can include all of what you both have been sharing in its complexity and contradictoriness. Out of that, you might discover something you—as in the relationship—want help with to grow in this moment."

Mark tries a third take: "I just finished creating what I think is my best film work yet. I've been doing this for ten years and I feel like I broke new ground. I didn't plan on it going this way, but the film became an expression of my and Francesca's journey together as husband and wife and how our relationship has grown. The star of the project is a woman that I have had a crush on, and of course making a film is intimate work between director and performer. Francesca has been aware of this crush and the woman is a dear friend of ours. Upon seeing the film, Francesca shared her regret of not starring in the film and has said how hurt/uncomfortable she is with my doing a project that doesn't involve her at all. I wish she could appreciate how I poured myself into exposing and expressing our love. I feel like we're stuck now. I even know she's not trying to be unsupportive, but it's hard to hear anything other than that I should feel guilty for doing this without her."

Commentary

Notice that the focus of this session could have been on the crush, or on discussing rules or boundaries of ethical non-monogamy. The coach chose instead to look at *how* they were talking with each other, in ways that created distance, in ways that got them stuck.

While these clients had never before reperformed a telling of a "what happened" story, they did have familiarity with the metaphor of performance, and previous experience of trying "new lines" with each other. In this case, the coach decided to introduce "takes" to support listening skills. This exercise allowed the couple to explore what goes on emotionally as they do a new "take" and for them to have the experience that they can recreate their telling/sharing/seeing of their story. They could do so as many times as they find helpful.

Take three is not the right way to say it; it is a re-creation of all the conversation proceeding it, a saying something new out of what Francesca, Mark and the coach had given. Take three was an offer to be built with and a new way of *how* they are talking together.

Francesca concluded the session by saying that she was no longer satisfied with the "first take" of their hard conversations and wanted her and Mark to find ways to try second and third takes.

Only Asking Questions

The coach has been seeing a married couple for three months who are deeply unhappy. This was their third attempt to find someone to help them. They were stuck in being angry and blaming each other. They remained committed to being the victim of each other's meanness. The coach has been waiting for an opportunity to push them to do something other than victimization during the session.

Susan opens the session by saying that her husband, Manuel, keeps saying the same things about wanting sexual intimacy, which has not occurred in some time.

Wondering if this kind of conversation is even possible with this couple, the coach offers, "Are you up for doing the work to create the environment in which there is the possibility for sexual intimacy?"

While the couple agrees that they are up for the work, they also immediately return to blaming each other for their lack of intimacy. The coach interjects, "Here's what it would mean to do this work: No blaming, no accusing, no interrupting. What are we going to do together if you are not doing that?"

Silence.

"Here's what just came to me. What do you think of this? We are going to speak in only questions. No one is answering the questions. There is no order of who speaks. You can throw a question out to our group at any time and it does not have to connect. The main thing is that you are not answering any question." The couple reluctantly agrees to try this.

The coach starts by putting out a slew of questions, to give an idea of the exercise: "How are we even going to do this, given how hard it is for you two to not blame each other?"; "What is it like for you, Susan, with the surgery you had?"; "Are you able to have intercourse?"; "Do you feel desire?"

Susan, Manuel and the coach speak in only questions for several minutes, until the coach ends the game. Susan immediately pushes back: "What was the point? That was just an improv game. That's not how people talk in real life. I do not like improv games. I want to have a serious conversation about this topic."

The coach replies, "In my opinion that question-asking activity was the most intimate conversation you have had here in three months." Manuel agrees. The coach urges him to say more and to "try to say it in a way that Susan might be able to hear how come you experienced the conversation as intimate."

"It's the first time it included both of our desires. We slowed down. I felt less reactive to Susan. I shared the things I wonder about in my head."

Susan builds on Manuel's comment: "I felt like I listened more. I would like to hear about your desire, and what you want."

The coach interjects, "Susan, can you formulate that into a question, maybe adding something like, 'Are you open to sharing that with me?'"

She imitates the line.

Manuel quickly responds, sneaking in the beginnings of blame: "Are you going to remember? Or write it down?"

This time, the coach offers another line to Manuel: "How about including yourself in your response, like, 'I would like to, but I am worried that you will not remember and then I will feel upset.'"

"I will write it down, I guess," responds Susan begrudgingly.

"Wait a minute," says the coach, "did you notice that Manuel just said something in a new way? He just reorganized what he said so that it included what he felt and his worries, rather than blaming you."

"Yes, I did notice that."

"What did you notice?"

"That Manuel didn't blame me. He responded in a different way."

"Can you let Manuel know that you noticed?"

"I appreciate what you just said, and that you reorganized how you just responded to me."

Manuel starts to say something and the coach pauses him, "Hold on. Did you notice that Susan noticed you did something different? How fantastic!"

Commentary

There was a minute left in the session. The coach was pleased to leave the question of desire unanswered, as the conditions had not yet been created to touch the subject. Thus, there was no effort on the part of the coach to get them to understand each other or compromise around sex.

Instead, the coach kept the focus on the activity of question-asking, slowing down and being curious. The coach's direction was for couple to do the activity of creating something together. In this "scene," they created intimacy by way of asking only questions, being uncomfortable (together) and taking the risk to say hard things, things that had previously only been said in their heads. Speaking in only questions bounced them out of their tired old scripts of each other. With the coach, they created an environment in which it was possible for something new to emerge. Nobody knew beforehand that it could be created. With the coach's support, they saw that not only could they converse in new ways, but also that they could create environments in which it is possible for new kinds of talking together to emerge.

I Already Know What She's Going to Say

This couple has been together 25 years. Their kids are newly out of the house and tensions are rising without having that mediating force.

Celeste begins talking and Matthew cuts her off: "I already know what she's going to say."

The coach is curious and asks them both, "How do you know, Matthew? Celeste, do you have that experience that Matthew gets you and reads your mind? What is your experience of these incredible powers?" They chuckled and respond by debating successful and unsuccessful mind-reading moments.

The coach adds, "Well, I have no idea what Celeste is going to say and I am here and part of this relationship we are doing right now."

The couple somewhat acknowledges that they were not considering the coach in their argument and ask, "What are we supposed to do when we have been together this long and know each other so well?"

"Well, if you already know what the other is going to say, what is there to learn and discover? Maybe you've heard 90% of it a thousand times over the years. There is the 10% that's brand new. Don't you want to hear the new part? Aren't you here with me because you'd like to hear something new? I want to support you to hear something new from your partner. I invite you to be curious. Perhaps you could imitate me in the ways I am curious. Let Celeste say whatever she was going to say and let's see what we can discover."

Commentary

The coach provided leadership here by insisting on being included in the conversation. Deprivatizing the relationship in this example involved the coach making a demand that the couple could follow (allowing Celeste to speak). The coach also found a creative way to challenge the knowing certainty with which we all speak, listen and operate by inviting Matthew to imitate the coach and perform just as curious about the 10%. Bringing in development—the possibility that something new can emerge—is key to creating a space unfettered by age-old assumptions.

Somebody's Crying. Now What?

Intense emotionality can show up in all forms of coaching. Here is a look at one way crying and other forms of emotionality can be related to by the coach.

"I feel like I am being ignored and I feel so alone in the relationship," says Joan as she begins to cry. "I am going to go crazy in the house by myself. I don't know what to do. I feel rejected by Michael."

The coach asks Michael what it is like to hear his wife say that.

"Frankly, I just shut down. I feel like I have to do something when she cries in order to get her to stop. It's manipulative. And then I feel super guilty that I did something terrible. I tend to stay away from her because I hate that feeling." Michael continues for some time, adding how rational he is and how his therapist tells him to be more empathetic.

"Are you interested in hearing my response to Joan's crying?" the coach asks.

"Yes."

"Why don't you ask me."

"What?"

"How about you performing the line, 'What was it like for you, coach, when Joan was crying? You are here with us, what was your experience?'" Michael imitates the coach's lines.

"Thanks for asking and inviting in another perspective. I am responding to Joan's emotionality as a giving to the relationship. She is taking a risk to say something hard to us. I see it as an opening to create with. Perhaps we could come up with a "Yes, and . . ." line. How does that sound to you?"

Michael and the coach go back and forth on how it was possible to see Joan's crying as something to create with, rather than to withdraw from, ignore or get reactive to. Ultimately, they co-create a "Yes, and . . ." line that Michael performs to Joan and the coach. Everyone explores how it was to say and hear the new line as well as the impact speaking this way might have on the relationship. The performed conversation continues as each spouse tries new lines that have been co-created with the coach and later to be co-created by and with each other.

Commentary

Relationality, imitation and completion are all at work here in the coach and the couple creating a new, more intimate way of communicating. When a thought or emotion is no longer "mine," but rather can be related to as "ours to build with," new possibilities emerge. What ensued in this example was a *performed conversation*. The coach invited Michael to invite the coach into the scene. Michael accepted the invitation and imitated the coach in performing the line ("What's was it like for you, coach . . .?"). In doing so, he discovered that: a) it is possible to ask such a question of another person; b) he is able to say those words to someone; c) he can handle the response to his question (i.e., it is possible to receive a response that is not judgmental or blaming and can be built with); and d) inviting others (in this case the coach) to give how they are seeing what is happening can be refreshing. There might be other ways to respond that he had not considered.

We have another note here on intense emotionality, in this case, crying. In American culture, strong emotions are often given special meaning (in this case, Michael saw it as a powerful way for Joan to manipulate him) rather than being related to as more ordinary discourse. The coach could have *explained* this to the couple but instead chose to direct a performance of it. The coach radically accepted Joan's crying as an offer with which to build and create more emotional intimacy. In the process, the size and shape of Joan's crying transformed.

Doing New Performances

In couples work, the metaphor of performance is particularly helpful. The coach can guide clients to both be in the scene, and see themselves as they perform the scene. This allows for the possibility of choosing another performance. Clients learn that they can choose to perform as a non-yelling, slower-speaking person, even as they want to "be themselves" and let loose a tirade. Couples also learn that they can decide together what kind of performance to do in all kinds of situations.

Continuously Deciding Together

These five-year life partners have been seeing the coach for about a year. Very sensitive to falling into roles and scripts, they decided to radically reorganize their relationship.

"*We* get to decide how we are together!" the couple tells the coach excitedly, as they announce they will consciously separate for two months.

A year prior, Tiffany sought out the coach to help facilitate the couple's conversations. They both felt confident of the partnership's foundation, but the relationship had been feeling stuck as of late.

Over months of weekly, then bi-weekly, sessions, the coach, Christopher and Tiffany worked to create an environment in which everyone could be vulnerable and take emotional risks with each other. The couple regularly asked for help and was inviting of the coach into their relationship. At times the sessions were very intense, focusing on feelings of jealousy, anger and frustration at their partner for being withholding.

They worked on feeling unworthy of love, finding it hard to be given to (without having to reciprocate) and overcoming obstacles to being more giving emotionally. Even though the session would start out with the couple being affectionate, it might end in tears, with each partner at opposite ends of the couch.

In the beginning, the couple had looked to the coach to advise on rules, boundaries and agreements to follow so that they could avoid their typical scenes or relying "too much" on the other for emotional support. However, the coach challenged this way of thinking and stressed that the three of them together were creating how the relationship was getting organized. Over the course of the year, the couple got more comfortable wandering around in the messy middle where nothing was determined, neat or clean.

Together, all three came to see the ways that Tiffany and Christopher were producing the typical scenes where one felt controlled and the other felt manipulated. They decided an area of growth for both of them was on expressing their wants and needs. In general, if someone was able to express a want or need, the other supported it, "If that's what he needs to become who he's becoming, I support it." Yet sometimes one spouse would be ahead of the other in asking for or responding to the other's expression of need. In those moments someone would feel anxious or reactive and hold on to old ways of being in the relationship.

Tiffany continues recounting for the coach what had transpired since the last session: "At first, I was overwhelmed and devastated by Christopher's mention that we consider separating. I thought he meant it as a road to ending our relationship. As we continued to talk and think about it, I saw the possibility that it might be helpful to us. We have not been apart from each other more than a few days in five years!"

It turns out that buying their first home was providing an opportunity for them to live apart for two months. Christopher would live in and renovate their new apartment. Tiffany would stay in their rental until the lease expired.

"That thing that I do of not expressing what I want, then not getting it and then getting victimized and blaming of Christopher, it's just not me anymore. It's not the kind of woman and partner I have ever wanted to be. But now that I have been growing it's really not me." Tiffany recounts that, while out with friends recently, they did something totally different: One partner went home earlier than the other, instead of making the other leave with them. "It felt like it was my choice to stay out," notes Christopher. "Yeah, and I was fine with it," adds Tiffany.

The coach completes them: "From what you are saying, this decision to consciously separate for a while has had an immediate impact and freed you both up to do new things. Without knowing beforehand, making the decision to consciously separate is creating space to discover other ways to be together. That's fantastic. In our work you often relate to your 'pattern' as a fixed entity that causes things to happen. But what I hear you both telling me is that you have blown the pattern up! I am so moved at your decision and courage to reorganize your relationship and who each of you is in it."

The couple thanks the coach and gives how much of an impact their work as an ensemble has had on them together and individually.

"Now what do we do coach?" A conversation ensues exploring how they might do the separation. Rather than give advice, the coach tries to offer methodological support. "You'll likely know much better *after* your two-month separation what it was that you had needed in order to do it. That is the nature of this kind of decision. It's unknowable how it will go down. Have you considered the emotional responses you might have to not being together?" The couple indicates that they have not considered that. "How would you want to handle when one of you misses the other? Or doesn't miss the other?"

The couple finds this helpful; it immediately challenges their idea that this would be an easy project or a matter of only planning and logistics. "Oh yeah, we get to decide how we do our relationship in a macro way, and we can keep creating how we do this conscious separation while we are doing it."

"Exactly! You might decide to not talk and send each other love poems, or a daily photo, or you could choose to have coffee now and again or you could discover that you want to stop the separation."

The main thing everyone decides is that Tiffany and Christopher get to decide how they are together!

They excitedly continue to play around with variations on what they might want to have happen during the separation and what kind of emotional support they are organizing from key friends. They look forward to the next meetings with the coach (both as a couple and individually) to co-create/co-recreate how the separation is going.

Commentary

This more longitudinal example traces the road to a couple's realization that they do not have to follow a script prewritten for them by society, their family, their liberal urban circles or their internal mantras. One important note is that they decidedly built their relationship with the coach and included the coach in their decisions along the way and were very open and vulnerable. They also included select friends who were able to champion the relationship and not get caught up in judgments or anxiety about the couple's choices. In that kind of environment—in which the relationship is not private, nor a precious thing to hold onto— the coach was able to give the couple *a lot* of support. The couple carried the relational and emotional tools developed from coaching sessions into their home, work, circle of friends and family life.

When One Member of the Couple Is Developing

It is not uncommon in couples work that when one member of a couple starts to grow—embody more emotional elasticity, build up other areas of their life (friendships, hobbies, volunteering), do a new performance with their partner—the other begins to feel fearful, threatened or rejected by the change in the relationship.

Martin and John have been together for twelve years. They connect as science nerds. Both successful engineers, they have relied on each other for support in a field where there are few models or alliances for queer people. As their relationship began to grow more distant, they leaned into where they felt most comfortable with each other—their shared intellectual pursuits. When that could no longer sustain the partnership, they sought out help working with a coach.

"We started coming to you three months ago because we were both lonely in the relationship. You have been asking us to be more emotionally present with each other. I feel like I have been more emotional with John and he is just not responding." Martin goes on to share how working with the coach is opening up the pain of the abuse and discrimination he has alternatively ignored or powered through in his life.

"I have been crying, like ugly crying. It's embarrassing, though I am glad I am doing it. But John can't handle it."

"John, how is it for you to hear Martin give this to us?"

"I don't know what to do when he gets emotional."

"I hear you. Do you have an emotional response to Martin saying he's having new emotional experiences and that he doesn't think you can handle them?"

"I am kind of pissed, to be honest. I don't understand what he's going through. Though I can see he's changing."

"Thank you for giving that to us just now." The coach decides to challenge both John and Martin's tendency to be analytical: "Does John have to *understand* Martin in order to build intimacy?" Everyone philosophizes for a bit on this. The coach reminds the couple of the time John gave Martin a big hug when he came through the front door after a stressful day at work and Martin melted in John's arms: "Did that act require understanding?" They agree that it did not.

The coach restates their earlier question in a slightly different way: "John, how do you feel that your partner is doing new performances, feeling new feelings? You can go slow in responding. Take a breath, feel your body and your gut where you hold your stress. What's going on for you right now?"

After a long pause, John replies slowly, "I feel out of control. Kinda panicky. This is all a little scary."

The coach replies to them both, "Yes, it is scary. New things are happening. Martin is taking emotional risks with you and in other parts of his life. He's growing. He's inviting you to do things that you, John, have never done before—that you both haven't done before—like be there emotionally for each other. Doing things you have never done before is part of the journey of growing your relationship. John, are you open to being more out of control *here* with me and Martin?" John is unsure, though he likes the idea of growing the relationship and helping it get unstuck.

The conversation continues. They explore what being "out of control" means for John as well as Martin's experience of John on the rare occasion that he has been out of control. Building with what they have given, the coach, Martin and John discuss what kind of support both men might need (from the coach and each other) to create new performances together in the scene formerly known as, "Martin Gets Emotional and John Gets Panicky."

Commentary

The coach completed the couple in pointing out that one of them is growing. With the coach's help, their work together centered on Martin and John embracing—radically accepting—where they were both at (one partner more open to trying new things and taking risks to grow emotionally, the other sticking close to what is comfortable—even if doing so is painful and keeps the relationship stuck). The coach also invited them to keep investing in growing the relationship, which would include John doing new things with/when feeling out of control.

Collectively creating a new idea of what it means to "understand" and be "out of control" opened up the possibility to move "around and about" (à la Wittgenstein) the problem (John's inability to be emotional with Martin). It created the conditions for John to be more honest with what was going on for him, thus giving more material for the coach and couple to create with. These activities empowered the couple to try new ways of creating together without knowing beforehand how to do it or what the outcome might be.

Performing Other than Oneself

This couple has been operating in more traditional roles and getting stuck.

"We keep getting reactive to each other and I don't know how to stop it," Paul says.

The coach responds, "What is the question?"

"What can I do to stop getting so reactive? About simple things."

Cynthia chimes in, "He just gets reactive, thinking that I am interrupting his story when I just add something because I am passionate."

"Exactly. I came from a really quiet family, so when I tell a story, I am not used to being interrupted. I get thrown off when she interrupts. I lose track of what I was saying and then I get pissed off. The whole thing is really annoying."

"And for me, I am just talking with him and telling him what I think. I am a southern girl and with my girlfriends we are always talking over each other, back and forth. To me, that is intimate."

"So, what would be a developmental question for you and the relationship?"

"I just want to have fun and be more intimate, like with my girlfriends."

The husband makes a face. "I don't know what that would mean for me. I can't be like her girlfriends."

"Why not?" the coach challenges.

"What are you saying? I am a guy."

"Does that mean you can't imagine what it might be like to talk with your wife like a girlfriend? Aren't there times where you have to speak in way that is different from your 'natural' self?"

"Well yes, when I go into making a sale at work, I always think about talking like my mentor."

"Great. Will you play a game with me? What about performing like your wife's girlfriend? It sounds like talking with each other in this way might be fun and playful. It might relieve you of focusing on the functionality of getting information across, which can be more mechanical."

The husband replies thoughtfully, "I'll consider this, even though I have no idea what that might be like."

Commentary

Relating to making conversation as a performance or an improv scene can be enormously freeing to couples once they try it and come to appreciate playing together in this way. To do so means letting go of the Truth referentiality that often pervades conversation. Truth referentiality means being more concerned about and committed to the "Truth" of the message, i.e., getting the story right. This tends to show up often in male-oriented activities. Though we all buy into the belief, men have a deeper history of having to be "Knowers," which is a premium skill for being successful in modern society. Women more often find themselves in situations that demand greater comfort with unknowability and chaos, e.g., managing a home, career, family and children all at once. In this case, once the husband was encouraged to perform speaking like one of his wife's girlfriends, he was able to be more playful. The couple began creating new performances of talking with one another.

Giving a New Performance Direction

Kyle and Rebecca came into coaching to work on the challenges of childrearing together. However, even before their two children were born, they were critical of each other. Now they are contemptuous, defensive and hostile. This is their second session.

Kyle kicks the session off. "I would like to communicate better with my wife. We only talk about the children and the logistics of raising them."

Rebecca adds, "I would agree with that. The way he talks drives me crazy. He's very judgmental of everything I do." Kyle gets defensive: "Well, she's just as critical. We end up angry and we stop talking. There must be a better way to communicate."

"OK," says the coach, "what do you mean by communicate? Are you asking me for a formula for safe communications? Because I do not have any formulas, unfortunately."

"Well, we don't know how to talk to each other. We have such different personalities and so little in common. At least that has been true since we had the kids."

The coach is curious how they understand having different personalities and so little in common, when after all, they did marry and have children together.

Rebecca shares her understanding of their differences. She grew up with her father trying to control every little thing she did. He would get furious when she wandered outside of the rules he had set up. Rebecca learned to shut down in his presence and secretly kept doing the things he did not want her to do.

Kyle states that his family life growing up was very different. It was traditional. He openly broke the rules and chose a different path than his brothers. He hung out with the school rebels.

The coach offers, "I am hearing a commonality in what you both are giving, can I share it with you and we can see how it lands with you?" The couple agrees and the coach continues, "It sounds to me like you were both rebels. You both refused to bow to authority, even though you did it in different ways. Rebecca, you refused to submit to men (your dad) who were critical and aggressive with you. I applaud that. Kyle, you refused to follow a traditional path with traditional values, and here you are wanting to raise your daughters with openness and collaboration, rather than rigidity and control."

The couple is surprised and agrees to the shared value of rebellion. They remember the ways they admired each other for their rebelliousness in the beginning of their relationship.

The coach suggests to Kyle and Rebecca that they try a new performance together right there in session. "What if you re-perform one of your typical angry conversations, and instead try relating to each other as rebels?" To their surprise, this exercise helps Rebecca and Kyle speak more slowly, listen more and become more collaborative, rather than adversarial.

"What is it like for you both to discover another way of communicating?" asks the coach.

"Well, it is not what I expected. I thought you would help us with a roadmap of better things to say in the heat of the moment," Kyle confesses. Rebecca adds, "Somehow, seeing the rebel in Kyle, that part of him I really love and admire, allowed me to connect to the conversation in a new way."

"This performance stuff is weird, but it is helpful!" they conclude.

Commentary

When couples raise that they want to better communicate, the underlying understanding is often that, if they (or their partner) only knew the "right" way to say something, the tension in the relationship would disappear. While changing the words or tone of communication can indeed be helpful, more often than not, there is a lot more going on in the relationship that could be worked on.

The coach wasn't sure but decided to relate to the couple's explanation of communicating poorly (having different personalities and little in common) as an offer. Perhaps there would be something in their responses that could be built with. As it turned out, their shared history of standing up to authority offered a possible commonality through which they could create different kinds of conversations, rather than each of them seeing their rebelliousness as a private act. It allowed Kyle and Rebecca to reshape and redirect the total scene. They were freed from having to know the right way to talk and could improvise in their performance as being on the same rebellious side.

Jealousy: The Problem Vanishes!

Jeri came into couples work with her wife, Samantha. They have frequently fought due to the intensity of Jeri's feelings of jealousy, manifested through teases, taunts and digs about Samantha's relationships with other women. Samantha has been distressed and feels like she has to walk on eggshells when they talk about her friendships, her past and her workmates.

Samantha says, "I don't know what I can do. It comes up all the time. Sometimes Jeri tries to be humorous, but often I find it very controlling. We get along well and have a good relationship. But this kind of behavior is spoiling it for me."

"What's going on for you, Jeri?" asks the coach. "And how do you feel about what Samantha is saying?" Jeri acknowledges the issue: "I know it is a problem but I can't help myself thinking about her with other women." Jeri continues, "I still think about her sleeping with another woman early in our relationship."

The coach inquires, "Do you feel Samantha betrayed you?"

"Not really. I mean, we were barely dating. We did not make any commitments to each other at that time. I do feel we are committed now. And Samantha has never cheated on me, at least as far as I know."

"OK, thank you for giving that. Perhaps it would be helpful to hear what you mean by jealousy. What does it look like for you?"

"I just think about how much fun she has with other folks. I usually wish I could be a part of it."

"So, you imagine Samantha having fun?"

"Yes, she is terrific at making friends and being the life of the party."

Samantha responds, "Yes, I do like to have fun with friends. And Jeri and I have fun together as well. At least we do when she is not jealous."

"I feel badly that my jealousy brings everything down. And when you get mad at me, Samantha, I get worse. I don't think that you should just stay home and not go out with your friends. I like your friends, actually."

The coach pursues this. "OK. You don't want Samantha to stay home. Do you get jealous of her spending time with her family. Or if she is playing with her dog?"

"No."

"Maybe you could give more of when exactly the jealously occurs?"

Samantha offers up a thought on Jeri's behalf: "It usually occurs because I have something to do, and she doesn't. I am good at planning events. Jeri is not. Sometimes she joins me and that is fine. But sometimes, I am just going out to have some girlfriend time."

Jeri concurs: "Now that you say that, yes. That is how it happens. I don't usually go out because I have nobody to go out with." Samantha challenges Jeri and points out that she has plenty of friends, but does not initiate plans and tends to wait to be reached out to by them.

"I am shy about initiating. I feel kind of ashamed about sitting at home while Samantha is out. I admire her ability to do that."

The coach offers, "Given what you both are saying, how do you know that what is going on is jealousy? It sounds to me like admiration at times, and at other times like Jeri's response to feeling shame or other times like you are missing being with Samantha while she is having a good time."

"Yes, that sounds right to me. Come to think of it, I don't feel I want to hold Samantha back. I guess I wish I were more like her. But instead, I chide and tease her about it."

"That is interesting to hear. I was wondering if you might try something right now. How about sharing with Samantha how wonderful it is that she organizes going out with friends. That you may envy her ability and may even want to learn from her to do the same. Let's see what it's like to say something like that."

Commentary

This scene illustrates the new possibilities that can emerge when we challenge the notion that our emotions are fixed, known and deserve primacy over all else. The coach here stays in the paradigm of jealousy until a window opens, provided by Samantha, who completed Jeri. Jealousy, the emotion, vanished. A discovery was made in the process of creating a more honest and vulnerable conversation in which Jeri could take the emotional risk to expose her envy and shame and how she covers that up by chiding Samantha.

Notes

1 For more on Wittgenstein and social therapeutics see pp. 97–103.
2 See pp. 47–51 on completion.

PART IV
APPLIED SOCIAL THERAPEUTIC CASE STUDIES

We conclude this practical guide to social therapeutics with a look at its innovative application from a sampling of social therapeutic practitioners in the US and Mexico. The nine authors who write of their work offer a glimpse into the elasticity of the method—leaning into relationality, not knowing, improv, language play and emotional growth—which can support all kinds of group and community work. Some of these six groups we are about to share have been operating online or in-person since before 2020. Others came into being in the wake of that year's events, including the global pandemic, the murders of George Floyd and Brianna Taylor in the US and the severe repression of young people's protests against police brutality in Nigeria.

We begin with a look at two short-term, topic-driven groups. While we have argued in this book for the power of heterogeneous groups, we feature these "single-issue" groups as illustrations of seeing and working social therapeutically with the diversity within the group, including the diverse levels of emotional development of the participants.

Dementia and Alzheimer's afflicts a growing number of people living with varying stages of the diseases. By extension, it also affects those in their lives and their caregivers. The case study *Creating With Dementia: Emotional Development Groups* includes a mix of all these stakeholders. A significant part of the work of the group co-leaders is to help the group in giving their emotionality around letting go of the need for memory and knowing what really happened/is happening. These groups are at once playful and intense.

Uncomfortable Independent Conversations invites participants to explore the power differentials of race and class in the US. A Black-led multiracial team of coaches guide participants of diverse backgrounds in creating an environment in which it is possible to take uncomfortable risks together and work to hear "the other" in new ways. These conversations are designed to neither teach nor correct, but rather to create with the messiness of our assumptions and judgments, for that is part of the actual work required to materially and permanently transform systemic racism.

The next three case studies focus on international groups. In *Launching Social Therapeutic Groups in Latin America* practitioners share how they grappled with if and how to apply/adapt/evolve social therapeutics to conditions that differ greatly from the US context in which social therapeutics was created. The group leaders decide to include the group in the grappling. They discover together and collectively make meaning of the activities of "building the group" and "growing emotionally."

Young People Building Community Around the World showcases how to creatively play with chaos and to follow the lead of youth. Emotional Support Sessions for teens and young people grew out of the isolation and loneliness experienced during the Covid quarantine. Connectivity issues impacted many, so the coach and teens decided to shift to the messaging app WhatsApp, and run the group sessions via text, shared images and recorded voice memos. Incredibly, young people from West Africa, the Middle East, the US and Europe build community through expressing their emotionality and their hopes without seeing and hearing each other in real time.

The final example of international work features ongoing weekly groups whose participants span four continents. *Developing Across Borders: Building with Differences as an Antidote to People Feeling Alone in Their Responses to the World and to War* shines a light on groups that, by and large, are made up of performance and political activists with a connection to the East Side Institute. The work (as always in social therapeutics) is to build the group. In this case study, the coaches share how they work with conflict both within the group and between the group and coaches.

The final case study, *You've Got the Smartest People in the Room, Now What?* brings us to an example of social therapeutic corporate team coaching. Here, a global team of top-level professionals *grows as a unit*. Through improv exercises and the metaphor of performance, team coaches and the corporate team lead work together to create an environment in which high performers stretch beyond their usual "I've got it all together" corporate performance. That stretching becomes the material for building the group and for growth of the team and the individual members of it.

A couple of final notes for reading this section. First, the authors of each case study took a unique approach to showcasing their work. Rather than editing for consistency of form, we opted to bring their expression directly to the reader. This remains in keeping with the organic growth of social therapeutic practitioners in diverse areas of the world. Second, all the authors have trained with and/or are affiliated with the East Side Institute, located in New York City. We have referred to social therapeutic founders Fred Newman and Lois Holzman and the Institute throughout this book. Finally, all names have been changed in these case studies to assure anonymity, with the exception of David Ezekiel, who gave permission to reproduce his poem as part of *Young People Building Community Around the World*.

9

SIX CASE STUDIES

Topic Groups

Creating with Dementia: Emotional Development Groups

By Helen Abel and Eileen Moncoeur

Since 2019, we have been leading *Creating New Performance of Memory Loss, Dementia, and Growing Older*, a four-week short-term group grounded in social therapeutics. The genesis of this work was a 2018 workshop held in Oakland, California, *The Joy of Dementia (You've Got to be Kidding!)*, created by our colleagues at the East Side Institute, Mary Fridley and the late Dr. Susan Massad.

The groups range from 8 to 20 people and are open to everyone: People living with dementia and their care partners (spouse, family, friends), health care providers, people grappling with aging and everyone interested in transforming the dementia experience from stigma and fear to growth and joy. We have found the heterogeneity of participants makes groupwork more powerful. People are clearly speaking at/from differing levels of development—cognitively and emotionally, and exploring our human capacity to create meaning that does not depend on memory or cognition.

We draw heavily on social therapeutics' understanding of the human ability to perform, pretend, play and improvise as key to emotional

DOI: 10.4324/9781003326465-15

growth. A diagnosis of dementia is often experienced as a catastrophic event for everyone, characterized as a loss of self and capacity to create. We disagree with this kind of problematizing. We have seen time and time again in our groups the possibility of not only continuing to create our lives, but even to create joy! Sometimes joy looks like the discovery that a new relationship is possible and is being created with a loved one living with dementia. Other times joy is the experience of literally playing with and performing dementia in new and positive ways.

We usually begin each session with a simple improv game involving everyone, such as a mirroring—in which people follow and imitate someone else's movements—or tell a collective story with everyone initiating their line by saying "Yes, and . . ." as a way of radically accepting and building with previous lines. This immediately accomplishes two things: Participants experience themselves as part of building an ensemble; and, they feel freed up from the worry of making a mistake or forgetting a piece of knowledge or a word. There are no wrong answers in improv!

We then invite people to share whatever they would like. Often people speak about memory, care-giving issues and concerns that come with growing older. They share with the group their pain, sadness, anxiety and worry. We then invite the group to respond and create something new together.

This work is highly emotional and we have been challenged to explore our own fears as they relate to dementia and growing older. As coaches, we include those subjective responses into how we lead the group. We feel it is an important part of getting closer to people's pain and creating an environment for growth.

People do grow emotionally in our groups, including people living with dementia. People's experiences of shame and isolation get transformed into feelings of connection and new possibilities.

LETTING GO OF THE TRUTH

As a continuous practice of method, social therapeutics does not need a Truth reference in order to help people grow. That is particularly valuable in working in this space. Part of the tragedy narrative of dementia is that the person who lives with it "goes away" because they no longer have access to memories and sometimes language. In one group a woman felt she was losing her mother to Alzheimer's and that she needed to let go. The group asked what she meant by "letting go" and asked if she was willing to explore what their relationship could become now, given her mother's Alzheimer's. She had never considered the possibility that she could have a new relationship with her mother that did not depend on her mother's memory.

In response, a different woman shared that her life partner often does not recognize her. She talked about the moment-to-moment choices she makes and that she is grateful for their relationship, even as it is difficult emotionally and physically. She said of the group, "I want to be with people where we can openly talk about what the hell we're going to do with our lives at this stage," adding that she felt memory loss calls for creativity from all involved. Her partner, who was in the group and living with dementia, responded by saying how hard it was to "not know."

A different group played with the idea of breaking out of the paradigm of Truth and exploring new ways of relating to people. One woman expressed her frustration when her husband cannot remember what they have been doing in the last hour. A different man in the group, who himself had early-stage Alzheimer's, suggested that she respond to him using improv—that she did not need to hold onto "Truth" and could respond in a playful way. He felt they would have more opportunities for connection in their relationship. The woman found it enormously helpful.

BREAKING OUT OF ISOLATION

People living with dementia and their care partners often participate in our groups because they have been feeling isolated and are in pain. One man commented, "I have been feeling very isolated, having difficult physical issues and struggling. I was very moved by people being so intimate and sharing their conflicts and feelings. I feel less isolated and alone after being in the group."

One couple had never participated in a group before. The husband was diagnosed with Alzheimer's and he had become isolated and quiet. During one group he shared that he had been feeling "useless" since his diagnosis. He had been a fire captain and very active in community projects. His wife responded that she wants to be his care partner and is happy to do so at this point in their marriage. She felt terrible about how her husband was feeling. The group asked the husband about his feeling useless and reflected back that they experienced him as being very generous and responsive. As the group spoke, he cried. He gave that he was immensely happy to be in the group. His wife also felt relieved and moved that this work was even possible, saying that in recent years he had shut down and would hardly speak.

The Possibilities of Dementia

The improvisational and performatory nature of building the group creates opportunities to literally play around with dementia in new ways. One man with early-stage Alzheimer's loved pushing the group to be more philosophical, asking questions like, "If I can't remember who I am, will that be hard for me? It's possible that I will enjoy my life even more." He later told the group joyfully that he now uses three times as much deodorant in his life simply because he cannot remember if he had already put it on or not. He joked that he is the sweetest smelling man around, much to the amusement of the group.

A different woman shared that she has felt more given to and more loved by her husband after his diagnosis. Her husband responded, saying that he realizes his diagnosis has changed him. He now fully accepts that he has Alzheimer's, and he feels lighter. It has become an opportunity to be even more present and unencumbered by memory.

In a follow-up survey one person responded to the question "Did you learn anything new about yourself by participating in the groups?" with "My mom is in the last stages of dementia as we speak. I learned to play and accept where she is. I learned how to enjoy her and to give her much more. I also learned how to listen and learn from folks in all stages of dementia and in care-giving roles."

A different woman in the group who is just starting to experience memory loss said that she was moved beyond words at the work the group was doing. She said it felt like a privilege to be part of these conversations and she was feeling less isolated in her life as a result.

Conclusion

Six million people were living with dementia and Alzheimer's in the US in 2022. The numbers are expected to increase to 13 million people by

2050. *Creating New Performance of Memory Loss, Dementia, and Growing Older* groups are part of a growing movement of practitioners and clients across the globe challenging the tragedy narrative of dementia. Reimagining Dementia is a network of 775 people from 31 countries advocating for play and performance and creating positive alternatives to traditional psychology.

Helen Abel and Eileen Moncoeur are both on staff at Life Performance Coaching. Helen is a member of the Reimagining Dementia Steering Committee. Eileen serves as Executive Director of the Sabal Foundation.

Uncomfortable Independent Conversations

By Dr. Raquell Holmes

I am a scientist and consultant trained in social therapeutics. In 2020, as people and organizations around the world created ways to publicly respond to the brutal police killings of African Americans, most notably George Floyd and Breonna Taylor, my fellow scientists called on me for direction. My response was for us to create an environment in which people who are very different from one another could get closer in ways that create something new. Thus began Uncomfortable Independent Conversations (UIC).

The structure of the UIC has grown out of the experiences and expressed needs and desires of the participants, myself and my co-leads. Its primary structure is a three-week Zoom series with weekly 90-minute group sessions. Groups range from 6–15 people, diverse by race, class, political affiliation, profession, age, gender, geography and sexual orientation. I am a Black, queer, cisgendered woman. My co-leads are Carrie Sackett, a coach, white cis woman, and two young African Americans: Andy Anderson Jr., cis man and Makalia Benson, cis woman. We come from divergent backgrounds: Poor, working-class and affluent. Importantly, we have all been building socially therapeutic environments for many years.

We invite UIC participants to build and inspire something that America desperately needs: New ways of coming together around race and class. We recognize that an essential part of the possibility and process of our country's development is our social and emotional development.

What follows is an excerpt from an interview with me by Carrie Sackett. In sharing the story in this fashion, I hope to give you a feel for the tone and voice that leads participants to playfully co-create uncomfortable, developmental conversations.

There is a growing number of initiatives to bridge the racial divide in the US. How do you see UIC's contribution to the work towards equity, diversity and inclusion? In other words, what is social therapeutic in this work?

Everyone is invited to participate in UIC. There is no litmus test as to people's views or understandings of "the other." Whoever is willing and wanting to engage in conversations on race and class with the intention of moving the country forward in fairness and freedom—for everyone, and particularly Black Americans—is welcome.

The power of UIC and social therapeutics in general is that our work is not about individuals. Although individuals who come to UIC often carry what they experience to be *their* individualized guilt, anger, frustration and upsetness. Yet, our "isms" [e.g., racism, sexism] in America (and everywhere) are socially and systemically produced. They are *ours*. Only together can we transform and dismantle them. Thus, by design, UIC participants grapple with "self," "other" and "system" in mixed company. For Americans, that in itself is uncomfortable.

Ah, that word, uncomfortable! Could you say more how you came to name these sessions Uncomfortable Independent Conversations?

In addition to the "uncomfortable" I just mentioned, there is a discomfort in creating new kinds of conversations that require stretching emotionally, socially, conceptually and practically. And in the case of UIC, there is the ever-present invitation of following Black leadership. Three of our four co-leads are African American, myself included. I chose "independent" to communicate the importance of building and innovating outside of educational, political and economic institutions, which, by their very nature, try to overdetermine how we see what is possible in terms of social justice and change. And by "conversation" in this context I intend the spirit of our needing to listen to each other and create an environment in which people can have their emotionality and give their emotional response to the world as it is currently organized.

Can you share an example of something uncomfortable in a UIC session?

David, a young African American man shared that he sees himself as a San Franciscan, not an American. Even as his family has lived seven generations in San Francisco.

Antony, a middle-aged white man and a second-generation Italian American remarked, "I find that hard to hear. That you identify with your local city and not your country. You are more American than I am."

Two older women, one Black, one Jewish, were visibly uncomfortable with the interchange. The following week they kicked off the session by giving their reaction: Antony was telling David how to experience himself in the world, that he should identify as American. They felt he was being racist.

We unpacked this as a group. What are we uncomfortable with now? Some people were uncomfortable with characterizing Antony's comments as racist. Some agreed that it was. Others were curious about the relationship David and Antony had built over the course of several UIC sessions together. Was there another way to go? What did the group want to do given people had different experiences/views. Did participants want to get closer to their different experiences of the group?

I could have responded to the uncomfortableness with, "Oh, my God! Are people okay? Does everyone feel safe? David, do you feel safe?" I think those questions come from very traditional psychology, which relates to each individual's pain as sacred and fragile.

What does it even mean to be okay, or feel safe, in this world? What I do is to continually invite people to appreciate, discover, even play around with our emotional responses together. Without the need to resolve them. We are in this world and our experiences of the world are different. And that is what we have to build with.

You mention a "playing with." How do you play in UIC sessions?

The explicit use of improv games in the first five minutes allows us to open with a playfulness that is not usually associated with the serious discussion of racism and classism in America. Everyone immediately experiences that we can create nonsensical meaning together, even in the face of very painful things. This helps to create the environment for the group's meaning-making around race and class as the session unfolds.

Another way we play is through the chat tool in Zoom. There will be a moment in group when people's assumptions of the other/what's really going on are strong. I ask people to share what they are wondering in the chat. This opens the possibility of shifting from knowing to wondering. Then I ask everyone to choose someone else's wondering from the chat and speak with the group on what resonates with them. This entire activity takes people through an experience of igniting their relational muscles and deprivatizing what is "in their heads." They have a glimpse of releasing the preciousness of *their* particular thought, *their* individual understanding, *their* fear of saying the wrong thing, *their* anger. An ensemble game unfolds with everything people contribute. There is no right way.

The "other" is materially present in UIC. Participants clearly are from different races and classes. How do you engage othering in UIC?

One of my favorite sessions was when one of the white female participants described how her father was racist, as if she herself were not. Susan was expressing, "I'm not them," as in, "I'm not one of the bad white people."

As a coach, I am not separate from the group. Giving my own emotional discomfort is part of building our group and our grappling with our racism. I acknowledge that we are all impacted by our experiences of race and class. In this case I shared my experience—my emotional response—of what Susan was saying:

"I feel uncomfortable in discussions on racism when I hear someone saying, 'I'm not like this other person.' We are all part of the racism in this world. We have all grown up with it. I don't think WE [all] can move forward as a community, country or world with a separating from, comparing, evaluative 'I am NOT THEM' posture. Of course, I do this too! I live in this world. I'm not suggesting that 'I am not you' and that I don't do that."

I did not know what would happen next after I said that. I did not know where the group would go.

A young African American woman spoke next. Lisa recounted that her mother always said dismissive things about other people and attributed those things to the person's race or ethnicity. Lisa felt her mother was separating herself from others, "We are not like 'those people.'" In giving this to the group, Lisa was creating a new identity. She built upon my comments and responded to Susan in a way that said, "We are in this together." It is mind-blowing that in sharing how they "other"—i.e., identify how we (one group) are better than those people (another group)—Susan and Lisa were able to create something more ordinary and not othering.

We created this lovely cross-class, cross-race, cross-age conversation. It was not abstract or intellectual. It was real women building an intimate conversation together with their lived experiences of othering and racism.

We did not end up with a definitive knowing conclusion and righteous judgment. The group and I could have said to Susan, "You are a racist. And you need to understand that you are."

In social therapeutics, we are neither interested nor invested in that somebody understands a particular anything. I find this extremely valuable when building these UIC groups. The goal of UIC is not to *get people to know* their or anyone else's racism. It is more like: "We are in this together. What can we create given who we are and what is here around us?" That is what builds intimate, hopeful, developmental groups.

You have often spoken of how this work is cultural, that ending racism or transforming racism requires a cultural shift. Can you say more about that?

We live in a painful world that divides people up by ethnicity, race and class. America has its own ugly history of this.

In one session we explored how is it for a mixed grouping, and especially white people, to be creating an environment in which Black women's emotional well-being is supported.

Where the group landed together was that it felt *integrating*, in that it had integrity—at both the individual and community level. I loved that for many reasons. One is that it created a new meaning of the word integration. That word has a very particular historical meaning. We know it in the legal sense as the laws passed during the civil rights movement. But here it took on a bottom-up, built-by-people meaning.

What the group was saying, the new meaning it created and how it got created, was cultural. Cultural transformation was something the civil rights movement was unable to effect. If it had, we would not be here today. This is the challenge of our times. Many are working at the cultural level today. I am proud that UIC is part of that movement.

*Dr. Raquell Holmes is the founder and director of improv**science**, the founding chair of Cultivating Ensembles, a public speaker and author.*

International Work
Launching Social Therapeutic Groups in Latin America
By Miguel Cortes and Majo Castrillo

About 15 years ago, one of us—Miguel—stumbled onto the work of the East Side Institute. He was curious and hoped they would have answers to his questions around innovation and education. He did not find answers, but something much better—the art of questions, the art of community and the healing power of group creativity. Since then, he has been a social therapy client and a social therapist on the front lines of discovering how to practice social therapeutics in Mexico.

The other of us—Majo—was born in Costa Rica and has been living in Mexico for five years. When she was about to finish her psychology degree, she became frustrated with its limiting and dehumanizing categories. In her global travels to find social innovators, she met and trained with the East Side Institute. Social therapeutics, with its revolutionary approach to human creative capacity, clicked for her.

Our relationship was created and fostered through collaborations with other social therapeutic practitioners from Costa Rica, Argentina, Guatemala, Nicaragua, Columbia, Venezuela, Brazil and Mexico. Recently we came together to create social therapeutic emotional development groups in Latin America.

We were very aware that we were experimenting with an Anglo-created approach to human development. There has been a long history of trying to fit European/American psychological approaches into Latin culture through modifying ideas and practices. Would we end up reproducing old colonizing tropes? Could we adapt social therapeutics into a culture that had no word for "performance," "emotional growth" or "becoming"? We wanted to avoid "tropicalizing," a word we use in academics for how cultural products from outside our cultures get rolled out in Latin America.

What we discovered is that social therapeutics cannot be tropicalized because by its own definition, it is not a tool to be applied instrumentally for a given outcome. It is, as has likely been said many times in this book, a practice of method, a tool-and-result[1] activity.

As English-speaking Latin Americans, we recognize that much of our participation with our international community is a privilege that not many in our countries can access. Throughout the years we have organized many Spanish-speaking opportunities for people to experience social therapeutics and collective development. We have been received with a certain degree of familiarity, given that historically much of our cultures are more collectively organized and less individualistic than in the US. Additionally, given that we live in contexts of poverty and oppression, people often come together to help and support one another. For example, when we are affected by a natural disaster, the first responders are ordinary people and civil organizations long before government assistance appears. So, it is no surprise that we have a sensibility towards group solidarity and activity. Yet, in creating social therapeutic contexts people often are challenged when invited to be vulnerable and open about their emotionality. Our ways of relating to each other are not free from the weight of our social problems: Machismo, poverty, corruption, violence, racism, inequity, etc.

Therefore, in doing social therapeutics in Spanish, we take much inspiration from Lois Holzman's assertion that:

> Cultivating and practicing this kind of development is like creating escape routes from our culturally produced and socially isolating prisons of pain. Without developing, without creating new things, we remain trapped (Holzman, 2022, September 6).

Es por esto que queremos cultivar y practicar en español.

Creating Something without Knowing How

We invited people to create something with us, without knowing how to do it or what would be the specific outcome. From the more philosophical to the more practical (duration, start date and pricing) we decided together the structure of the group. It can be intimidating to ask people to create something with you without the "certainty of knowing" what the result will be. However, we considered that giving people the opportunity to create the conditions for their own emotional growth is to relate to people as creators of their own lives and culture, something very rare nowadays in a society that tells us that we are supposed to be consumers and not creators.

We ran two six-week emotional development groups in Spanish with a total of ten people. We were proud of having members from different countries of Latin America (Costa Rica, Mexico, Colombia) as well as some living in the USA as immigrants or people living on the US-Mexico border. The members also had different professional backgrounds (artist, musicians, entrepreneurs, community organizers, educators and students). We were so excited and nervous to see what we could create with such diversity. Most had done individual therapeutic work, but not group work. No one had ever worked with two therapists at once (co-leads). Most had never heard of social therapeutics. Some came with the expectation of discovering what could be created. Others were curious (and maybe a little suspect) about how their different therapeutic motives (professional challenges, relationship challenges, grief, social anxiety and many others) could be met.

Which would be the best way to start? Did we want to play it safe and begin translating social therapeutic concepts from English? How would we express starting a work group in Spanish? Rather than explaining or describing, we decided to create fun, interactive yet intimate games to start us off. In one session we performed an out loud ruminating orchestra. Everyone was expected to simultaneously share our ruminations with different voices, speeds and pitch. In another session we selected music to dance to, which was appreciated by many who came to the group after work.

Over the six weeks, we continued to invite group participants to be intimate with strangers, to share their pain and emotions with them and to learn to ask for help! One group looked like this:

A client initiated, "I like what we do here, but sometimes I feel like we don't listen to each other when we are speaking. I am afraid to share because I think that people won't really listen." The group responded in various ways, "Has there been a time when we did that?"; "Yes, that sometimes happens"; "I don't recall a specific instance, but I feel it"; "Yes, sometimes Marianna talks and the group goes into all different directions."

Coach Miguel asked the client who raised how the group listens, "Do you have a sense of what it might mean for us to listen here?"

"I am not sure. I would like to know what the group thinks." Another client immediately followed, "Why don't we try it and see?"

Coach Majo sensed that diving in and trying might skip over the group continuing to build with what people had just been giving around their experience of the group. She saw an opportunity to support her co-lead, "I think we may be moving too fast. Let's go with Miguel's invitation to explore how we might be listening—or not—in this space." Coach Miguel built on Majo's direction, "Yes, thank you. I was wondering what goes on for people here that keeps us from listening to each other and to the group? Are we able to create that environment together?"

Group members started to share concerns and questions on how to do group. Different participants shared they were "trying not to monopolize the space"; "being careful not to say a wrong comment"; "being afraid of saying something offensive to someone"; "trying to help or give advice" etc. This opened up a rich dialogue on the experience of creating something new with new people, without knowing if they were doing it "right." Although this is a challenging activity, they were doing it; they were building the group and creating an environment in which it was possible for everyone to grow. As Fred Newman[2] liked to say, they were having the experience of building the boat as it was sailing across the ocean.

In the midst of this, we were also discovering how to work together, as this was our first time as co-leads. In the earliest sessions we tried subtle ways of doing that in the group, concerned that the group would be noticing us. However, after a while we decided to ask questions directly of each other and be more transparent in the group, e.g., "I have this thought about a way to proceed. What do you think?"

In our last session we invited the group to play with who we are and who we are becoming, as a group and individually. We used a Padlet (a virtual platform for education) to create a virtual collage with our experiences. About the becoming process some people expressed, "I arrived a little fearful of what was going to happen and I am feeling strengthened with all the support from the group"; "I arrived as a woman very afraid of sharing and I am leaving wanting to know more about everyone here and the world around me"; and "This experience of building together without a roadmap has opened me up to other ways of being with the people in my life." As practitioners we were surprised with the responses, mainly with the fact that people were articulating what social therapeutic environments are without us having to explain. It came from the vivid experience of creating growth together.

The group created a new culture, new emotions and new ways of being in the world, in community. It reignited people's creativity and relationality. Nowadays, with our current political, economic, environmental and social situation worldwide, we should be asking ourselves more *What can we do together?*"

Miguel Cortes is a psychologist and educator. He is the Director of the Fred Newman Center in Juarez, Mexico. Majo Castrillo is a psychologist and social entrepreneur. She is a staff member of the East Side Institute.

Young People Building Community Around the World

By Jennifer Bullock

I started working professionally with teenagers and young adults, as a social work advocate, mentor and counselor, when I was a teen myself. Young people have always been a significant part of my life. And they continue to influence me to this day, as I have become a solidly middle-aged therapist, coach and performance activist.

At 25, I met a unique community of world-changers who were innovating and practicing the approach that is the topic of this book, social therapeutics. This radically relational group approach transformed my work with young people. I went from seeing them as kids who needed my protection and advocacy to seeing them as collaborators and co-creators of our work together. No longer were parents the enemy. They became partners in building new ways of living together. No longer were young people to be listened to unconditionally. They needed to learn to be listeners themselves.

In 30 years of leading social therapeutic teen groups, I have seen clients learn from one another and practice with each other new skills for facing anxiety, depression, pressures of life and constant distractions. Then the pandemic hit. That changed everything.

Some of the everything that changed included that we went from in-person sessions to Zoom sessions. I asked the teens I was working with, "How do we work together now?" They came up with a warm-up for the beginning of the group. We created a collective drawing together on the Zoom whiteboard (of course, they had to teach me how to share the whiteboard!). One of us would start with a line, then another would add a squiggle, then another a circle. Before long, the group had created a dinosaur vaping, or a family photo or a conversation between two dogs.

These activities brought us together in a new way. There was a unique intimacy that we could not get in my office room together. For example, everyone could bring their pets on screen to join the session. Clients performed show and tell with favorite photos of friends and family. We discovered that being online together gave us a better platform to co-create the social therapeutic environment.

I love my work with clients. As these Zoom-driven discoveries were unfolding, I decided to act on a years-long desire to work with youth outside of the formal structure of a counseling office or nonprofit organization. I had been itching for something more experimental. I found it. Or rather, I helped to create it. Here is the story:

PART 1: CREATING COMMUNITY, CONNECTION AND SOCIAL CHANGE THROUGH PLAY

I consider myself a performance activist. Playing—creating new meanings together—can be an everyday way of living. Performance activism is an emerging movement, with roots in social therapeutics, that integrates and utilizes play, improv, clowning, theater and therapeutics into everyday life. This practice is a vital methodology for creating hope, possibility, emotional well-being and development. An international group of us performance activists (artists, performers, therapists, coaches and educators) came together virtually in 2020 to explore what kind of global platform we could create that would benefit people living through the crisis of the pandemic. From our perspective, everyone in the world needed support to express our human need to be creative, to love, to laugh, to cry, to be socially connected and to grow.

We decided to initiate a movement called Global Play Brigade (GPB) and began to offer free sessions on Zoom and WhatsApp where people of all ages from many countries would join together to play. Young people and adults were improvising, playing, storytelling and doing poetry-making sessions on the same screen. We were crossing borders of geography, age, diagnosis, class, race and language.

Part 2: How Can We Offer Support during the world's Pandemic and Social Upheavals/Crises?

During the outcry for social justice in the US and other countries in the summer and fall of 2020, GPB leaders including myself asked another question. While play and improv sessions are fun and even therapeutic, what would it be like to offer participants emotional support? Could we offer sessions for people who are experiencing upset or even trauma? For example, young people in Nigeria,[3] the US and around the world were protesting in the streets for a better world and were also scared during the pandemic. Some of these young people were joining either my therapy practice or Global Play Brigade sessions or both. They were feeling a mix of sad, overwhelmed and traumatized. What could we do together? Here was the opportunity for me and my GPB colleagues—the ordinary people of the world—to experiment with boundaries, borders, mental health and wellness.

Part 3: Can We Play with All of Our Emotions and Our Hopes and Dreams?

We started to experiment with what came to be called Emotional Support Sessions. Designed to create a space for teens around the world who wanted to grow in new ways and discover how to do that at the same time. The idea was to play with all of our emotions—especially with our pain, fears, anger, challenges and transitions—as a way to help us break out of our alienation and isolation. The Zoom and WhatsApp sessions are typically 10 to 20 people from all over the world. They feature improv exercises, collective poems and stories, and supportive, inclusive conversations that initiated with "How are you doing? How are *we* doing?"

When we were on Zoom, we would breathe together, share how we were doing, tell stories, make up stories and poems, cry and laugh together. However, internet connectivity was not reliable for participants in some areas of the world. So once or twice a month, we started offering sessions on WhatsApp, which is a texting platform. Now we were not only not meeting in person, but also we could no longer see or hear each other in real time. Once again, we were forced to improvise how we would build our group connection, and we had no idea if it would work. A session at any time could comprise of 16–22-year-olds in countries such as Morocco, Greece, Nigeria, the US and Brazil. After misunderstandings, chaos, trial and error, we discovered that we could use Google Translate for understanding each other's texts as well as post voice recordings and photos (a universal communication channel) to the group chat. This asynchronous communication opened up many possibilities.

To begin a session, I generally ask something like, "What's most alive for you currently?" Participants share they are worried about the future or are having financial struggles. They may be upset that a friend was killed or heartbroken over a breakup. I pick one of these and make it a theme for the session. For example, with the heartbreak topic, I then offer a prompt question for everyone to respond to, "What does your heartache look like, feel like, smell like, sound like?" and invite everyone to respond. Participants share stories, images, pictures and audio messages with one another through the group chat. We usually close every session with a collective poem. I start the poem with a title, for example, "Heartbreak, it's a . . . ." and everyone then adds a line. The poems are moving and powerful. The connection between participants has grown such that they have started an online community to be able to reach out to each other to check in, offer support and share good or bad news in between the sessions.

PART 4: WHAT COMES NEXT?

I cannot wait to discover additional new ways of working with clients that build community in our sort-of-post-pandemic era.

Impact statement from participant David Ezekiel, Lagos, Nigeria (age 20)

I got introduced to Global Play Brigade in Nov/Dec 2020 through Street Project Foundation and the experience since then has been an amazing one.

Prior to knowing about GPB, I struggled with not knowing how to express myself and what I felt in different gatherings, be it social or private. I would usually just go with the flow. But with the help and support of the Emotional Support Sessions offered by GPB, I was able to learn how to say how I feel and further express this in the writing of collective poems (usually at the end of every session).

I remember a time when I was ill, tired and not able to move much. But I was able to attend the Emotional Support Sessions on Zoom. I knew I would feel better if I was with a loving community, even through Zoom! So I brought myself to attend, and true to it, I explained how I felt. The amount of love I was shown brought me to tears. I was reassured of the love I knew was present in the community-now-turned-family.

Global Play Brigade, to me, is more than a community of improv leaders. It is a family of fun, caring and loving people all around the world

I want to thank the leaders for their unending support and love to all, especially me!

Moving Forward
Collective poem from a GPB Emotional Support Session
Baby steps
progressing
left, right, repeat . . . one foot in front of the other
baby dance steps
deciding
three legs but first two
bold steps
failing forward and learning as you fail
flip flap and fall.
tangled toes, inching toes
failing forward together
starting the race
here comes the tide, but we keep sailing
help help help, asking for it
cheese chaser
not learning to fail but learning in failure
dragging others along even while you are sinking

flaying arms in embrace of falling
laughing
picking pebbles, making bricks
dancing in the euphoria of banal living
breaking chains to flee
following the footprints of heroes
euphoria, banal
frayed hope living
striving
surviving
together
we move, not forging backwards, but blazing a new trail
baby dance steps
like a hawk, we soar with hope
in the end we move, not forging backwards, but blazing a new
trail

Jennifer Bullock, M.Ed., M.L.S.P., LPC. is founder and principal of The Philadelphia Social Therapy Group. She is also a facilitator with The Global Play Brigade.

Developing Across Borders: Building with Differences as an Antidote to People Feeling Alone in Their Responses to the World and to War

By Barbara Silverman and Melissa Meyer

This is the story of an ongoing virtual weekly social therapeutic coaching group—one of several such groups known as Developing Across Borders (DAB)—designed to create global, cross-cultural and social-emotional "development zones." DAB was founded in 2010.

Many of the 15 group members have trained with the East Side Institute (ESI) and/or participated in their international events. Many, though not all, are political, social justice and performance activists. They range in age from 20s to 80s and are from the US, Latin America, the Middle East and Europe. Everyone commits to attending weekly. Some join the Zoom sessions while starting their day with a cup of coffee, others are finishing theirs over a glass of wine. Some have been participating in group since its inception sever years prior, others joined more recently. With the support of the social therapeutic group leaders, clients are tasked with the challenge of organizing a developmental environment, deciding how and what they want to discuss.

What follows is a compression of group dialogues that took place over several months. While many group members participated significantly in this dialogue, we have highlighted specific aspects of the conversations for purposes of this case study. Welcome to a "scene" from Developing Across Borders.

SUPPORTING THE GROUP TO KEEP DECIDING

Shortly after the war in Ukraine began in 2022, a new member, Anna, joined the group. As the group gathered, members greeted each other. Coach Barbara Silverman began the group by saying "Let's discover how we are." Anna, a theatre director and political activist living in Western Europe bristled at the friendly tone and said, "How can you be smiling at a time like this? Your indifference to the Ukraine War is disgusting." Other group members were taken aback. Anna continued, "I can't believe we're going to discuss our feelings when there are tanks in the street."

Vesna, an intercultural youth exchange trainer and coach also living in Western Europe, who survived the Balkan War as a teenager said, "As the war in Ukraine begins and images of tanks in the streets dominate the news, I am going through déjà vu remembering how the region I lived in was so hated."

Anna looked around the Zoom screen and zeroed in on Carol, a political activist based in the US who works with families suffering from addiction. "You look so complacent in your leather chair. You Americans are so privileged!" Carol, blind-sided by this remark, responded that she felt attacked by Anna, and that as a Jewish woman she found Anna's comments anti-Semitic. Eduardo, a Latin American computer science researcher living in Europe, corrected Anna, "America is a continent that includes lots of countries. Carol is from the United States."

Henry, a youth development worker in the US, told the group he had something he wanted to say but was concerned that it might be unproductive for the group. Patrice's ears perked up. A European who founded a non-profit for radically inclusive intercultural transformation, Patrice replied to Henry and the group, "Henry, I'd like to hear what you have to say. You don't often make statements like that. Go ahead and don't worry about whether it would be unproductive." Henry took a slow breath and began, "Anna, I'm sick of your shit. Once again, you come in here judgmental of and belligerent to the group. You don't know where you are or who you're talking to!" Indignant and insulted, Anna declared, "I think I want to leave this group!" Sheldon, a leader in the performance activism movement who lives in the US, picked up on several group members' comments about the war, "Just because the world is going crazy, doesn't mean we have to."

This dialogue opened up a number of different attitudes and political and cultural questions. Sheldon and Alessa, a refugee activist living in Europe, questioned why the world was focusing on the conflict in Ukraine when there were devastating wars creating refugee crises in Sudan and Syria. Why wasn't the West welcoming these refugees? Quinn, a learning experience designer living in Europe, asked curiously, "If they are changing international border laws for Ukrainians, what other rules have we created that we can now do away with to help the world's people?"

For the next few groups, this intense conversation continued. There were developments and tender moments. Anna, who had initially attacked Carol, apologized to her. Carol responded that she was so upset over the incident that she had been thinking of leaving the group. The group appreciated Carol's opening this up and invited her to share more of what was going on for her and in her life. This particular session ended with Anna expressing appreciation of getting to know Carol. Carol said she felt the same way.

However, in general, emotions were still running high. Group members agreed on one key issue: *They were all angry at the group leaders for not intervening in these fights.* Was it possible to build the group with all the anger?

Silverman and her group co-lead Melissa Meyer said they appreciated what people were saying and that they were not interested in playing the role of police officers of the group. Some group members thought there should be a rule for when the group gets aggressive. Meyer said, "If you want a rule, then the rule is this: If you need something from Barbara and me, ask us," adding that the group's responsibility was to create the environment for working together, including having difficult conversations and even fights.

"What kind of relationship," Silverman asked, "does the group need to have with us so that group members *could* ask us for help?" Meyer added, "For us to change the world, we have to change it with *everyone* who is in it, including people with whom we do not agree or like. In fact, those very people might be helpful to us. Our differences with each other can be valuable when we work thoughtfully on how to create with each other." Several group members responded. One shared they were conflicted about asking the coaches for help. Another was irritated at the idea of relating to everyone in the group, including those they found to be a pain in the neck. Someone else wondered, "What was the possibility of creating an environment in which people could say hard things to each other in ways that could be heard?"

When Anna returned after missing several groups, Silverman asked how she was doing. Anna said she was having a rough time—close friends had died, and she was still upset by how fellow group member Patrice seemed to rejoice at Henry's statement to her. She stated that she thought young people like Patrice were not doing enough about the state of the world. "Don't write me off and my whole generation," responded Patrice. "I second that!" said Emilia, a European video educator working with an international peace and security organization. Anna said she was still angry at the group leaders for not doing anything to shut Henry down.

Manuel, a Latin American psychologist and group coach, said to Anna, "I think you are responding to the group as a victim." Anna got emotional and shared that she was learning something about herself. "I've always lived my life as a victim, even as a child," she said. "I'd like to do something about that, something different. I came here to learn." Silverman and Meyer thought Anna's comment was an important relational moment that emerged out of the group's collectively creating with each other's emotionality, life stories and political responses. Manuel added, "Anna, you've been losing loved ones, that sounds very painful. We could support you in dealing with that loss." Group members built with Manuel's offer, sharing moments of loss in their lives and ways the group had been there for them.

In spite of the intimacy of this conversation, Anna said she was still thinking of leaving the group. This time, however, several group members said they didn't want her to go. "We're learning from you," they said, perhaps to their own surprise. Anna has continued in the group, and the group has continued to grapple with complex questions, disagreements, beliefs and responses.

Epilogue

Ongoing group conversations such as the one we have provided here are challenging for members and group leaders alike. The Developing Across Borders groups are not designed to resolve differences but rather to help people create the conditions they need to grow emotionally. Lois Holzman[4] puts it like this:

> [I]t's not pretending the divisions don't exist or even trying to eliminate them. Rather, it's "building with what we have" (the very basis of development and growth) and making something new out of it. If what you have is deep divisions, then what you have to build with has to include them (Holzman, 2022).

Group leaders provide a structure that is nonauthoritarian. They do not mediate relationships or take value positions during challenging moments. In this conversation, the leaders had a variety of subjective responses to what people were saying, and they worked hard to *not* take sides. They thought it was important to support the group to develop these conversations *with everyone in the room and everything going on in the room*—the heightened emotionality, the experience of personal attacks and the difficulty for the group to make decisions in such a charged environment.

The group is building a place for heartfelt, difficult conversations. It is not a safe haven. It is a community-building activity where the group can continuously grow, even when they do not see eye to eye.

Barbara Silverman, L.C.S.W. is the founder Developing Across Borders and a member of the East Side Institute faculty. Melissa Meyer is the Associate Director of the East Side Institute and a social therapeutic coach.

Team Coaching

You've Got the Smartest People in the Room, Now What?

By Maureen Kelly

My co-worker, Gene, and I met in the Zoom room a few minutes be-fore 9:00 a.m. to get ready to begin our third coaching session with a marketing team in a global professional services firm—eight colleagues each responsible for developing the sales and marketing strategies for the managing partners in their respective regions.

Maya, the firm's Head of Marketing, shared that each member of her team led business development and marketing for a different regional managing partner. This is a high-pressure job with staff working mostly remotely. While she felt that team members were, as individuals, doing a good job, she believed that greater collaboration would improve the quality of the work, as well as make it a more nourishing work environ-ment. Team members, however, were not so sure. As one team member said, "Collaboration is a great concept, but we just do not have time given our workload." Across the board, there was skepticism.

After meeting with each team member individually, we designed a three-month team coaching engagement, which included six sessions with the full team, two one-to-one coaching sessions for each member, and leadership coaching for Maya. For this third coaching session, many team members were traveling, so Gene asked everyone to write their cur-rent location into the chat box, along with one word describing how they were doing that day.

We saw responses like "Austin TX, tired, long week"; "London, also tired"; "NYC, stressed about my region's Town Hall later today"; and so on.

Gene asked everyone to take a moment to read what they each wrote and say how they thought the ensemble was doing. The group was silent for a bit. After all, "How are *WE?*" is not a commonly asked question.

After about a minute, Theo said, "It seems like we're all over the map, literally!" Everyone laughed. Maya offered, "As an ensemble we're riding a roller coaster this week. Some regions' revenues are unexpectedly up, and others are unexpectedly down." Sharon said, "I think we're actually learning how to answer this question. Gene, remember how we looked at you like you were crazy when you asked, 'How are we?' a few weeks ago? You got nothing!" That got another laugh from the team, and Gene replied, "Yes, let's give our ensemble a round of applause for *that!*"

In our first two coaching sessions we had engaged the group in performing improvisationally together. We coach teams to perform, and in performing they can experience being part of and growing as an ensemble. I asked Sharon what the team was learning and why that was important. Sharon reminded us of one of the first improvisation performances they did where each took turns leading a slow, physical movement, and the others had to follow the leader, performing the exact same physical movement—as if they were one another's mirror. Sharon noted "It was excruciating to move that slowly, *and* it helped me to lead in ways that others could follow. And when I wasn't leading, I loosened up and let others lead. The question 'How are WE doing' gets me out of my own head, and I look around, and see that I'm here with my colleagues. It's crazy, but I often just dive into speaking, driving the agenda." Gene responded that driving an agenda isn't crazy; in fact, it's an expected performance at work. He continued that we are not trained to listen and to see and build the ensemble.

Elise said she found the question "How are we doing?" anxiety producing, and wondered "shouldn't we be getting back to work?" At that moment, Sita joined the call, apologizing for being late. Sita was one of the most senior consultants on the team, working with the Managing Partner who led the largest region. She had attended the first coaching session but left early and joined about halfway into the second coaching session. Gene welcomed Sita and shared what the group had been doing. Returning to his dialogue with Elise, he asked what she meant by "getting back to work"?

Elise said, "It feels a little 'touchy feely' to be taking this time. We are all so busy. And at the same time, I know that this session is about *how* we work together. So I guess I'm mixed on the value of doing this and whether it makes sense to invest the time."

Gene asked the group, "What do other people think about what Elise is saying?" Steven said he also wondered if they were wasting time with these exercises. Then he asked his family—a wife and twin 8-year-old boys—how they thought they *as a family* were doing. He noted that the kids spoke up more than usual and said they would like to go on vacation together as a family. He saw the value of that conversation, and, as he put it, "So now I think, maybe it *is work.*"

At this point, Theo asked Sita how her town hall went that morning. She said that it went well and added that although the revenue news was not great, "We surfaced our action steps to respond." Maya said that was great to hear, and thought that in the day's session, they could do some collective work on how they were prepping their managing partners post the Town Hall meetings. Sita said she would be happy to share her team's talking points, but that she could not stay for the whole session.

In our preparation with Maya for this session, Gene and I discussed that Sita's perspective had been that collaboration was not worth investing in. We agreed to embrace this as an "offer"—everything in an improv scene is an offer to be built with—including input we find challenging. Maya agreed and commented, "Sita is not the only person conflicted about this activity."

Gene pointed out that as an ensemble, this was a tough moment, and they needed to provide leadership to their clients. Maya thought there might be pulls to go fast, so the team might need to slow folks down, to help them stay on strategy. Investing the time to do this kind of work together is not easy. And in many ways, Gene noted, they were doing well without it. He proposed they do an exercise called "Slow Start," to continue to develop the group as ensemble. And in so doing, build the environment where they could make some discoveries about whether they wanted greater collaboration, and if yes, why; if not, why not?

Theo and Elise volunteered for the first exercise. Gene asked the rest of the team to suggest a location and relationship in which two people might find themselves. The group suggested that one of them be a tourist and the other, a tour guide in front of the Eiffel Tower. Gene's directions were that each could only speak one sentence at a time, with the other waiting at least ten seconds before responding to what their scene partner said. The cardinal rule of improvisation is that *everything* is an "offer"—what you say, how you say it, the emotions, the body language. Theo and Elise performed the scene, Gene coached them to keep going slow, and the scene ended with the group hooting and hollering their support.

Gene asked for two more volunteers, and Maya offered to go next, and asked if Sita would join her, to which she said yes. The team suggested they be two astronauts on the moon. Maya opened the scene with, "I'm glad we're finally here. It's beautiful." Ten seconds passed, and then another. The team could see Sita biting her lip, her face flushed. Gene suggested that Sita take her time and say something simple in response. Sita said, "I'm sorry, I just can't do this. Can we stop for a minute?" Gene said, "Absolutely. Let's pause."

When everyone came back together in gallery view, Sita said, "I'm sorry, this improv stuff just isn't me. I prepare." And with that, a tear came down her face. I responded, "I'm so glad you are giving this to us. I find it brave, and I appreciate it. Would it be OK with you if, as a group, we talk about what can make this exercise so hard? We could take a brief break, and then come back to chat."

During the break Sita reached out to me and told me, "Preparation is everything to me. It's how I work and why I'm successful. I just do not get why you are asking us to wing it."

I replied that I, too, deeply value preparation, and by no means was I asking her to not prepare. "What we're doing is building a muscle to complement preparation," I told her. "Seeing and being seen by the people you are working with. Sita, you are clearly a brilliant marketing strategist, and I believe you have much more than your brilliance to give to those around you. We want your brilliance, and we want you. Are you interested in exploring that type of growth with this team?" She said, "Possibly." I said, "Great! Let's explore 'possibly' with the team."

When we reconvened, I asked people to share their experience with this exercise. A few people said they were nervous to even try it. Elise said, "Sita, that so would have been me. I was impressed you said yes to Maya!" Maya agreed and said, "Thank you for trying this, Sita. Sitting in silence with you, I felt close. And I'm sorry if asking you do this put you too far outside your comfort zone." "No need to be sorry," replied Sita. "I think we all know I like to know what I'm doing. And *this* I do not know how to do. And I have a glimmer that there is some value in learning. I'm pretty impressed with what many of you can do in this context."

We used our remaining time to explore what it is like for everyone to do things, "before they know how." And that took us to the topic of collaborating as a team—a new performance that they did not "know" how to do, yet they were beginning to do it. They decided to hold a working session the following week to discuss how they were each approaching this disruptive period with their respective managing partners, and Steve suggested they kick it off with some roleplays that showed what these conversations look like now. Sita—who wound up staying for the session—said, "Great, I'll work on my script now." Everyone applauded, and she took a bow.

Maureen Kelly is the President of Performance of a Lifetime, a leadership training and organizational development consulting firm.

Notes

1 See pp. 56–57.
2 For more on Newman, see pp. 37–41.
3 In fall of 2020, Nigerians participated in mass protests against police brutality throughout their country. Nigerians in diaspora and others signed petitions and protested as well.
4 See Part I for more on Holzman and social therapeutics.

References

Holzman, L. (2022). Caste, Class & Gods: How Do We Go On with These Divisions? *The Developmentalist.* Retrieved from: https://loisholzman.org/the-developmentalist/#letters
Holzman, L. (2022, September 6). A Developmental Response to Trauma and Trauma Language. *Mad In America.* https://www.madinamerica.com/2022/09/developmental-response-trauma/

CONCLUSION

In these last chapters, the reader has adventured into over 30 scenes of social therapeutics in practice—in Life Development Groups, couples work and applied social therapeutics. Through this experiential activity we have attempted to share the culture of social therapeutic coaching—how coaches and clients lead, speak, listen, complete, play, imitate, create and make meaning together. We have attempted to show how relating to the group and building with what is emerging from the group's activity is a foundational part of how a social therapeutic coach leads. We have provided numerous examples of the coach discovering developmental possibilities together with their clients, creating alternatives to our modern tendency towards resolution, compromise, content-driven language and outcome-driven focus.

Across nearly all examples, the coach speaks in ways that are supportive of both the group/couple and the individual at the same time. And, in the spirit of there being no Truth or right way to practice social therapeutics, we have provided numerous options of what a coach might say in certain scenarios, while always stripping the story down to its social therapeutic methodological bones. Finally, we have showcased moments of our clients' emotional growth and group transformation. If you have made it this far, you have glimpsed the tremendous potential of social therapeutics for changing lives, supporting community-building and creating a better world.

From the elements we just outlined above, the reader can draw a throughline to some of the core competencies of coaching as defined by today's largest global industry associations. However, the most significant element—seeing and relating to the group as a whole—is the unique contribution of social therapeutics.

With 40 years of evidence of its success, social therapeutics is a methodological as well as an ontological break with what has come before in the modern history of addressing emotional pain. It works from the understanding that we are a social species, rather than an aggregate of individuals, and its focus rests on the *activity* of the group, rather than the content of what is being said. Co-founders Fred Newman and Lois Holzman fused and advanced discoveries in human development by drawing upon multidisciplinary threads whose components include:

- **Relationality:** An acknowledgement that we live *in relation to* others. Giving how we experience others and receiving how they experience us is key to making developmental discoveries of who we are and who we are becoming
- **The zpd:** The Zone of Proximal Development—radical acceptance that growth and transformation occur when people at different levels of development create together
- **Performance:** The human capacity to stretch beyond what we know how to do, be and feel; to create new lines to speak with others; and to create new ways to be, do and feel in the world
- **Language games:** The empowerment of people and groups to create language and meaning together

On our best days as practitioners, we challenge conventional assumptions of method, emotions and growth to create environments in which new possibilities can emerge. This continuous activity of building and creating with others is an improvisation liberated from the need to know. It empowers the coach and clients to co-create with the material they bring to group—their emotions, judgements, fears, history, philosophical questions and values. This creates the conditions for emotional growth and transformation and produces the growth at one and the same time.

The tool-and-result methodology of social therapeutics is a breakthrough in understanding human development.

This brings us back to the importance of the experiential. We have to *do* things (without knowing how), in order to *see* that they are possible. Furthermore, we have to *act* on this possibility to *experience* doing, seeing, feeling and creating in new ways. This is the *performed activity* that Newman and Holzman call for as a path forward.

We have written this book out of the desire to introduce this powerful approach to the growing global network of coaches and group and couples practitioners. In doing so, we believe we have made fresh discoveries about how to teach and show social therapeutics. We founded The Center for Group and Couples Coaching to provide immersive trainings and collegial oversight to those who want to deepen their understanding and practice of social therapeutics. We hope to see you there!

With deep appreciation and gratitude.

INDEX

Printed in the United States
by Baker & Taylor Publisher Services